LAST

CHAT

by

K. Allen

published by Flying Finish Press

ISBN 978-0-6152-0948-7

my adventures continue……………

Dedicated

to

Jim, Tim, Cam

&

Sherry,

Debbie

&

TJ
(rip)
my dearest friends

MAY
2007

May 1, 2007

After this month - no more parties. And the WWG will be disbanded. While I hope to continue knowing my friends - one never knows. The admin has just become too much. No more 'Vetting' - which was mainly for the parties anyway.

Activation of the dicta "If he wants you, he'll be with you; if he isn't then he doesn't." By your actions you shall be known. Take heed for I will move on though it may break my heart to do so.

Polo will continue but whether The Firehouse/Fire & Ice continues is another matter entirely. Also in this 'maybe' category is Stargazing. We shall see.

This is the season for changes.

The revised and expanded version of <u>Notes of a Dominatrix</u> as professionally proofed and edited, is now available for purchase at triple w dot lulu dot well you know, company.
Also now available, same place, is this little bit of comedic writing! Second in a series of three.

May 2, 2007

No Playtime post for you all today - the teddybears have been very, very bad. So, no fun for them!
Not that this stopped me from having fun, mind you! *EG*

Bach was precise, Mozart was frivolous, but Beethoven was PASSIONATE esp. in his odd-numbered symphonies. LOVE THE NINTH!
The 2nd of the 7th is a real heartbreaker too!
Just the stuff to crank up the volume on when dancing around the house naked in the early morning!

8

YIM Dialog:
image of Kitten pouncing upon Teddybear A
Wake up!! tee heeeeeee !!
I have my methods.

> lol
> not that waking up to Kitten would spur on time
> work arrival!!

there is that one little detail
hint: to wake up the Kitten - steal all of her blankets and
remove the teddybear(s)

> not a good way to keep Kitten happy!

yes, well, not the objective in this case; here trying to get
Kitten awake

> easier just to place sleeping Kitten paw on hard
> penis...

ssshshhhh no giving away secrets!

FEBRUARY = ATTITUDE
Abstract thoughts. Outgoing. Loves reality and abstract.
Intelligent and clever. Changing personality. Attractive.
Fun to be around with. sexiest out of everyone. A real
speed demon.
Has more than one best friend. Able to cheer anyone up and
make them laugh. Amazing smile. An awesome kisser.
Temperamental. Honest. A very good girlfriend/boyfriend
and loyal. Determined to reach goals. Loves freedom.
Rebellious when restricted. Loves aggressiveness. Too
sensitive and easily hurt. Gets angry really easily but does

not show it. Dislikes unnecessary things. Loves making friends Daring and stubborn.
Ambitious. Realizing dreams and hopes. Sharp.
Loves entertainment and leisure. Romantic on the inside not outside. Superstitious and ludicrous.
Spendthrift. Tries to learn to show emotions.
LOL! Thank you, K and W!

May 3, 2007
It was marvelous meeting you all! I had a very nice time and collected a few kisses. It was fun!!
Especially that bit out in the parking lot!

"It's not until you stagger into moments like this that you realize that your "independence" is a myth. That your best attempts to "control" your world are laughably inadequate. That, for all the effort you put into being "strong," you are more fragile than a Ming vase...."[1]

I have to agree with him. Several of my friends and I, myself, are dealing with just this sort of challenge as we sort through our lives, await events, and make decisions. Wish us good luck!

May 4, 2007
It looks so peaceful on the outside, self-pleasuring
Inside the lurid fantasy plays; rioting in the one last fantasy
The one you haven't done. The only one that still works.
The outward serenity belying the screaming tumult within!

mmmmmm and NO I'm not telling you.

---

[1] *J. Edmunds*

The Metaphysics of Sexuality (excerpt)
"Our moral evaluations of sexual activity are bound to be affected by what we view the nature of the sexual impulse, or of sexual desire, to be in human beings. In this regard there is a deep divide between those philosophers that we might call the metaphysical sexual optimists and those we might call the metaphysical sexual pessimists.

The pessimists in the philosophy of sexuality, such as St. Augustine , Immanuel Kant, and, sometimes, Sigmund Freud , perceive the sexual impulse and acting on it to be something nearly always, if not necessarily, unbefitting the dignity of the human person; they see the essence and the results of the drive to be incompatible with more significant and lofty goals and aspirations of human existence; they fear that the power and demands of the sexual impulse make it a danger to harmonious civilized life; and they find in sexuality a severe threat not only to our proper relations with, and our moral treatment of, other persons, but also equally a threat to our own humanity.

On the other side of the divide are the metaphysical sexual optimists (Plato, in some of his works, sometimes Sigmund Freud, Bertrand Russell, and many contemporary philosophers) who perceive nothing especially obnoxious in the sexual impulse. They view human sexuality as just another and mostly innocuous dimension of our existence as embodied or animal-like creatures; they judge that sexuality, which in some measure has been given to us by evolution, cannot but be conducive to our well-being without detracting from our intellectual propensities; and they praise rather than fear the power of an impulse that can lift us to various high forms of happiness.

The particular sort of metaphysics of sex one believes will influence one's subsequent judgments about the value and role of sexuality in the good or virtuous life and about what sexual activities are morally wrong and which ones are morally permissible."[2]

As you believe, so you shall do.

May 5, 2007
If he's not ripping his clothes off on his way to get with me - I'll find him insufficiently ardent.
Enthusiasm, please!

May 6, 2007
Driving to Pennsylvania Today!

May 7, 2007
These looong rides are so much more fun when there's someone congenial with you! Esp. when being good and obeying the speed limit. Who set these things so low??
Like a delicious teddybear, for example!

After drinking 4 glasses of scotch:
But, there were witnesses so nothing will come of my "ahem" increased interest in the opposite gender. Oh well!
All rev'd up and no one to do!

May 8, 2007
The operations was successful and she's back home now but, had to cancel the cabana boys to wait upon Mom hand and foot while she recuperated lounging in her chaise on the back deck because they kept her another day!

---

[2] http://www.iep.utm.edu/s/sexualit.htm

Apparently she had a stroke while on the table getting her stent put into her carotid. So! She's tired but cheerful today while the doctors compare her various CAT scans.
PLEASE Wish her luck!

May 9, 2007
This week:
Tonight = Opera night!
Thursday = Afternoon Playtime
Friday = Polo and The Firehouse
Sat = off to Alabama
Next Week:
Wed = back home
Thursday = Cat Toy Appreciation Day
Upcoming Events:
Memorial Sunday = Rolling Thunder
June 9th = Special Polo Match Ireland vs. USA
June 10th= Upperville Horse Show (escort needed)
June 20th (more or less) = Stable Tour (escort needed)
July 7th = apg Beach Bash
Anyone have anything else going on they'd like to announce?

"I certainly understand the inclination to feel protective of your woman. Being a guy yourself, you are all too familiar with man's predatory nature. So how do you distinguish between the dogs who are really out for your girl and those whose ill intentions are the product of your distorted imagination?"[3]
Your woman? "protective" - really? Sounds more like he's protecting himself, not her.
Try trusting HER a little bit!

---

[3] *www.askmen.com*

13

May 10, 2007

A group of attractive men willing to adore and serve in exchange for 'experience' not all of which would be sexual. Rather like that commercial where the women were at the spa on their chaise lounges and the first woman says "Here's lunch." and her friend says "And he's brought grapes".

And some wonder why we're called 'cougars'.

"Tosca is an opera in three acts by Giacomo Puccini to an Italian libretto by Luigi Illica and Giuseppe Giacosa, based on Victorien Sardou's drama, La Tosca. The work premiered at the Teatro Costanzi in Rome on January 14, 1900. One of the most dramatic of operas, Tosca is, according to Opera America, the eighth most performed opera in North America."[4]

In spite of the 'romantic' over tones - this is a political opera. Corrupt official, unlawful arrest, torture, betrayal, and underhanded dealings - those are the main themes.

I wanted to smack Tosca all throughout the opera. What a wimp! I mean, really, believing the man she hates and fears while doubting the man she loves? Jeez!

Well, at least she killed the bad guy.

Orchestra good, scenery SUPERB! costumes quite nice except for that pink gown in the beginning.

All in all - a very nice time. This was my first opera too! *checks another item off the list*

Seven willing and very skilled men, gentlemen all, are available in a woman-centric, reverse gb environment. Do you think the women rush to enjoy these men? NO, they

---

[4] *Wikipedia*

don't. In such a site as this too. This is why this is going to be my last sex party. The ladies just aren't "stepping up". Now why is that?

May 11, 2007
Engaging in sexual activities with a mute lover is just not fun. You don't have to say anything intelligible but, please moan, groan, even scream! Perhaps a gasp of pure pleasure? I'll even accept a purr. It isn't that I don't enjoy your quivering flesh - I do, I do! It is just that I enjoy your verbal responsiveness as much as, I hope, you do mine.
Can you do that for me, darlin'?

The Good Soldier
Gunfire in the street
Where we used to meet
Echoes at a beat
And the bass goes "bomb"

Right over my head
Step over the dead
Remember what you said
You know the part about life

Is just a waking dream
Well I know what you mean
But that ain't how it seems right here, right now

How can this be real?
I can barely feel
Anymore

I am trying to see
I am trying to believe
This is not where I should be

I am trying to believe

Blood hardens in the sand
Cold metal in my hand
Hope you understand the way that things are gonna be

There's nowhere left to hide
'Cause God is on our side
I keep telling myself

I am trying to see
I am trying to believe
This is not where I should be
I am trying to believe

by Nine Inch Nails
from the album Year Zero

How it goes. Now I'm off to 'Bama where I'll have to do the staid and sober - RESPONSIBLE - thing. (Only three good things happened this week - Tosca, the testride, and polo.)
If only they had any idea how often I'd love to put my fist through a wall.
Yeah, not my best week.

May 12, 2007
Long, long - beautiful scenery - too many semi's and slow people in the left hand lane - took 9 hrs and 38 minutes - have to change the cds in the cd changer - but best of all other than making it here in one piece = NO TICKETS!!!!! YES!! I can drive on the highway and NOT get tickets!!!

Granddaughter Report:
At first a little shy but she warmed up and we had a great time making odd noises at eachother. She was up way past

16

her bedtime and had a good case of the "pre bed maniacs" going but we got her settled down - eventually.
I warn you, I have pix and I WILL SHOW THEM TO YOU!!

May 13, 2007
Beach Bash YES!!
I will be there and I'm expecting great things and LOTS of FUN!
How many teddybears fit in one king size bed?
Want to help me find out??

May 14, 2007
Everyone join in welcoming Vivian to the world!
Born today circa 1pm and weighing it at 8lbs; length 20.5 inches; with an excellent Apgar of 9.9 !!!
HURRAY!!

I'd like to post one for you HOWEVER the teddybears have been conspicuously absent. One even missed THREE playtime opportunities last week! Can you imagine?!?!
BAD BAD TEDDYBEARS!!!

May 15, 2007
I do hope you all filled up yesterday, as I did. But if you're gonna be stranded somewhere tis ok to get enough to get you where you need to be.
The rest of you - bypass the gasoline/diesel pumps today!

May 16, 2007
1. Tell me WHY must people be in the left hand lane in FRONT of ME and doing the speed limit?
2. Why is it always faster going than returning?
3. Best ads seen:

a. HEAD DOWN. LEFT ARM STRAIGHT. (NO NOT NOW) - for a golf center
and
b. picture of fork with the two center tines folded down - for the Hard Rock Cafe
and now -
NUNC EST BIBENDUM

May 17, 2007
One WILD Cat Toy Appreciation Day! I'll tell you about it later.
I am busy!!

May 18, 2007
"5 Female Sex Secrets
There are many things that men don't know about women's wants in the bedroom. It's not because men don't care, it's just because the subject either hasn't come up or she's too shy to offer you this information. While every woman is different, there are some things all women can generally agree on when it comes to sex.

Because couples who communicate their needs and desires have far better sex more often, you should encourage her to talk about the things she wants. In the meantime, to get you started, we're giving you five feel-good secrets she's been hiding.

secret 1:She likes period sex
Generally, this is true, but there are rules. It can tend to get very wet very quickly; throwing a sausage down Niagara Falls may be a more appropriate description. And make sure you are both showered and clean. The other problem you may face is temporary vaginal dryness. If she uses

tampons, expect a little uncomfortable friction after she removes it to have sex, and prepare by having some lube handy. She will warm up pretty quickly, but dry sex is painful and unpleasant, so don't blow your future chances by being too forthright in the entering department. The bonus of period sex is she is likely to be quite randy -- hormones make this a positive (but obstacle-laden) time for nookie. Don't try to go down on her unless you have a death wish or share morbid vampire fantasies because she will knock you out of the way faster than you can say "What's that taste?"

secret 2: She doesn't like never-ending sex
This is faking-it territory. Don't believe the hype: Being the man means being a man and knowing when to just sit back and relax and enjoy the fruits of your labor. A happy girl on your hands is great, so don't blow your own rep by trying to prove yourself. Yes, love machines exist, but aren't they wired to just keep on pounding away? Aren't they made of plastic and rubber? Women want a lover, not a love machine. Women adore orgasms as much as the next man, but one is good -- just make it count. Two is a bonus (but the bonus need not include strenuous and lengthy attempts to achieve) and after that, well that all depends on the situation. Know when to relax into her arms and enjoy the smell of her hair. No doubt, if she is still up for it she will -- in no uncertain terms -- let you know.

secret 3:She thinks fingers can be unpleasant
When using your digits to pleasure your woman, just remember that the entrance to the vagina has a large number of nerve endings compared to deeper inside the vagina -- use this knowledge to your advantage. The point is to give her pleasure, so keep to the pleasure zones: the outside entrance to the vagina, just inside the vagina and

the G-spot. When manually stimulating her start off with one finger, and after tickling the outside entrance, gently and wetly enter her body. Start stroking in a come-hither motion on the front wall of her vagina. Here you will find her G-spot. Be gentle; if she wants you to go deeper or harder she will show you by pushing herself onto you. It can get a little uncomfortable for her to have half a hand jamming and slamming away, so always ask before putting another finger in and avoid trying to reach her cervix. Clean, trimmed fingernails are lovely; mucky claws and paws need not apply.

secret 4: She likes trying new things
There are many things she has always wanted to try, but may never have felt comfortable enough to ask for or to initiate. Things she may be afraid of include: anal sex, anal fingering (you or her), bondage, fisting, outdoor sex, and role playing. None of these are as hard core as you both might think; ordinary people do them all the time with very nice results. A fun and easy way to find out what new things she wants to try out is to swap a sexual to-do list with her. Each of you writes a list of things you would like to try together, then swap it and get busy.

secret 5: She's horny in the morning
Guys and morning wood have been waking sleeping women since the dawn of time. Generally, it can be safely ignored by the not-so-keen woman by pretending to be asleep. If you want to try a different tack, try sliding your moist erection gently between her thighs, just brushing her vaginal lips. Take a little bit of time, and sure enough, just like a beautiful flower, she will (hopefully) open up and let you in because you are unobtrusively enticing her. The trick to morning sex is getting her from sound asleep to highly aroused before 8 a.m. Oral sex also works very well,

but the thigh trick is less effort; do what works best for you. A tip is to moisten your penis before doing anything with it. Saliva or lube works; it takes the hard work out of it for you and replaces that "I just woke up and you're mauling me" feeling with "Oh, that feels nice." Not everyone is a morning-sex fan, so if your girl isn't too keen on an early morning rise and shine, there are some easy steps you can take to encourage her without making a scene.

sexy secrets
There are many other things that women secretly like or dislike, but every woman is different and so are her secret loves and hates. Another way to find out these secrets is to play games. There are board games that encourage some out of the ordinary interaction; this is great for learning how to communicate better with your partner, and for finding out things you would never have thought to ask. Don't forget: The best sex is always had by partners who can honestly discuss what they want."[5]

As for me I do not have periods; never-ending sex depends upon his skill level; fingers hurt only if dry or inept; I not only will try but have tried most things; I hate morning sex - am not alive let alone awake before 9am.
TALK with your partner!

Notes of a Dominatrix is now 'out' and available for purchase online. You have the choice of a dust-jacketed hardbound book, a softcover book, and via download.
The next book that will be openly available will be an UNEXPURGATED biography.
BTW anyone want to act as editor for THAT one?

---

[5] www.askmen.com

EG Yeah, it's THAT hot!!

Party Report:
Oh my, yes! Very sensual and caressive. I got to play with some of the Toys with some of the toys from my brown leather backpack. Just a small taste of kink and of a fantasy. It is difficult to concentrate when someone's doing you while you're doing another but we managed quite well.
Semper Felines!

May 19, 2007
The Contents of my Playbag
collar - two, different sizes
leash - three
large multi-purpose strap - one
cuffs, padded - two pairs
leather hole punch - one, in case some size adjustments are needed
body lotion - two, different kinds
body oil - one
lubricant - one
body spray - perfume
matches
Nicorette
condoms
comb and hair brush
wipes
blindfold - one
sundry makeup items for running repairs if needed
mink tail - one
leather glove - one
nylon stocking - one
vibrating anal probe - one, silver
extra batteries
petroleum jelly

nipple clamps, adjustable - one set with chain

and other items as desired
Now you know!

May 20, 2007

Just because the needle on the speedometer tends to creep up on my way to naked frolicking - and heaven help anyone in front of my truck - I do not think it makes me a 'sex addict'.
I like men. I enjoy sex. I have a healthy libido.

The flip side is, if you think I'm "too much" what does having that opinion say about you?
(a very evil grin inserted here) No, I am not going to say them but I do have some ideas.

And here men are always complaining they don't get enough sex!
HAH!

"Hello sensuous and sexy woman,
I saw you on cam you're very special so sexy. My dick went very hard for you, was so excited wow, wow.
I cum was so good. So bad we can't exchange and see your nice figure. You seemed, like me, have an appetite for exploration that could not be sated. Like me you drop inhibitions with respect. The bedroom and cybersex is the adult's playground its only rule is endless invention. Would like to warm you with my tongue or work my fingers. Sex lives beg to be in state of constant reinvention.
Would like chat cam2cam with you. Here is my personal msn(messenger)

Communicate your preferences and desires like never before. How far are you willing to go for pleasure, with respect?"

Since I have NEVER been on any cams ever, this email was obviously NOT meant for me - but he sent it anyway. If he had read my profile, perhaps he would have known better then to send me something so inept?

and as the runner-up we have this one:

"can you stay up at least 3 days nonstop yes or no if not ok"

and why would I want to? Can you, a 53 yr old man, keep it up for at least 3 days non-stop; yes or no?
Your turn! What dumb emails have you gotten recently?

May 21, 2007

Handling Confrontation:
We all know anger and distress. What most do not know is how to effectively and positively deal with it Whether it is yours towards another or another's toward you.

First is the question of legitimacy. Is the anger/distress based upon a legitimate complaint?
While the true issue may lie beneath the verbiage - there is a reason for the anger and distress. Know what it is.

Second is the question of "brakes". The choice of language used must be carefully judged. It is usually best to say less and limit your statements to "I feel....because....and I'd like you to...". If you are on the receiving end, asking why they feel that way is a good beginning. There may be additional factors involved that do not pertain to you that are fueling the fire.

There does come a time when the one receiving has to say something along the lines of "You cannot ask me to go to a wedding with you one minute and then dump me the next." addressing the behavior, not the person, in a reverse confrontation.

Delaying confrontation because you, alone, do not want to deal with it now, only escalates the issue. Silence is never good. The only reason to delay a confrontation is to give both parties a chance to step back from the fray giving each side the chance to review their position. Neither party should use violence.

Finally, consider the desired outcome. Assigning blame is a waste of time. What do the sides want? Can both outcomes be achieved? What would be required? Then do it. If both desired outcomes cannot be attained for some reason, what outcome would give each side most of what they both want? Look for the "win-win" solution.

It is in there somewhere.

Nessun Dorma
sung by Lucian Pavarotti

The Prince:
No one sleeps, no one sleeps...
Even you, o Princess,
In your cold room,
Watch the stars,
That tremble with love
And with hope.

But my secret is hidden within me;
My name no one shall know, no, no,
On your mouth I will speak it*
When the light shines,
And my kiss will dissolve the silence
That makes you mine.
Chorus:
No one will know his name
And we must, alas, die.
The Prince:
Vanish, o night!
Set**, stars!
At daybreak, I shall conquer!

Quite possibly the most Romantic aria ever!

What Word Truly Describes You.....
What Means The Most To You......
What Couldn't Ya Live Without.....
What Makes Ya Happy....
What Makes It All Worth While...

May 22, 2007

No Stress Here!
 received a lovely letter from the IRS, long may they wave, recalculating my 2006 return - and NOT in my favor. Oh joy!

There's another professional exam looming on the horizon and I have not studied for it.

I got tapped for jury duty. Ridiculously low compensation, spending time with people I didn't select, hearing things I'd rather not.

Slow days at work and half-hearted men who you just want to kick-start. *EG* Nice concept but I do not play that way.

Further delays in a few areas in a continuing saga of "yes, but not yet". While it costs me money in the form of missed opportunities and time-value while they wait.

Another pair of ventures on hold until the "issues" are resolved. More about those later.

Certain persons taking umbrage for things not meant for them. Yes, you do not have my respect because you haven't done a damn thing to earn it. Suck it up and go away.

Besides all of that, the SRM is being a huge PITA!

That's what is on my list. What's on yours?

UP FOR AUCTION!
One well-worn husband, 6 ft 4 in, 245 lbs, 52 yrs, has his hair and teeth, car guy, excellent around the house, handyman, also cooks and likes cats. Good sire, previous offspring available to view. Decent in bed. Well-paid, comes with truck, healthcare for life, two Harleys and one partially rebuilt 1969 Jeep CJ 7 with the big 8 cylinder engine. Bad back, bad knees, snores, unsocial, miserly, prone to depression and being a PITA. He prefers long-legged brunettes but the highest bidder gets him (regardless of her appearance) and half his assets.
This week - I'm kidding! But next week...........................

May 23, 2007

Some Smartypants...He told me he was waiting until I came up for auction. This got me to wondering what my auction catalog entry would say. So how about it?

Tell me what you would write to get me to "sell".

Keep in mind that full disclosure of all major flaws is required.

Flaws include:
unfortunate driving habits
unfortunate spending habits
too fond of the written word
non-reproductive
hates housework
non-monogamous
Machiavellian

Comes with:
$2000 per month
free healthcare for life
far too many books
1974 1/2 MGB Roadster
1998 Ford Expedition
and half of all the assets

Grab hold of your courage and let's see what you can do!

contest ends June 1st
winner will be announced herein

Contestant 1 sent in this entry:

Available to the highest bidder subject to her personal approval:

Sleek, sophisticated, statuesque, sexy, enlightened, dynamic, polyamorous with a fondness for the written word, both her own and the classics; this independent lady of means graces her lucky partner with sensual expertise rivaled by no one. Preferring the social arts rather than domestic, you are more likely to find her driving her antique MGB in search of a great Scotch, or cruising to the polo grounds in her Expedition rather than slaving over a vacuum cleaner. Her domestic preferences favor the epicurean and garden arts and balance her natural tendency to race to the next event. There is no fear of offspring; and hers are grown and out of the house. She knows her own mind, secure in herself, and seeks others who thrive in her presence. Not for the faint of heart or frugal of purse; this dynamic lioness will challenge her mate intellectually and sexually, but the journey is well worth the trip. Photos and statistics are available to only the serious bidder!

Contestant 2 sent in this entry:

SERIOUS BIDDERS ONLY PLEASE:

Seeking motivated buyer for a Classic 1955 Hybrid (cross-over sports/utility). Well used, but in purrfect condition and professionally maintained so all you DIYers need not respond. The bumper-to-bumper extended warranty includes all major components as well as scheduled maintenance items. This sleek, high demand model offers the best in both drivability and comfort. Loaded with all power, Bose sound (for Puccini or Led Zeppelin), GPS, Corinthian leather abounds throughout to wrap you in buttery comfort and for "restraint" when needed. Equally adept for an evening at the Kennedy Center or an afternoon of being driven hard on "twisted" country roads. This is the last of its kind off a now closed assembly line. The well above Blue Book asking price includes life-time asset protection (hers not yours). Pet friendly (especially felines-- meeoww).

May 24, 2007

I cleaned my office and will now attempt to clean my desk! Pay few bills maybe. File some papers maybe. I have to call Frank later on, get in some groceries and buy a pair of yellow high-heeled sandals but for now, I'm here doing this. *EG*
I hate 'housework'!
What's on your agenda for today? Anyone having fun?

May 25, 2007

One has to learn to enjoy the simple art of breathing, of the blood rushing through, and the nerves firing down their pathways. Life i.e. never meaningless nor hopeless. Life is infinitely mutable.
"This is glorious in our eyes!" to quote Elizabeth I.
Breathe deeply and tell me, how are you today, REALLY?

I constrict better than a boa, cum like Noah's Flood, and sound like a symphony to his ears - not to mention the biting and clawing if he likes that sort of thing. Totally unbridled!!
P.S. you'll also need a 5 point harness to stay on.

"Here, where the sea shines
and the wind howls,
on the old terrace
beside the gulf of Sorrento,
a man embraces a girl

after the tears,
then clears his throat
and continues the song:
I love you very much
very, very much, you know;
it is a chain by now
that heats the blood inside the veins,
you know...

He saw the lights out on the sea,
thought of the nights there in America,
but they were only the fishermen's lamps
and the white wash astern.
He felt the pain in the music
and stood up from the piano,
but when he saw the moon
emerging from a cloud,
death also seemed sweeter to him.
He looked the girl in the eyes,
those eyes as green as the sea.
Then suddenly a tear fell
and he believed he was drowning.

I love you very much,
very, very much, you know;
it is a chain by now
that heats the blood inside the veins,
you know...

The power of opera,
where every drama is a hoax;
with a little make-up and with mime
you can become someone else.
But two eyes that look at you,
so close and real,

make you forget the words,
confuse your thoughts,
so everything becomes small,
also the nights there in America.
You turn and see your life
through the white wash astern.
But, yes, it is life that ends
and he did not think much about it,
on the contrary, he already felt happy
and continued his song:

I love you very much,
very, very much, you know;
it is a chain by now
that heats the blood inside the veins,
you know..."

"Caruso"
sung by Luciano Pavarotti
(translated from the original Italian)
So good it makes you forget you're all dressed up with
nowhere to go.

May 26, 2007
Further discussions are NOT taking place but at least he's
off the couch and NOT watching television. He's mowing
the lawn. Why? Because according to him, I do not do it
correctly. This is also why I do not wash cars. You will also
recall that I'm not any good at axe-swinging either. I'm
entirely ineffective with an axe. (That should make some
men sleep more soundly.)
However, if he continues leaving rooms when I enter
them.....

May 27, 2007

Rolling Thunder Report

We left at 10am; only one hour late so not too bad. We cruised on up 95 and hooked up with the 'two by two' pack on the HOVs around Springfield. But they all scooted past the Pentagon (why?) and we roamed around DC before making our solitary way back to the Pentagon. (Who organized this mess?) We arrived last, parked, got a bite to eat and roamed about looking for my brother, my sister-in-law and their friends. (Some people do not answer their cell phones.) We found them and were enjoying ourselves. Then I went back to the bike to get a soda and found that, yes, they had begun moving off - taking us late people first! So I was standing all alone by the bike frantically trying to get someone to answer their cell phone and send my SRM back to me. (The last shall be first.) He showed up and we hopped on and joined the parade (hatless) and, yes, I showboated on the Memorial Bridge standing up on my footboards and waving both arms. (You should have been there, baby!) Slapped a few palms, waved a lot, did fists and V's, smiled - had a good time! Took a break just past the WW2 Memorial and then led some visiting bikers back to 95 south. A good time was had by all - including the sunburnt SRM. The bike ran very well and it wasn't raining!

All of those lovely, lovely motorcycles! It is quite a sight! I hope you were there and enjoyed yourselves!

May 28, 2007

I am running one contest - Some Smartypants........ and one poll - The Sex Addict Poll in this blog.

Both end June 1st - so, please, get your vote and your entries in ASAP!

Thank you!

I am working on several biographies:

thus far up to my mother's marriage
and
to my first day in kindergarten - after which I am told, I informed my mother "that was done and I'm now ready to go to college".
Nothing if not precocious!

I am also continuing work on the following:
Designs & Scribbles
Aunt Agatha Answers
Escape Velocity
The Last Chat
and a family calendar for 2008

Yes, I do find the time to sleep.
The teddybear hunt has been put on hold for the moment as the teddybears currently retained sort themselves out. Ah Me!
And business has been s-l-o-w. Egad!
What have you been up to, lately?

May 29, 2007
Fakes: those who are not what they pretend to be.
This covers the full gamut; from those males pretending to be couples, those males pretending to be females, women who pretend they want to, fake or old pix; all of that and all the way to those who stand you up.

There seems to be several reasons why some people do this:

1. CHILDISH - they have not yet grown up and still delight in "faking out" others.

2. PATHOLOGICAL - they simply can NOT be truthful.

3. COWARDNESS - they want to be here but are afraid of being "found out" (which may be partially legit but jeez!)

4. CRIPPLES - emotional or psychological who are not sure about what they want/need but are sure they want/need something.

5. THE USERS - the predators, the hookers, the stalkers, et al. Those whose motives are not good ones.

Most of us just fulminate and move on - but really, is that the best we can do? Can we not report such people to our host? Our host is a private company, I remind you, who are offering us a service. Some of us pay for more service than others it is true but we all should be able to expect some level of "quality control" if nothing else.
Suggestions, please!

OLDER MEN
More skills, more empathy, more life experience both good and bad, more baggage, more money, more history, more issues: just more of everything! There's a lot 'more' for a woman to have fun with when she gets with an older man. There's just more to explore. And I even like the 'grumpiness'. What can I say! LOL
There's usually also a lot "less", as in a lot less vanity, a lot less 'groundless self-satisfaction', and a lot less in the way of expectations. It seems that once a man's been run over by life a few times, he actually begins to think a bit.
Yes, some younger guys may have their attractions - but give me an older man who "gets it" without me having to spell it out in words of one syllable and in all caps!
Thank you!

May 30, 2007

"Your material has unbelievable results. After reading your book and newsletters, I am finding myself in a dilemma of needing to let some of the women down in order to make room for others.

The problem is that they keep wanting to fill my schedule and I haven't learned how to let these women know that like yesterday's newspaper, I have read and prefer to read current events as opposed to rereading the same newspaper over and over. I guess I am being a Wussy in this regard because I just do not know how to say "See ya."

"Yesterday's news" huh? Gee thanx, I love you too.

This is a penis-centered attitude. When you get a guy like this, you have to drop them after calmly pointing out that that penis of his, of which he is so very proud, can easily be replaced with bigger, firmer, with vibration, color, twirling bits and that it will last as long as the supply of batteries holds out. And, as an added bonus, she then doesn't have to put up with any masculine BS.

The "fuck 'em and forget 'em" approach leaves a male completely unprepared for a decent relationship with women. He learns nothing and this attitude is a trap for him I do not recommend this attitude.

Summer drinks should be simple and refreshing because who wants to work all that hard in this heat? Make by the pitcher-full.

You need:

tequila, vodka, rum, and Pimm's No. 1

Keep them plain and light so they mix well.

Mixers needed:

Coca-Cola (reg & diet), Full Throttle, Collin's mixer, ginger ale, vermouth, margarita mix.

For those who do not know, you can now make:
Rum n Cokes, vodka martinis, margaritas, vodka collinses, and if you mix the Pimm's and the ginger ale over ice you have a light summer drink for the whisky and scotch drinkers. Add the vodka to the Full Throttle, pour over ice and he'll have the energy for the next round *W*
Enjoy!!

"Slade may have never truly caught on with American audiences (often narrow-mindedly deemed "too British-sounding"), but the group became a sensation in their homeland with their anthemic brand of glam rock in the early '70s, as they scored a staggering 11 Top Five hits in a four-year span from 1971 to 1974 (five of which topped the charts). Comprised of singer/guitarist Noddy Holder (born Neville Holder, June 15, 1946 in Walsall, West Midlands, England), guitarist Dave Hill (born April 4, 1946, in Fleet Castle, Devon, England), bassist Jimmy Lea (born June 14, 1949, Wolverhampton, West Midlands, England), and drummer Don Powell (born September 10, 1946, Bilston, West Midlands, England), the group originally formed in the spring of 1966 under the name the In-Be-Tweens, playing out regularly with a mixture of soul and rock tracks. Several attempts at cracking the U.S. market came up empty (with track listings between their U.K. and U.S. full-lengths differing), although such albums as Slade Alive! and Slayed? are considered to be some of the finest albums of the glam era.
Despite the change in musical climate, Slade stuck to their guns and kept touring and releasing albums, as the title to their 1977 album, Whatever Happened to Slade?, proved that the group's humor remained intact despite their fall from the top of the charts. A large, dedicated following still supported the group as they offered a performance at the 1980 Reading Festival that was considered one of the day's

best, resulting in sudden renewed interest in the group back home and Slade scored their first true hit singles in six years with 1981's "We'll Bring the House Down" and "Lock up Your Daughters."

Slade received a boost stateside around this time as well, courtesy of the U.S. pop-metal outfit Quiet Riot, who made a smash hit out of "Cum on Feel the Noize" in 1983 that resulted in a strong chart showing for Slade's 1984 release Keep Your Hands Off My Power Supply (issued as The Amazing Kamikaze Syndrome in the U.K. a year earlier). Slade then enjoyed a pair of U.S. MTV/radio hits, "Run Runaway" and "My Oh My." Holder and Lea also tried their hand at producing another artist around this time as well, as they manned the boards for Girlschool's 1983 release Play Dirty. Despite another all-new studio release, Rogues Gallery, and Quiet Riot covering another classic Slade tune ("Mama Weer All Crazee Now"), Slade was unable to retain their newfound American audience or rekindled British following and they eventually faded from sight once more, this time without a comeback waiting around the corner."

~ Greg Prato

Best tunes:
"Mama Weer All Crazee Now,"
"Cum on Feel the Noize,"

"Sly & the Family Stone harnessed all of the disparate musical and social trends of the late '60s, creating a wild, brilliant fusion of soul, rock, R&B, psychedelia, and funk that broke boundaries down without a second thought. Led by Sly Stone, the Family Stone was comprised of men and women, and blacks and whites, making the band the first fully integrated group in rock's history. That integration shone through the music, as well as the group's message.

Before Stone, very few soul and R&B groups delved into political and social commentary; after him, it became a tradition in soul, funk, and hip-hop. And, along with James Brown, Stone brought hard funk into the mainstream. The Family Stone's arrangements were ingenious, filled with unexpected group vocals, syncopated rhythms, punchy horns, and pop melodies. Their music was joyous, but as the '60s ended, so did the good times. Stone became disillusioned with the ideals he had been preaching in his music, becoming addicted to a variety of drugs in the process. His music gradually grew slower and darker, culminating in 1971's There's a Riot Going On, which set the pace for '70s funk with its elastic bass, slurred vocals, and militant Black Power stance. Stone was able to turn out one more modern funk classic, 1973's Fresh, before slowly succumbing to his addictions, which gradually sapped him of his once prodigious talents. Nevertheless, his music continued to provide the basic template for urban soul, funk, and even hip-hop well into the '90s." ~ Stephen Thomas Erlewine

Best tunes:
"Family Affair,"
"Hot Fun in the Summertime"
"Everybody Is a Star"
"Everyday People,"
"Stand,"
"Thank You (Falettinme Be Mice Elf Agin)"

May 31, 2007
This is it! Your final opportunity to enter the contest Some Smartypants........ and to vote in the poll The Sex Addict Poll. All of writers and/or all of you with any libido at all should get in on these!

At midnight TONIGHT the tabulating and awarding of prizes will begin!
Good Luck!

JUNE
2007

Jun 1, 2007
We have a Contest winner!

Congrats to: G

His winning entry:

"Available to the highest bidder subject to her personal approval:
Sleek, sophisticated, statuesque, sexy, enlightened, dynamic, polyamorous with a fondness for the written word, both her own and the classics; this independent lady of means graces her lucky partner with sensual expertise rivaled by no one. Preferring the social arts rather than domestic, you are more likely to find her driving her antique MGB in search of a great Scotch, or cruising to the polo grounds in her Expedition rather than slaving over a vacuum cleaner. Her domestic preferences favor the epicurean and garden arts and balance her natural tendency to race to the next event. There is no fear of offspring; and hers are grown and out of the house. She knows her own mind, secure in herself, and seeks others who thrive in her presence. Not for the faint of heart or frugal of purse; this dynamic lioness will challenge her mate intellectually and sexually, but the journey is well worth the trip. Photos and statistics are available to only the serious bidder!"

Poll Results

40 respondents
Admitted Sex Addicts = 24 or 60%
Conditional Sex Addicts = 9 or 22.5%
There was one person who is a sex addict but wishes they weren't

There was also one person who apparently has never had sex and does not know what it is.
Two people want to be sex addicts.
Three people are not sex addicts and are happy about that.

Now you know! 82.5% of people here are to some extent addicted to sex! HURRAY!

My Blog Stats
Yes, well, I do like to know. It is a form of feedback.

Total number of Watchers = 306
Total posts = 700
Total comments = 3083
Average comments per post = 4.40
Average views per post = 562
Time to reach average post = 1 week

This is nothing compared to my beloved Blog Divas, but, hey, I am happy!
Thank you all for your support!
I now return you to you regularly scheduled blog.

THE MEN I SEEK
Those whom the gods love....who also bleed freely, heal quickly, and need not answer for marks left upon them.
Currently seeking a LTfwbR with a suitable man who meets the criteria below.
Males must be between 45 and 55 years of age, eager, 6ft tall, furry, witty, able to withstand my ardor, kneeling, sincere, nearby, and possess more than half a brain.
Waivers to any of the above are at my discretion.
Please do not beg.
"Bad boys" need not apply.
No drug users, thank you.

(Founding member of The Wicked Woman Group)

Jun 2, 2007

Men use language differently than woman do. This is not news. Most men are more than well aware that women seem to speak another language altogether especially when the ladies get rolling with their meta-messages and nuances.

However, I do not mean to insult you guys when I say things like "I always listen when men say that." If you had said it, I would have listened to you. But this guy over there said it, so I listened to him. I did NOT mean to imply that you were not a man.

TRUST ME - if I HAD meant to insult you - you would be in no doubt. My insults tend to be very, very clear even if the word scrophulous is used.

Now, it being Saturday - I am off to make my bed (but not to lie in it just yet) and do some shopping.

Busy! Busy!

Jun 3, 2007

Spent the day being lazy, reading the newspaper, <u>hanging out with the guys here</u>, and just generally fluffing around the house wishing the sun would come out.

Kittens don't like cold rain.

What did you do all day?

DANGER, DANGER...

My beloved feline, now aged 15 years, is NOT doing very well and may require euthanasia.

You may experience some irrationality and irritability from me. I dislike losing those I care about.

Oh DAMN.
I need a hug again.

Spent the late afternoon in your arms. Ah! So very, very
good to be with you. Furry, skilled, and with such an
imagination when it comes to sexual adventures. Wow,
what a trip! Wow, what a man! More nirvana sex and then
you went one better! By shower time I had no bones left
and was purrrrrrrring all over the place wearing a very silly
grin!
Thank you!
I just love giving away the contest prizes!

Jun 5, 2007
..got an earful of my flaws and mis-steps from the SRM.
Stress level right back up to where it had been. A little
support would be nice, fella! It isn't like I'm NOT putting
forth the effort! Please notice that I am not retaliating in
kind by pointing out his errors to him.
But I'm telling you: STRANGULATION is looking REAL
good right about now!
More Scotch?

The deed was done. My feline has gone to her reward -and
this just SUCKS!!

Jun 6, 2007
Today would be a good day to just lie in the sun naked,
drink, smoke some cigarettes, and ponder a few
ponderables with the occasional dip into the hot tub for that
aaah! factor.
ALAS!
I'm only half-way though cleaning off my desk and I have a
phone call to make - which I am dreading. I am also
awaiting phone calls.

HOWEVER
There is my lunch appt., and the M&G in Richmond this
evening to look forward to and to enjoy.
Will you be there?

In addition to the clitoris, and the G-Spot (fanning self
here), there is also a third spot no one should miss in their
rounds of pleasure aka sexual escapades. It has no name
and you will not find it listed in the brochure or on a map
but it is in the area of the posterior fornix. This is one
where you have to learn by doing. A bit of "hands-on-
training" as it were. Find the cervix (gently!) and then go
down below it and waaaay in the back. It helps if she's
nicely loosened up from the first 15 orgasms - see what you
can do about that. Then press downward (with her on her
back) and caress back and forth (in and out if using a
penis/dildo to stimulate). You'll have to experiment to find
exactly the right 'touch' to use as it will vary between
women.
Works for me!*EG*

Jun 7, 2007
Some, mostly women, people on here and similar sites have
some sort of issue with moving on. "No dating others I
might know or have as friends until 30 days, 4hours,
2minutes, and 16 seconds after we have broken up", for
example.
Once you have parted, he/she is a free-agent and can do as
she/he pleases. Get over it.
This praising someone to the skies and then saying "but
you can't have him/her" is not because you "wuv" him/her
or that you "cannot bear to see her/him with anyone else"
(stop whining), it is your pride that cannot take it. Of
course, they could just be doing it from malice. The "I'll

46

make sure no one touches her/him ever again" thing. Poor, baby! Vengeful little beast, aren't you?

All of which only debases you and doesn't harm the recipient.

If you are being subjected to this sort of thing, call them on it! Right then, right there and do not pull your punches. There is no need to yell but, be forthright and honest. If they are doing this publicly, then reprimand them publicly. No one should have to stand for this kind of stupidity.

If you witness this behavior, discredit it. Understand that it is his/her pride, vindictiveness, and jealousy that is speaking. Anything she/he may say is most likely false.

If you are doing this - stop. Realize that you are not doing yourself any favors by behaving this way. Just stop. Harming others or seeking to harm others, does not help yourself.

Jun 8, 2007

The Irish Georgian Society is Ireland's Architectural Heritage Society.

The Irish Georgian Society was founded in 1958 by the Hon. Desmond Guinness and his late wife, Maria, for the protection of buildings of architectural merit in Ireland. The Society aims to encourage an interest in and to promote the conservation of distinguished examples of architecture and the allied arts of all periods in Ireland. These aims are achieved by education and grants, planning participation, membership and fundraising.

Jun 9, 2007

Ambassador and Mrs. Fahey were the kindest of hosts. They served Bushmill's, canapés, and honeyed, very 'Irish' humor while we all mingled and said hello. You would not have recognized me in my "twin-set and pearls" guise. I love that cadence the Irish have to their speech! The Knight of Glin presented his new book on Irish Furniture to the Ambassador. The embassy itself is absolutely a gem. Beautiful architecture with a small but choice garden. The library is particularly noteworthy.

Was an arena practice session out at Chetwood Farms. We were roughing it as they hadn't scrubbed the viewing area and no chairs had been set out yet. We drank Pimm's & gingers and nibbled lots of light picnic fare. Hazel was particularly interesting out there in the arena. She had no backhand. Nevertheless, she scored a good number of the goals. The chant was raised - "Hazel! Hazel!".

Hot, sweating; nevermind, you are delicious! Very desirable! Nice that I got to be on top, getting you all so very wet!

all of this talk about polo and embassies has given SOME people the idea that I'd be "slumming", or would have trouble with it if I attended their parties.
You don't know me very well.
As long as the scene does not resemble the movie "Deliverance" or involve drugs - I should be fine.
Lagavulin and lots of Diet Coca-Cola also helps. Good music, friendly people - no problems!
If you REALLY wanted to ensure that I have a good time - just invite a group of comely and willing teddybears!

Jun 10, 2007
Wherever did you get the idea that polo was "la ti da"??
Most common injuries are broken bones (shoulder, arm, wrist, collar and neck) and that's to the riders. To play polo well, you have to aggressive - that's AGGRESSIVE, fast,

48

sly, and hard-hitting. And you cannot fall off the horse who has to be just as aggressive as the rider.

"The horses are loitering on the field and with intent - they brought their sapiens with them."

Unlike croquet mallets, polo mallets are flexible. If you have ever been hit by one- well, there's another bone cracked or broken.
This is not a game for the faint-of-heart.
If you want to stay safe - go play rugby.

On to The Polo Report

Ireland versus the USA
Ireland won in the final chukkar 5 to 4 after a vigorous slugfest all over the field. While there were moments of finesse it all came down to who had the fastest horse, the strongest arm, and the best hand-eye coordination. The teams were well matched and consisted only of amateur players this time.

I and my escorting teddybear, tailgated - and were photographed because of our splendid turnout - nibbled fried chicken, supped on pears and drank chardonnay. This time we really did tailgate as I had driven the Ford F150, complete with every bell and whistle possible, to the game. The sun shone and it was hot but a light breeze made it very pleasant.
I hope your Saturday was just as fun!

Jun 11, 2007
Sexual Civility Survey
What is your number 1 sexual pet peeve?

Please abide by the following rules:
1. one peeve per man
2. it must be a manners issue
3. it must be something you have actually experienced - no hypotheticals

Results will be codified June 20th.

How to deal with feminine irrational irritability:
Just go over, and give her a big bear hug and do not say anything at all. But do not let her go. Just hold on to her firmly and she'll cry on your shoulder and all will be well. Just remember - shut-up. When she stops crying then you let her go and very quietly say "I'm sorry, darling." Then shut up some more.
Got that? *EG*

Jun 12, 2007
LONDON - A father who ordered his daughter brutally slain for falling in love with the wrong man in a so-called "honor killing" was found guilty of murder on Monday.

Banaz Mahmod, 20, was strangled with a boot lace, stuffed into a suitcase and buried in a back garden.

Her death is the latest in an increasing trend of such killings in Britain, home to some 1.8 million Muslims. More than 100 homicides are under investigation as potential "honor killings."

Mahmod Mahmod, 52, and his brother Ari Mahmod, 51, planned the killing during a family meeting, prosecutors told the court. Two others have pleaded guilty in the case. Two more suspects have fled the country. Sentencing is expected later this month.

The men accused the young woman of shaming her family by ending an abusive arranged marriage, becoming too Westernized and falling in love with a man who didn't come from their Iraqi village. The Kurdish family came to Britain in 1998 when Banaz Mahmod was 11.

She was my present, my future, my hope," said Rahmat Suleimani, 29, Banaz Mahmod's boyfriend.

During the three-month trial, prosecutors said Mahmod's father beat his daughter for using hairspray and adopting other Western ways. Her uncle once told her she would have been "turned to ashes" if she were his daughter and had shamed the family by becoming involved with the Iranian Kurd, her sister 22-year-old Bekhal Mahmod testified.

Banaz Mahmod ran away from home when she was a teenager but returned when her father sent her an audio tape in which he warned he would kill her sisters, her mother and himself if she did not come home, her sister said.

She was later hospitalized after her brother attacked her, the sister told the court. The brother said he had been paid by their father to finish her off but in the end was unable to do it, said the sister, who testified in a full black burqa. She said she still feared for her own life.

The years of Banaz Mahmod's abuse were compounded by police officers who repeatedly dismissed her cries for help.

She first went to police in December 2005, saying she suspected her uncle was trying to kill her and her boyfriend. She sent police a letter naming the men who she thought would later kill her.

On New Year's Eve, she was lured by her father to her grandmother's home, where she suspected he planned to attack her after he forced her to gulp down brandy and approached her while wearing gloves. She escaped by breaking a window and was treated at a hospital.

Police dismissed her suspicions, and one officer, who is under investigation, considered charging her with damages for breaking her grandmother's window.

Laying in her hospital bed after the escape, Mahmod recorded a dramatic video message saying she was "really scared."

The videotape, taken by her boyfriend at the hospital, was shown to the jury during the trial.

After she was released from the hospital, she returned home and tried to convince her family she had stopped seeing her boyfriend.

But friends told the family they spotted the couple together on Jan. 22, 2006.

Soon after, a group of men allegedly approached her boyfriend and tried to lure him into a car but he refused. It was that event that prompted Banaz Mahmod to go to police again. This time officers tried to persuade her to stay in a safe house. She refused, believing that her mother would protect her.

But her mother and father left her alone in the house the next day. Her boyfriend alerted police after time passed in which she failed to send him text messages.

Her body wasn't discovered until three months later after police tracked phone records.

Britain has seen more than 25 women killed by their Muslim relatives in the past decade for offenses they believed brought shame on the family. More than 100 other homicides are under investigation as potential honor killings.

Some Muslim communities in Britain practice Sharia, or strict Islamic law.

"We're seeing an increase around the world, due in part to the rise in Islamic fundamentalism," said Diana Nammi with the London-based Iranian and Kurdish Women's Rights Organization.

There is nothing more shameful than the wanton abuse and murder of your own child.

If you or someone you know is being treated this way -
GET OUT OF THERE!
Damn such persons to HELL!

Government Sex
"I must return to optimize, utilize, facilitate, and enhance."
"Ooooooo, baby!"
"Oh yes, baby, optimize me again. Yesssssssssssssssss!"
"We can utilize each other to facilitate the optimal enhancement of our mutual pleasure."
"God that makes me hottttt!"

LOL

Hey! Did you file a 3310 stroke B declaration of intent-to-consummate along with a disclosure statement enumerating erogenous zones eligible for this encounter?

I thought not.

Now get back there, fill out that paperwork, and start over. (Harsh, I know. Terribly so. Making 'em repeat all that hard work...hard sweaty work...uh..ummm...excuse me a minute.)

Jun 13, 2007

Profile

Tall, lithe, blithe, and elegant domme' who bewitches alpha males, and only alpha males, into becoming willing cat toys as they succumb to their own desires.

I am a soft domme and do NOT do pain, abuse or indulge in humiliation. Basically I want wild, rampant, skin-on-skin, full body contact sex on my terms with someone who can accept himself as he is.

My Ideal Person:

Those whom the gods love....who also bleed freely, heal quickly, and need not answer for marks left upon them.

Currently seeking a LTfwbR with a suitable man who meets the criteria below.

Males must be between 45 and 55 years of age, 6ft tall, furry, witty, able to withstand my ardor, kneeling, sincere, nearby and possess more than half a brain.

Waivers to any of the above are at my discretion.

Please do not beg.

"Bad boys" need not apply.

No drug users, thank you.

Founding member of The Wicked Woman Group

Looking For: Men for 1-on-1 sex, Discreet Relationship or Group sex (3 or more!)

Please note: LTfwbR = Long Term friends with benefits Relationship.

If you are meeting me please be aware of a few items:
1. I will ask about your previous relationships.
2. I will ask about your sexual skill level.
3. I will ask about your desires.
4. I will note your etiquette.
5. I will note your attitude.
You can talk to me about anything even if I disagree with you. Yes I am not into country-western music or rap, Nascar is not as much fun as rally motorsports, and my idea of fishing is for marlin but hey, I can deal with it if you can. A lively sense of humor without being malicious or "cocky" is a HUGE plus with me! As is the courage to grab hold of me and shuffle around the dance floor. Yes, I won't win any dance competitions but that's not the point now is it?
If your idea of feminity or womanliness includes shy, timid, demur, modest, self-sacrificing, undemanding, or submissive - go annoy some OTHER woman, thank you very much.
Yes, I'm not making any friends here but you know, I won't hurt you.............much.
LOL

June 14, 2007
Results of the Favorite Position Poll
34 votes total
7 female superior
8 from behind
1 spooning
1 side entry
15 for all positions

and
2 for other - but they didn't specify
So:
44.1% are indiscriminant as to which position they favor, they like sex however it comes.
20.6% prefer female superior - girl on top for you non-technical persons
23.5% prefer from behind aka doggy style
2.94% prefer spooning and also the same for side entry
5.88% prefer some other position
Now, you know!

Goodbye.
I will damn the day I met you. I will never forgive myself for loving you as you are. I have always felt your pain, understood your reasons and supported you. I have that kind of courage and strength of heart. You have betrayed me in ways you cannot comprehend. Another failed relationship. And all your talk about caring deeply was simply talk.
I will truly love you until the day I die.
But I am tired of being unimportant, unvalued, unloved, unworthy, and unconsidered.

Jun 15, 2007
Friday:
Polo at 7pm
Fire & Ice M&G at 9pm
Rt50 in Fairfax Va
Saturday:
a wedding at 2pm
I hear L is holding a party at her place near Lake Anna.
Contact her for info.

also g is hosting a hotel party in Richmond at the ESW
Hotel circa 7pm - they need couples! But single women can
come out too. Contact them or s for further info.
Sunday:
a boat party! always fun!
and I guess the rest of you are resting up
Have a good weekend!

"being drawn to a keyboard and computer screen for hours
on end; an addiction to believing that real feelings can exist
in a virtual world."
Being a writer and thus compelled into expression as my
friend above is - I have to disagree with him.
The only reason why real emotions exist in a virtual, or
indeed in any realm, is that humans are involved.
At the end of that electron stream is a human being. A
human being prone to emotional responses.
Writers very rarely get immediate reader feedback. This is
why blogging is so addictive. That immediate feedback
from your readers - writers LOVE getting comments, both
good and bad - gives a writer, so often solitary, a
connection with other people.
This is but a small part of my friend's post, "It's Hard". I
encourage you all to read it in full.
My friend, I am here. Call on me at need.

Jun 16, 2007
WYSIWYG
There are those who are more wary in chat than in IRL.
There are those who play games, test out various personas,
act up, and act out. Some even "come out" in the chatroom.

Too much like work!

Then there are those who prefer to play it cool IRL as opposed to chat because IRL you could get hurt.

The old "sticks and stones rule" you understand.

But with some others, and this includes me, what you see in chat is what you get in real life, unless I lose my temper whereupon all bets, and the gloves, are off.

If I don't like your persona in chat, I will not bother to speak to you IRL. If you, in effect, blow me off when we are IRL, well, I'm not going not be exactly friendly thereafter.

Holding up one finger so you can interrupt our conversation to participate in another and then forget to return - excuse me? What's up with that?

This whole thing revolves around being reciprocal. We'll be interested in getting to know you if and when you are interested in getting to know us. No one gets a 'free ride'.

WYSIWYG

Jun 17, 2007
2 phone calls, 2 yim's, and 1 email - and no reply.
Well, well = guess I was right after all.

According to stats recently published in an article by Dr. Henry S. Lodge:
1. married men live 5 years longer than unmarried men "mostly the result of coasting on their wives' coattails" as the ladies connect with others.
and

2. a widow's life expectancy increases over and above her married life expectancy after the first 4 years of widowhood.
Now if we combine those two stats.... (insert an evil grin here) ......ladies, our husbands are sucking the life out of us! and here, the men have been saying it was us to them!
LOL

Jun 18, 2007
Like most weekends, there was both good and bad.
Friday: no polo - I have no idea why.
Saturday: A married H on the grass behind her parent's house on their farm in Warrenton. It was a wonderful time! They are well suited for eachother! Congratulations!
Sunday: A boat party! Excellent weather! Good people. But someone was missed. Oh well. There was one man who simply would not leave me alone - he stuck closer to me than my tan! Such a pest!
How was your weekend?

Jun 19, 2007

On my own again!
Let's see what I can get up to!
maybe I'll tell you all about it later

Be sure to get your sexual pet peeve of the manners variety mentioned! Results will be codified tomorrow and reported on the 21st.
Women use Sexual Civility Survey #2 WOMEN ONLY
and
Men use Sexual Civility Survey #1 MEN ONLY

Jun 20, 2007

Most men are aware that there are some topics that others, both men and women, will not find funny. Some men are aware that the type of humor you deploy does matter. This is to say maliciousness never wins no matter how witty it is. Even if she's a friend there are jokes you do NOT ever use when doing that 'friendly bashing thing' that guys tend to do.

Do not tell jokes involving the following - ever!
No. 1 Abuse.
example: "What's black and blue and hates anal sex?" "The girl tied up in my basement."
This sort of joke just CREEPS women out and they tend to react violently against those who tell such jokes. If a man happens to be a father of daughters, he might very well also react against such jokes.
You must be aware that many people have been abused, had family members/friends who were abused, or deal with/date/love those who have been abused.
No. 2 Issues you know are sensitive.
If she's sensitive on a certain topic (weight, for example)- do not go sticking a knife in there. Yes, I know guys like to "cruise for a bruise" every now and again but seriously, you'll hurt her or anger her. Either way, the outcome will not be pretty.
Some women are tough, have thick hides, and few inhibitions about slanging you in return. Remember that women usually have a much better command of language than men do. Are you sure you want to lay yourself open to her fire?

Humor is good, even black or morbid humor can be funny and well-received, but if you use humor with intent to kill - no.
What "joke topics" are your personal least favorites?

Freak Test!
Scoring.......... 0 - 50 Average man or woman (need to be a little more adventurous) 51 - 100 Beginner Freak (keep up the good work) 101 - 150 Big Freak (your heading in the right direction) 151 - 200 Professional Freak (you could charge for your services) 201 - 250 King or Queen Freak (others will never forget you) 251 - over SUPER FREAK (you could write the book, teach the class, and hang the certificate on your wall, or get help!!!)
My score = 280
Life is a daring adventure or it is nothing at all!

"By this time, I had gone through several men and one woman. There had been Duesreal, the ice cream/short order cook who put me into the hospital, the taxi cab driver who practiced coitus interruptus, the couple with whom I tried the threesome, the owner of several nursing homes who was really into music, and a psychiatric nurse (male) who was a real sweetheart and drove an old BMW. He gave me a wind chime as a going away gift when I went off to college. There was also the special effects man whose truck didn't have a working reverse gear. That was the only time I really caught it from my mother. I had stayed overnight. This was unacceptable. Remember the young man at MIT? The only guy my own age was an aborted attempt in the music classroom with Tony, a very handsome black kid. I saw him several summers ago and he had not worn all that well but now he was an established family man, well-employed with children and he was happy. Philip, whose knee I would caress during physics class, I do not count since I never did anything with him other than sexually torment him by getting him aroused when there was nothing he could do about it. Everyone in my class still

thought I was a virgin since they had never seen me with anyone and I was not popular enough for anyone to care." Someone had entirely too much fun, dontcha think?
Jun 21, 2007

Sexual Civility Results
Not altogether surprisingly, most people regardless of gender wanted an expressive, responsive, and physically clean partner whose attention was focused upon them and not on themselves, their cell phone, the tv, or some mythical standard of performance.
The message to all is:
Participate!

Jun 22, 2007

Schedule
Friday:
polo
Fire & Ice

Saturday:
Thunder in the Valley
up in Pennsylvania on the motorcycle

Sunday:
drinks at Mike's at 2pm

Monday:
tee heeeee!

Tuesday:
more fun at noon

Thursday:
Hunting fireworks! Wanna come along?
Followed by - more fun!

Have a good weekend too; will you, please?

A polo buddy is now required. Must clean up well and
provide some edibles, other than himself. Should meet the
criteria in my profile. I'll drive, thank you!
<---inquire within for full details.

Jun 23, 2007

I must inform you that another teddybear has passed away.
This one only lasted 6 months! But one eye is hanging on
by a thread, there are distinct teethmarks showing nibbling
on one ear and there's stuffing coming out the left side
where the seam split.
But they begin to past-think.
They begin to future-think.
And the present gets shot all to hell.

Jun 24, 2007

"I don't wanna have to 'pay' for this.
I don't want to know the lover at my door,
Is just another heartache on my list."

-R. Thomas

Not a heartache - a heart attack! *EG* Like me and enjoy
what we do, but don't love me.
Can you do that, baby?

Thank you, BHL - it was fun!

Check it out at An Interview With The Seductively Sexy
EvilEvilKitten1 From Northern Virginia!!! !

Jun 25, 2007

Why s/he may not like sex.
1. Medical issues – these can range from influenza to low
hormone levels.
2. Physical issues – tired, stressed, overworked, just had a
baby, or sprained/broken something
3. Psychological issues – may think sex is 'dirty',
'degrading', etc and so forth or may have been previously
abused
4. Relationship issues – you two may be unsuited
Some of these can be cured or fixed and some require
medical assistance. But no one should have to live without
a decent sex life as that corrodes your soul.

Jun 26, 2007

"My grades ran the gamut that first year. Then came
Organic Chemistry and it was time to change my major. So,
no longer a chemical engineering student, I went back and
began again. Given the courses I had already taken, I didn't
need another science course – ever. I also did not need to
go further with a foreign language, having studied Russian.
The problem with being an English major, apart from being
generally unemployable, was the amount of writing you
had to do. The good thing was you didn't have to buy any
of the textbooks. One trip to the library solved your book
problems most affordably. Yes, I was a poor college kid. I
lived in dives, wore my clothes to shreds and made one can
of Campbell's Tomato Soup, costing 25 cents, last for two
meals."
25 cents! That was a while ago!

As we age, life takes its toll upon us. Being understanding will go a long way to building your relationships with your men. Erectile spongy tissues in both sexes fill with blood during arousal. Poor circulation, nerve damage, hormone imbalance and performance anxiety may cause inadequate blood flow. The erectile tissue of the clitoris is much larger than previously thought. Deteriorated spongy tissue may allow blood to leak out, sabotaging male erection or female arousal. Hardening of the arteries, high cholesterol, hypertension, diabetes, and diet can produce fatty deposits that constrict the inside diameter of genital arteries and restrict blood flow. This can also impair function of the spongy tissue. Sensory nerves may lose sensitivity with aging, low sex hormones, physical injury, or surgery. Nerve impairment may occur with diabetes, smoking, hypertension, or athletic injury. Male nerve damage may occur with surgery of the prostate, bladder, or rectum. Female nerve damage generally occurs with childbirth, hysterectomy, or surgery of the bladder or rectum. Nerve function is necessary for arousal response, ejaculation, and orgasm in both sexes.

The choices we made in our youth, such a motor-cross, will have a negative impact upon our bodies when we age. Yet, not taking risks makes for a very dull life. Being kind, gentle, and understanding is necessary to building a good relationship. One can work around physical ailments and conditions or one can deal with them medically. But they should not get in the way building and enjoying a joyous sexual relationship. Some drugs taken for medical reasons do have a negative effect upon a person's sexuality. This may require a performance enhancing drug to counteract the first drug. Alternatively, one can just accept it and move on to other methods. For example, Lipitor requires the male user to also use Viagra or Cialas in most cases. Taking Lipitor may, on the other hand, have no effect upon a person. You will just have to investigate each partner's needs individually.

You, yourself, may not the terror you once were either. Are you prepared to deal effectively with your own liabilities? Fair is fair after all. One can only ask for what one is also willing to give. Care and consideration in even the Mistress/slave relationship goes both ways. Will you permit him to care for you should you need it? Consulting appropriate medical professionals may be required.

Safe Play Practices - If the submissive says stop, the play stops. Limits are never to be tested or pushed. Dominants must earn trust, not demand it. You earn trust by being trustworthy at all times. The only proper punishment is to ignore the erring submissive. Never leave the room while play is ongoing. Do not ever leave a submissive tied up in any fashion for longer than 45 minutes at one time. If you wish to try something new and different, discuss this with the submissive beforehand and give him/her time to consider it and decide whether to participate.

Jun 27, 2007

Usually when role-playing, one has a safe word. Once the submissive has used the safe word they are released, aided, and all play stops -immediately. No questions asked.

When choosing a safe word, make sure it is nothing you'd normally say in 'the heat of passion', and is easily articulated. Having to yell out something polysyllabic or partially unpronounceable is just not going to work well.

The trouble with safe words begins as soon as a gag is involved. So one cannot rely solely upon safe words to keep oneself safe.

This is why I also recommend prior discussion and NOT pushing limits - see my previous post.
I also do NOT always role-play with my lovers. After all, even dommes like a bit of variety.

The 10 Worst Jobs in Science:
A salute to those men and women who do what no salary can adequately reward!

10. Whale-Feces researcher
9. Forensic entomologist
8. Olympic drug tester
7. Gravity research subject
6. Microsoft security grunt
5. Coursework carcass preparer
4. Garbologist
3. Elephant Vasectomist
2. Oceanographer

and the absolute worst:

1. Hazmat diver

-from Popular Science, July 2007

Preferred Order of Operations
From an informal poll of suitably experienced women:
Kissing
Basic foreplay
Manual stimulation
Oral stimulation

Oral with manual stimulation
Penetration
Cuddling

REPEAT
The consensus is that if she gets hers, he should get his so
either 69 it or take turns.
Are you okay with that?

Jun 28, 2007

Entertaining Me:
Hmmmmmm
how about candle light, heavy metal music playing softly in
the back ground, a very, very good single malt scotch, a
very very good cigar for you to smoke while wearing
nothing but a collar and a smile?
Purrrrrrrrrrrrrrrrrrrrrrrrrrrrrrrrrrrrrrrrrr
W

Jun 29, 2007

YES and No:

YES
1. I am active and I play.
2. I am 'for real'.
3. I have permission.
4. I really am dominant.
5. All adventures depicted herein really happened as
written.
6. I live a very scheduled life.
7. They really are my pictures.
8. I do like men.
9. I do know what I want.

10. I can be 'nice'.

NO
1. Younger men.
2. Bad boys.
3. Begging.
4. Pain, abuse or humiliation.
5. Spanking.
6. Public sex, Cybersex or Phone sex.
7. Women.
8. I am not your mother.
9. Drive-bys or booty calls.
10. Exclusivity.

I am not indiscriminate.

Jun 30, 2007

Here's the problem, men want to know they have a chance and yet they want to feel that they're special and not just one of a crowd, NSA notwithstanding.
Just how 'fun-loving' should a woman be?

Women walk a fine line between being too easy and too difficult. Women also want to feel special but for them it usually isn't a numbers game. It is more a question of enthusiasm. So they test his eagerness.
How many tests are too many?

Rather than trying to read your minds, I thought I'd ask.

Shopping List:
Milk

Fresh Veges
Polo Snacks
ProVeal
Froz Lunches
Froz Juices
Clausen's Dill Pickles

Saturday:
shopping, see above
laundry
dusting
vacuuming
Richmond M&G

Sunday:
polo

Half domestique and half wicked woman.

JULY
2007

Jul 1, 2007

Firecrackers! Mortars! Bottle Rockets! Sparklers! Roman
Candles!
The more BOOM the better!
What are you doing on the 4th?

Jul 2, 2007

"These people have such massive egos and are so
narcissistic that they believe that other people would be
interested in reading their pointless ramblings. Even more
disturbing is the fact that many people have such boring
lives that they have nothing better to do than to read these
stupid online diaries. They just feed the egos of the
"bloggers" and encourage them to continue posting
nonsense."

Some 99% of all human communication is...GOSSIP. Yes,
really! Social scientists have done research. The main point
of communication is all about forming connections with
other people - so you, and I, are not alone.
Face it - look at where you're at, baby! A sex site and why?
To form some kind of connection with other people, of
course! Accept it! Embrace it!

I know, I know - most of you would only be too happy to
embrace a few others! *very evil grin*
Me too!

Today was THOR's first ride real car ride and I have the
scratches to prove it. Yet, there he ended up, sitting
comfortably in my lap as I drove along. He relaxed enough
to lick his paws and purr a bit as well.

72

We went plant shopping, which didn't go terribly well, but we both survived the experience. We are here now to unload the truck and take a break before heading out to the V -E -T.
Shhhh, don't say it out loud!

BTW
What about ALPHA, NOT SUBMISSIVE MEN do you NOT get?
They don't submit; they comply to our mutual benefit, baby!
Come on and get sophisticated. This is "graduate education" here.
(she said with a wave of her tail)

Jul 3, 2007

"I'm very sorry, ma'am, but their system is down right now. Please call back tomorrow. Then we can help you. I'm very sorry we could not help you to resolve this problem tonight."

The guy from the call center, tech support, in India - naturally, was so very patient. He kept apologizing as if hoping to escape wrath - but the wrath didn't come. I held on the line. I didn't fuss or snarl. I went over and over the problem. Tried all of the 'solutions' suggested. None of them worked, of course, but I typed it in and pressed enter like a nice woman.

But you know.......
......I really did want......
.....to reach out and strangle someone.

Jul 4, 2007

Steaks on the grill and explosives in the air!!!
Aaaaah! The smell of cordite!!

Independence Day!!!

Jul 5, 2007

be very, very quiet
sneak up to her bedroom
and
POUNCE

dammit Thor!

so there I am, naked in bed, watching a 2 and 1/2 pound
furry purring bundle of destruction trying to eat my hand

pesky males!

Jul 6, 2007

All you really need to know about The Pension Protection
Act is Title VI which says that your employer may now
retain financial advisors to provide advice and counsel
about 401(k)s to their boards, and their employees.
HURRAY!
I say: go for it!!

Jul 7, 2007

To improve a woman's mood and temper - provide
orgasms. Tends to change her entire outlook on life.
At least it works for me!

74

Probability of Retirement Ruin

a = 2xER+2.773/MRL
Vol x Vol=0.6931/MRL

β = 2 x Spending
Vol x Vol=0.6931/MRL

ER = expected return %
Vol = Volatility %
MRL = median Remaining Lifespan in years
Assumed nest egg = $1 million

Alpha
/Beta 0.25 .050 0.75 1.00 1.25 1.50 1.75 2.00 2.25 2.50 2.75

Alpha/Beta	0.25	.050	0.75	1.00	1.25	1.50	1.75	2.00	2.25	2.50	2.75
4.00 0%	0	1	2	4	7	10	14	19	24	30	
3.75	0	0	1	3	5	9	13	18	23	29	35
3.50	0	1	2	4	7	11	16	22	28	34	40
3.25	0	1	3	6	10	15	21	27	33	40	46
3.00	0	1	4	8	13	19	26	32	39	46	52
2.75	0	2	6	11	17	24	31	38	45	52	58
2.50	1	4	9	15	22	30	38	45	52	58	64
2.25	1	6	12	20	28	37	45	52	59	65	70
2.00	3	9	17	26	36	44	52	59	66	71	76
1.75	5	14	24	34	44	52	60	67	72	77	81
1.50	8	20	32	43	52	61	68	74	79	83	86
1.25	14	28	41	53	62	69	76	81	85	88	90
1.00	22	39	53	63	71	78	83	86	89	92	94
0.75	35	53	65	74	80	85	89	91	94	95	96
0.50	52	68	78	84	89	92	94	95	97	97	98

from Research, Apr'07

Jul 8, 2007

After a slow start this past Friday (excellent appetizer
however!) this past weekend was TREMENDOUS FUN!
The Beach Bash was 780 persons all bent upon having a
wonderfully sexual time of it and we all did our best to
uphold the "open door" policy!
I am seriously going to have to work on my "room decor"
for next time!
Black curtains anyone? *EG*

Jul 9, 2007

Laying down on my big wide bed wearing a blindfold. Feel
my hands spreading, slowly, spreading scented oil over
your body, massaging, first one arm into a cuff, then the
other arm. Kissing you knightly and running my lips gently
over yours. slowly sliding, slowly caressing, slowly kissing
down your naked body, and pulling your legs to ease your
knees before bending down to nibble and suck on your
cock. Just enough to get a taste and keep you nice and hard
as I unroll the condom onto you. Sliding back and up and in
while lightly raking my claws down your sides before
riding you.
Aaah! Such fun!

Jul 10, 2007
Thinking of a new "describe yourself" for my profile:

Ancient, gnarled, and gravely debilitated domme with
humpback and only 3 teeth and no hair.

Well, according to the people (two men, one woman) trash-
talking me during their elevator ride - like I knew them? -

76

that is what I should put on there. Sorry, you scrophulous offal-eating pidiculous toads but you were overheard. Nice to know you're not judgmental!

If you don't swing this way; you don't swing this way - no harm, no foul. But there's no need for that sort of behavior.

Finding Mr. Right:
When you first meet a man, whether it's online, at the grocery store, at a bar, at school or at your job, you should feel that he wants you.

Soon after meeting him, you should discover that he has appropriately achieved in at least one area of his life.
He will never make plans for the future that he does not intend to back up.
If you are in the right relationship, it will feel reciprocal and mutual.
If he's the right guy for you, he will have good friends and you will like who he is when he's with them.
He will like you for who you are.
He will never view you as unconditionally bad or make you feel terrible about yourself.
He has a learning curve.
He will seek his own solutions.
He will not try to have power over you."

To apply to Ms. Right, simply switch the genders.
Generally sensible, if generic, advice.
Don't you think?

Jul 11, 2007

"I think I've lost my libido. Really! No shit... and I'm really not making light of what is likely something that other men go through sometimes; it's just that, well... I just... shit, this isn't easy to admit. I guess I'm embarrassed to say that my body seems willing enough (that morning wood has to be coming from somewhere!) but my mind, or heart, or both, just isn't in it."

Women are often confused and disheartened when men seem reluctant, hesitant, or are in fact unable but it rarely has anything to do with the particular woman at hand. More often the cause is something going on in his head or the medications he's taking for this or that. I am not advocating the "praying mantis method" of removing the cause of his distress. What I am advocating is relaxing and showing men the same courtesy we expect from men when we're not in the mood. Remove the pressure to perform. Lounge around talking nonsense. Perhaps cuddle a bit. Give him bear hugs, smooches, and tell him he's cute.

He may not believe you. He may think you're just being nice and sparing his feelings. Nevertheless, being kind cannot hurt.

Jul 12, 2007

Found some delightful women who say they'd like to attend parties. May have to re-activate the party group. Nice to see some interest from women.
But will they show up and play?
That's the question!

There's another huge party coming up and I have to be ready so I'll begin planning now.

The trouble is a suitable theme. This is in honor of Halloween so costume and macabre is permitted but it has to be SEXY!

I can do the whole black leather biker/domme thing.

I can do the Venetian Renaissance Carn-e-val thing.

Both of which are undeniably sexy. But you all have seen those costumes before.

Suggestions please, people!

Jul 13, 2007

Stress is killing your sex life.

1. get proper rest
2. get lots of exercise
3. learn to take life lightly and gently - think serenity
4. get more massages
5. tackle all problems head-on after giving them due thought

Now go get naked and tease your lady by dancing just beyond her reach.

Jul 14, 2007

Had a GREAT time at Friday's evening practice match between the Vodka Team and the Martini Team! We all impartially cheered and yelled out advice from the sidelines "Keep your mallet up, Sara!" and so forth as required. Lots of fun and very good natured harassment from all sides! Nice to see Martin back up on a horse doing his coaching from the saddle. Julie was AMAZING esp when you consider she's never held a mallet before. But the best was

Jeanne mounted up on Rubia - that girl can really play polo! Irish and Rubia were the best ponies - each of them knowing exactly what to do and loving it!

Then we had a feast! Wine, chicken, steaks and a dessert as well as the usual snacks! I contributed a large bottle of Sauvignon Blanc to the festivities!

I still need a Polo Buddy!

Jul 15, 2007

Yes, I know you all are iPoding it nowadays but the SRM just loves his furry harmonics so we had the Sansui AU-D9 cleaned up and checked out and we are now putting it back into the mix. Also got new speaker wires so the Klipsch sound good. BTW we also run the television through the stereo.
Now if only we could figure out where to plug each wire in. Hmmmmmm.

That sound you hear overhead is Thor dashing from one side of the room to the other in pursuit of his newest cat toy.
Thor remains obsessed with climbing but has given up lying on the dirt in the potted plants pots. I had several inches of sharp marble shards put in to cover the dirt.
He has learned to beware the feet of humans, that soda cans are easily toppled, that bottles of nail polish do not roll very well,, that brown paper grocery bags make excellent caves, and the Mom doesn't want kittens climbing her curtains.
He has discovered, like most males, that pouncing upon women when said women are naked in bed results in some fun.
SIGH

Jul 16, 2007

It seems that I will have plenty of time to catch up on my writing, look after my business and house, and to play with Thor - do lots of 'feline-bonding' since the teddybears are playing hide 'n seek - but mostly 'hide'.
Is it 'feast or famine' with you as well?

Kittens & Society
The normal feline social unit is a mother and her kittens. Adult males lead lives separate from the family unit because adult males will kill nursing kittens who aren't their offspring to induce the mother back into heat. The mother, who has invested time and effort into those kittens, does not want to lose them so she keeps adult males away from her kittens. Kittens, therefore, do not understand the concept of "daddy".

When the kitten enters a human household, he/she tries to fit the humans into this feline social pattern. Thus, women become "Mother" and the children become "littermates" or "siblings". The men remain a problem. If the man is a nice to the kitten - the kitten will classify the man as an "overgrown littermate". If the man is not nice to the kitten - he will be seen as "an enemy" or as "a threat". As the cat ages - all humans will eventually be seen as 'staff' even the one "special person" the cat selects as "their's".

Kittens reflect back what they receive, so if you want a happy, well-adjusted cat, you have to be happy and well-adjusted toward the kitten. This does not mean that you do not set boundaries for them nor does it mean that you do not discipline kittens when it is necessary. Strong words are usually sufficient punishment but if more stringent

81

measures are called for pick up the erring kitten, place
him/her onto the floor in a curl and then roll him around
beneath your hand - as a mother cat would do to correct her
erring kittens.

Older kittens and young adult cats, say 6 months to 1 year,
can have bean-bags, paperback books, and pillows thrown
at them or can be squirted with water bottles. By now they
should know the rules of the household, so any breach of
those rules is a deliberate act of defiance and we are not
permitting anything like that here, thank you. You can now
be more human and less feline since by now the young cat
would be out on its own and leading an independent life.

Adult human males are also considered by kittens to be
rather clumsy creatures - but it was amusing to see the
SRM, who is a huge man, try to levitate when he felt a
furry creature beneath his bare foot when he stepped out of
the shower and onto Thor who was not injured having
scooted out of harm's way at the last moment.

BTW I have LOTS of "kitten stories" so if you want to save
yourselves - a suitable teddybear will have to be offered up
as a sacrifice!

Jul 17, 2007

Picture this: the SRM, naked, with a broom in hand, a cat around his ankles, at the top of a flight of stairs in a 3' by 2' space, 3 am, with a bat fluttering around his head while the cat yells advice to him.

The SRM finally swept the bat down to the cat who promptly killed it, gave it to the SRM, and then wandered off - "his work here being done". The SRM put the corpse into the trash and then called me at work to tell me all about it.

I collected the most amusing stories when I worked the night shift.

"U.K. schoolgirl loses 'virginity ring' court battle. Lydia Playfoot says ring should be exempt from school ban on jewelry since it is an integral part of her faith."

A silver ring worn on her left hand, yes, on the ring finger, like she was married, to show to all that she is committed to retaining her ignorance, ahem, excuse me, her virginity, until she is really married. Talk about your mixed signals! She's on a date while wearing that ring?

Sorry honey, but being a virgin is NOT an integral part of being Christian, else all of the married Christians would have to leave and become adherents of some other faith. Then there is the whole continuation of the species thing. Betcha some man thought this whole virginity thing up.

Jul 18, 2007

Grrrrrr

Went to the clinic about my knee - something snapped inside and now it is very unstable - only to be told to "come back tomorrow".

My appt with a teddybear has been cancelled tonight - ARGH! - for all the fun I have been having lately I might as well be male - sorry, feeble joke, but there it is - I do feel for you fellows! But if you cancel there's nothing to feel, ya know?

I shall now go away and cry in my scotch! Ciao, babies!

Nevermind what you thought.

Each "partnership" is different. Hell, even with the same person - each time is different! Yes, I would know, having been with the same man for 29 years now. Do not expect the same activities to occur with you as they might with me. It simply will not happen. And your perception of my reality is NOT necessarily correct to begin with. Open your mind to other possibilities.

To be blunt: I am a domme of doms.

Even so, get rid of the cartoon / comic book stereotype - there are no whips being used here and there never were. There never will be. I am NOT a whip-swinging sister. I do not ask for obedience, merely a temporary and limited compliance.

And to continue with your education, it is really the one complying who TRULY has the power because at a word from him (or with other doms, her) - it all stops. Immediately. No questions asked. No argument given. PERIOD. FINI.

I go one step further, he knows beforehand what will happen. He can modify any part of the planned scenario. Full disclosure with time to think about it and the option to say yea or nay to any part of or even all of any scenario. If you have been paying any attention to my blog posts, you will also notice that I am not being dominant ALL of the time. Why? Because it is boring as all hell to having to always do all of the work, okay? Do you mind if the lady takes a night off? Thank you. About damn time! I needed a break.

Just as I need a break from always being dominant (now, do not be thinking I go sub because I don't - we just make it

84

vanilla), so too do some men want a break from being dominant. A man's entitled to a night off as well. Think about this. Men spend so much of their time, trying to get women interested, trying to get women alone, trying to get women into bed, trying to please her once she's there (so maybe she'll want to come back or even stay), that they end up exhausted or cynical or even depressed.

How nice would it be to have a woman approach you, ask you into her bed, have her focus all of her attention upon you, explore the nuances of your body and your desires - repeatedly, and also have that woman really be truly unbridled so you do not have to ask if she was pleased with you because, DAMN!, she SHOWED you how much she enjoyed you? I even turn PINK if I am pleased! It is unmistakable!

Are we all clear on this now? I hope so.

Don't make me have to speak to you all again on this topic.

Jul 19, 2007
MEDICAL REPORT
Blood Pressure = 100/71 which, considering how much I smoke, is phenomenally good!

Weight = 160 which is approx 19 lbs gone in 3 months without dieting - just stress. Not bad for 5' 9" and 50-some.

Now for the X-Rays:

After being told the machine's up, the machine's down, and then having the supervising radiologist chase me down saying "it's up, it's up, come back!"...

I had Osgood-Slatter's Disease when I was 11 or so but that was old news. A touch of arthritis in the knee which is no surprise. But no damage to the bones, meniscus, or cartilage. The doctor consulted with the orthopedist to make sure.

So after walking back and forth and moving this way and that and holding my leg over there and here...

The Diagnosis: you strained but did not break any tendons, ligaments, muscles, etc and so forth. Take these crutches, drink 3 glasses of milk a day, take these pills and come back in two weeks if not better. "Then we'll do an MRI." Free medical care - ya gotta love it!

What I am going to do *EG* is to have a certain person who shall be nameless come and open my hot tub (not who you might think), drink scotch, and chit chat with my buddy who also feels herself to be in need of de-stressing. But you knew I'd do the scotch and hot tub routine didn't you?

What I Want to Hear

....in addition to "Please.", "Yes, ma'am!", and "You're a pain in the ass but I love you anyway!".....

are honest questions to which you want honest answers.

that if you have an issue with me, you discuss it with me.

that if you know me, you give me the benefit of the doubt. Why? because I do not want to be "blamed" afterwards for things which are not my fault and most issues can be cleared up if one would simply confront them head-on after due thought with the person with whom you have that issue!

so let me close by just saying..

"You're a pain in the ass but I love you anyway!"

Jul 20, 2007
RELATIONSHIP AGREEMENT

The following persons, (XXXX) and (YYYY) freely enter into this relationship agreement, which will begin _____ 20__, extend for a period of one year, and terminate on _____, 20__. We are defining our relationship as a(n): (Open Dyad). At the expiration of this agreement, we may choose to reconfirm or renegotiate our agreement. Or we may choose not to continue our relationship and to part from each other peacefully, respectfully, and as whole and free persons.

(Name)(Name) Dated: _____, 20___

I freely enter into this contract, choosing to live in the NOW with you and remaining open-hearted to future expansion of our family. We know nothing is guaranteed and "happily ever after" exists only in fairy tales. Love and relationships take conscious, consistent effort to maintain and to flourish.

I am free to make commitments and I accept responsibility for my actions. My freedom comes from the personal expression of my own power. No one can take away my power to be myself. I choose to help empower you, not to own you nor possess you. I choose to love, honor, and respect you.

I will be as truthful and reliable as I can be. I will not agree to do things with you unless I truly want to, yet I will be respectful of, and sensitive to, your needs and feelings. When I want something from you, I will ask clearly, not hint or expect you to read my mind. I will not create expectations in my head concerning you or your actions then blame you for their unfulfillment. I will share my love, joy, and caring with you.

I will never use your words against you nor divulge your private thoughts and actions to others without your consent. I will communicate to you what "privacy" means to me, and I will accept your definition of "privacy" for you. Any actions or words that relate to something the two of us said or did together should be considered private unless we have discussed it and agreed to reveal our actions or thoughts to others.

I will care for you when you are sick or hurt even if it means you want me to do nothing at all for you. I will respect that, in most instances, you know what is best for you, and what you need from me. However, I will not let you purposefully hurt or destroy yourself without attempting to persuade you otherwise. You may count on me for strength and emotional support when you are down and I expect the same of you.

We are separate and unique individuals who choose to enrich and cherish each other. Ultimately, though, only I can choose to be happy or not, fulfilled or not. I am equal to you, not more nor less. I will not compete with you and play "I win, you lose" games. I will enjoy your different qualities and work towards "win-win" situations. I feel proud of you and will not take you for granted. I will accept you as you are and not try to change those aspects of yourself I am uncomfortable with. I will endeavor to keep my mind open and my boundaries flexible. I will support your growth processes. I will not attack you in public or private when something occurs that I don't like. I will instead accept it as a part of who you are and rationally discuss it with you in private in order to more fully understand who you are. I will remember your love and constancy and communicate this to you. I will not judge you against my past relationships, good or bad. Nor will I hold on to issues or grudges. I will enjoy sharing hopes, dreams, and plans for the future with you now.

Our time together has a high priority in my life. I value our time and will make conscious efforts to ensure we have as much time for each other as we need. I also recognize that we need separate and alone time, too. I will respect your right to be apart from me, and I expect you to respect my right to have alone time also. I have friends and interests that are not in common with you; you also have friends and interests not in common with me. I will not be possessive or jealous of your time away from me, recognizing that the fulfillment and joy you receive benefits me as well. I will be open to uncommon experiences with you though. Our careers are also important to us and I will be understanding when job demands temporarily take a high priority in your life; I expect the same from you.

When problems occur, I will work with you to resolve them as soon as possible. When I am upset or conflicted, I will center myself, clarify my feelings, and determine my issues before confronting you. Only then will I approach you to discuss my issues. I will never make threats of breaking our commitments to each other, leaving you, or asking you to leave. I will never intentionally physically harm you nor threaten to. I will not expect either of us to be perfect. Occasionally I will get frustrated and stressed and disappointed, but I will not reject you nor attempt to control your individuality. I accept that I will have times of anger, sadness, fear, and pain and will want your emotional support. I will not feel you are attacking me when you express frustrations or bad feelings.

I use sexual intimacy as a way to express my love and inner self to you. I will not withhold sex to punish you nor use sex to control you. I value our sexual intimacy and will be open to your sexuality and need, as well as my own. I may not agree with every desire you have and I will be open to new experiences. However, I will not do things I am uncomfortable with, nor would I force you to do that which is uncomfortable for you. I will not be intimate with another unless you are comfortable with it. If you feel threatened, I will show you my love and reassure you and listen to you. However, I will not let you control my actions if you have unreasonable fears or a need to have power over me.

I will be responsible for supporting myself, and I will share what I can with you to the best of my abilities. I have personal property and I will respect and care for your personal property, as well as our common property, as if it were my own. I will make agreements with you concerning mutual financial matters. I will not control you with money, nor will I be controlled by your money. I also will consult with you before attempting to change our place of residence.

I commit myself to growing and changing and creating a conscious future with you. I will do my utmost to live up to the spirit of this agreement. We may revise or renegotiate this document as we deem suitable.

_____

Dated:_____, 20__

Witnessed by:_____

from:polyamorysociety.org

Sounds good to me. What do you think?

The Collar Contract

I like to keep things as simple as possible so my contract is short and, well perhaps not sweet, but it isn't too onerous.

1. I come first. Meaning that you are to value this relationship.

2. Wear condoms with all others. After having tested clean for me, of course.

3. Keep me informed. So I do not knit my schedule which we all know I am prone to do

And that's it! That is all there is too it.

Considering other collaring contracts I have seen - this one is NOTHING!

Trust me on this. You do NOT want to know the details of those OTHER contracts!

Comment Received = "Very lenient from what others have told me of theirs."

Jul 21, 2007
PSAS
Resources:

Leiblum, S.R. & Nathan, S.G. (July 1, 2001). "Persistent Sexual Arousal Syndrome: A Newly Discovered Pattern of Female Sexuality". Journal of Sex & Marital Therapy 27 (4): 365-380.

Finger, William W., Lund, Margaret and Slagel, Mark A. (Jan, 1997). "Medications that may contribute to sexual disorders: a guide to assessment and treatment in family practice". Journal of Family Practice 44 (1): 33-43.

Goldmeier D, Leiblum SR. Persistent genital arousal in women - a new syndrome entity Int J STD & AIDS 2006; 17:215-6. PMID 16595040.

"Persistent Sexual Arousal Syndrome", Boston University Medical Center Institute for Sexual Medicine, 3/1/2004. Retrieved on 2007-05-04.

Also affects men but that is called priapism.
A very real and very debilitating disorder but NOT my issue - Sorry, fellows!

The Skippy List

For those who do not know of The Skippy List, here's the preamble/explanation:

"Explanations of these events:
a) I did myself, and either got in trouble or commended. (I had a Major shake my
hand for the piss bottle thing, for instance.)
b) I witnessed another soldier do it. (Like the Sergeant we had, that basically
went insane, and crucified some dead mice.)

c) Was spontaneously informed I was not allowed to do.(Like start a porn
studio.)
d) Was the result of a clarification of the above. ("What about especially
patriotic porn?")
e) I was just minding my own business, when something happened. ("Schwarz...what
is *that*?" said the Sgt, as he pointed to the back of my car? "Um....a rubber
sheep...I can explain why that's there....")

To explain how I've stayed out of jail/alive/not beaten up too badly..... I'm
funny, so they let me live."

as an example of the kinds of things you will find on the list:

33. Not allowed to chew gum at formation, unless I brought enough for everybody.
34. (Next day) Not allowed to chew gum at formation even if I *did* bring enough
for everybody.

and then there are Skippy's issues with his uniform:

43. Camouflage body paint is not a uniform.
55. An order to "Put Kiwi on my boots" does *not* involve fruit.
56. An order to "Make my Boots black and shiny" does not involve electrical
tape.
68. I may not line my helmet with tin foil to "Block out the space mind control lasers".

72. May not wear gimp mask while on duty.
73. No military functions are to be performed "Skyclad".
80. Not allowed to wear a dress to any army functions.

There's plenty where these came from! Just Google The Skippy List!

Jul 22, 2007
After twisting me knee and all of that silliness, I went and baked 6 dozen cookies: oatmeal raisin and chocolate chip - 3 dozen of each. Mmmmm cookies! The Breakfast of Kittens!

On to this week's schedule:

Mon = Thor's next vet appt
Tues and Wed = some fun
Thursday = might actually have to work!
Egad, how did THAT happen?
Friday = 10am memorial service and then polo

Then a quiet weekend at home. (j/k)

What is on your agenda?
Anyone baking cookies?

The Last Harry Potter -
A quick and fun read even with the cat, Thor, lying across the pages ("move your paw!"). A great many Nazi overtones, a bit of The DaVinci Code, even a hint of The Freemasons - not bad.
The line between good and evil was never blurred. Evil stood forth clearly delineated as did the rewards of doing evil. Regardless of the magical trappings, I recommend the series to all parents - for their children, of course.

Jul 23, 2007
FLOW
A new free game I have been playing - and it comes
without instructions so I thought I'd tell you all what they
were. This is an extremely elegant game.

You begin as a baby worm thing whose job is to eat its way
down the water column growing arms and legs and
becoming bigger. It is an evolution sort of thing where
jellyfishes and manta rays of various sizes try to eat you
before you eat them. Gradually you become long tailed
trilobite with gaping jaws. After you defeat the centipede at
the bottom of the water column, you evolve into a jellyfish
and do it all over again.

You have to eat the bright dots on the various creatures -
for example: there are 3 on the big manta ray and they
change positions within the creature so you have to swim,
swim, swim - all the while avoiding the manta's mouth -
and eat the 3 dots. Once defeated, the creatures break down
into various bits which you then eat in order to evolve.

To move up and down the water column you swim toward
the blue (up) or the red (down) eddy to find the diatom -
eating the diatom moves you up or down the water column.

Creatures who take a bite out of you can automatically
shove you back up the water column. Here you regroup and
try again. Certain levels are all about food - eat as much as
you can as quickly as you can.

Creatures that turn orange are trying to eat you. Creatures
turn blue while you're eating them. White creatures are
neutral.

94

Hope this helps: ENJOY!

-for August, I shall lounge on my library deck, listening to music, enjoying the sun and the hot tub while drinking Pimms and ginger and trying to rewrite my books so it doesn't seem like a left-handed, blind, touch-typing orangutan wrote them in the middle of a bout of influenza- and an update to this week's schedule - Thursday now will also be fun - HURRAY!
Iffen you'd care to join me - just let me know and I'll consider it.
Cat Toys always welcome!

THOR REPORT
Thor: the Destroyer of Worlds, after womanizing his way into various feminine hearts at the vet's office, taunting two dogs for being lesser creatures, and sneering at two other dogs, clocked in at 3 pounds 14 ounces and in perfect health. Part Two of the Kitten Package is now complete. Next appt is Aug 15th when he will complete The Kitten Package in its entirety.
He is napping beneath my chair as I type this. So cute!

If I strangle my husband - promise me you won't tell?
(just because you had a bad day at work - do not come home and pick a fight with me, dammit! Pesky male!)

Jul 24, 2007
The Wicked Woman Group is now online on its own.
Let me know what you think of it, please!
C Ya

<-ancient, gnarled, and gravely debilitated domme seeks alpha males to be my sex slaves, must meet my specs - inquire within

Jul 25, 2007
It is hard to do anything with a kitten in your lap!
So I'll blog later.

Playtime with Teddybears
WOW
Oil slowly being spread over my back with a gentle, caressive hand; arms, legs, rump. The slow entwining of me in your arms. Snuggling into your fur. Then the oiling continues over my chest down to my mons and thighs followed by your lips. Gentle orgasms for now induced by hands and mouth. Kiss me, darlin'. Oh yes! A bit of edge play for you as we keep moving together until you have orgasmed twice. You roll to your right and I scoot to my right to move our injured knees from the danger zone. We'll talk about anything during these interludes - tonight we discussed Hitler's plan for America during WW II and what he should have done if he hadn't been insane. Some pinot noir. Gradually I crept closer to you. Yes, I saw your smile. You knew what was going to happen. Purringly straddling your body and sliding you inside - I love it when you lie there and "take it like a man" - so erotically charged! Fast, slow, fast, fast, slow; upright then lying on top of you and always moving: back and forth, up and down. Add a twist for more torque. Gushing all over you! Lord how I came and came again and again! Oh wow! So nice that you enjoy getting wet! Rolling about and ending up with my legs over your shoulders and your lips kissing my ankles! Yes! We collapse laughing. Wow! You are just sooo much fun! and my knee seems to be healed! It is a miracle!

Comment Received = "Even an old gnarled teddybear with some of his stuffing knocked out of him, can still be a favorite play toy for an enterprising kitten."

Jul 26, 2007
The Heart of Terrorism
"The intensifying to anger of the natural scorn of youth for the mess their elders had made of the world. The desire to punish violently the objects of scorn. The death of love for parents. The permanent sneer for all forms of authority. The frustration of not being able to scourge the despised majority. And after that, the deeper, malignant distortions...The self-delusion that one's feelings of inadequacy were the fault of society, and that it was necessary to destroy society in order to feel adequate. The infliction of pain and fear, to feed the hungry ego. The total surrender of reason to raw emotion, in the illusion of being moved by a sort of divine rage. The choice of an unattainable end, so that the violent means could go on and on. The addictive orgasm of the act of laying waste." -D. Francis, Trial Run

"Protest is when I say this does not please me. Resistance is when I ensure what does not please me occurs no more." - Ulrike Meinhof

Malignant distortions sums it up perfectly.

PILLOWTALK
Our 'pillow talk' mainly consists of word games: alphabet animals and prefix/suffix.
Alphabet animals = "Aardvark, badger, cat, dog...." taking turns, you have lost if you cannot come up with one.
Prefix/Suffix = "cat, precat, precating, proprecating, proprecatingly..." if you mess it up, you have lost.

Just too cute!
What's your 'pillow talk'?

Jul 27, 2007

The essence of submission is to yield, to give, to accept, to trust. The essence of domination is to bear the burden of that trust. You have remember that you have a person "between your hands" to whom you are obligated.

Interesting how that works, don't you think *EG*?

Jul 28, 2007

Profiles.

Sad to say, most are very off-putting.

Errors:

1. using tech-speak such as r for are
2. using ghetto-speak such as wazzzup
3. misspellings
4. poor grammar
5. wrote an encyclopedia
6. has too many requirements
7. has too few requirements
8. is angry, demanding, or disrespectful
9. is depressed or needy
10. there is no wit to it

and yes, often times those of women are just as bad esp when it comes to error number 6.

Recommendations:

1. lead with your best - what is the first thing others notice and LIKE about you?
2. keep it concise
3. tell the truth
4. say exactly who you are looking for ex: bbw
5. say exactly what you are looking for ex: LTR
6. sound like you're a good time
7. be non-threatening esp if you are a big male
8. check your spelling
9. check your grammar
10. English is a great language - use it!

and a clever and attractive picture helps - but there you have to go with what you have - if your face is not your best attribute, well, then you have to use something else or be artful.
You can post superb pix that tell you all you need to know without showing a face - try something along those lines for your pix.

Mmmmm, tasty!
I like mature, witty teddybears - so sue me - not that you'll get anything because I have given it all away to charity and you know what they're like. But I digress. I cannot say precisely why I am so attracted to teddybears. There's just something about them I find impossible to resist. If you have a chest like this one, see photo, expect to find a Kitten upon it in the near future.
So all of you mature, witty teddybears out there - watch your backs!

BODY WORSHIP

The following is a detailed account of how body worship is done. Either gender may do this to their partner or you can both try to do this simultaneously to eachother, which is a blast and lots of fun.

begin with your partner naked and lying face down onto the bed, using an edible oil, lightly begin massaging neck and shoulders and arms and slowly work him/her over from head to toe, then repeat using heavier and heavier hands, a woman doing this to a man may have to use her full body weight here, while also nibbling, kissing, licking, biting, scratching, caressing in agonizing slowness everywhere you had previously massaged. Use your body, your hair everything to lightly trace arabesques all over your partner's body mixing it up between heavy touch and barely felt, between pleasure and just a hint of pain. Take your time with this. Then slide back and have him/her roll over.

Do the same on the front as you did on the back but DO NOT TOUCH his/her genitals. Save those for last. Once again take your time, be slow, slow, slow and lingering - you want to drive him/her mad with lust. Then when he/she is at your mercy, then you may engage in sexual intercourse beginning with oral sex and progressing through to earth-shattering multiple orgasms for both partners.

When I say all of his/her body I do mean all of his/her body including nibbling fingertips and sucking toes. Breathe on his body hair to ruffle it. Feel free to experiment - does he/she like it when I do this? Lick scars. Kiss the outer corners of his/her eyes and lips lightly with just a hint of moist tongue tip. Slide your fingers in between and up

along his/hers. Do several things at once in an attempt to provide sensory overload. It is all good. the more adventurous can add in vibrators for P-Spot/G-Spot massage as well. Please note that no equipment is required. You do not even have to use the oil. The only caveat is NO TICKLING.
wandering off looking for the nearest teddybear
"Touch of Grey"
Words by Robert Hunter; music by Jerry Garcia
Copyright Ice Nine Publishing; used by permission

Must be getting early
Clocks are running late
Paint by number morning sky
Looks so phony

Dawn is breaking everywhere
Light a candle, curse the glare
Draw the curtains
I don't care 'cause
It's all right

I will get by / I will get by
I will get by / I will survive

I see you've got your list out
Say your piece and get out
Yes I get the gist of it
but it's all right

Sorry that you feel that way
The only thing there is to say
Every silver lining's got a
Touch of grey

I will get by / I will get by
I will get by / I will survive

It's a lesson to me
The Ables and the Bakers and the C's
The ABC's we all must face
And try to keep a little grace

It's a lesson to me
The deltas and the east and the freeze
The ABC's we all think of
Try to give a little love.

I know the rent is in arrears
The dog has not been fed in years
It's even worse than it appears
but it's all right.

Cows giving kerosene
Kid can't read at seventeen
The words he knows are all obscene
but it's all right

I will get by / I will get by
I will get by / I will survive

The shoe is on the hand it fits
There's really nothing much to it
Whistle through your teeth and spit
cause it's all right.

Oh well a Touch Of Grey
Kind of suits you anyway.
That was all I had to say
It's all right.

I will get by / I will get by
I will get by / I will survive
We will get by / We will get by
We will get by / We will survive

Jul 29, 2007

Please note:
"Being a challenge" is a huge turn-off for me because life is just too short to have to put up with that.
Thank you.

The Ladies are getting togethor to machinate and formulate while hot-tubbing, drinking wine and listening to music.
Anyone's ears burning yet? *EG*

Jul 30, 2007

This week it is time to tackle the piles of paper that have been scattered about the floor by my "feline office helper".
I'd rather be doing other things but the teddybears all tell me they're busy!
Guess they just are not into sex as much as I am.
SIGH

The Dreaded Single Male - well, I for one say: Hurray for single men! And based upon recent research, some other women feel as I do since there are times when you just don't want to deal with the wife. What can I say. In addition, there are times when you like him, hate her or hate him and like her. How it goes sometimes.
But with the single man - you generally know where you're at and it is nay or yeah as the case may be! Hence:
HURRAY FOR SINGLE MEN!

I know you agree with me, right?

Jul 31, 2007

There's some word out there that I do gangbangs and enjoy them. The answer is Yes if they are conducted on MY terms. Of course! Who's the domme here? Damn well had better be on MY terms.

1. The men had better be up for it and skilled.
2. If I want you here doing this - comply.
3. Do not ever spank me.
4. Condoms mandatory.
5. You will be respectful before, during and after.

This latest offer consists of two men.
ROTBLMAO
Certain people know why I find that amusing.

AUGUST
2007

Aug 1, 2007

Ah! Summer is here and with it come all of the parties: house parties, boat parties, pool parties, beach parties, polo parties!

You do understand that I love parties, dontcha?

(Esp those where no clothing is worn and I can pounce upon as many teddybears as will hold still for it.)
Yes. I am sure that comes as a great shock to you!
Nevermind - you'll get your chance to pounce too!

Aug 2, 2007

You do realize that I need a week's notice before anything can be done. So if you want to see me - call today for an appt next week. Only a few select persons can get instant appts. Sorry but you have to save something for those who are special to you.
Also I do have a process. Any attempt to circumvent the process will result in instant disqualification. Sorry but I have my reasons.
Thank you for your cooperation.
Your call is very important to us so please hold and your call will be answered in the order it was received.

Aug 3, 2007

Here's a testimonial for my new website:
www.wickedwomangroup.us

"OMG! It was awesome, I had him melting under my fingertips, I have had him whimpering in the past but JESUS, he ate it right up. I asked beforehand if he completely trusted me and informed him that I had a plan. When he came to bed last night, I basically just ambushed him. Thanks for the direction, I really like this form of satisfaction!" -from ToWild2Tame

Fun, fun, fun!
but it does require courage on the man's part to cede control like this - and they earn my respect by doing so

Profile for EvilEvilKitten1
Tall, lithe, blithe, polyamorous, and elegant domme' who bewitches alpha males, and only alpha males, into becoming willing cat toys as they succumb to their own desires.

My Ideal Person:
Currently not looking.
I am a soft domme and do NOT do pain, abuse or indulge in humiliation. Basically I want wild, rampant, skin-on-skin, multi-orgasmic, ejaculatory, full body contact sex on my terms with someone who can accept my unbridled sexuality.

Aug 4, 2007

Such a sneaky and sly Kitten. You'll find out soon enough but there is a surprise awaiting you!
You'll enjoy it too!

Don't you just love receiving delightful surprises?

Aug 5, 2007

HURRAY FOR NAKED POOL PARTIES!!
WE SHOULD HAVE MORE OF THEM!!

THANK YOU D & R & A!!
and may I have copies of the pix, please?

Aug 6, 2007

I began this list and it was getting far too long so I have
deleted that post and am now embarking upon another. Try,
try again.

Essentially, the one thing that immediately and irrevocably
sends me from a man's side is FEAR. You simply must
have courage. Because I will ask you for it in matters both
large and small.

I will ask that you step outside of your comfort zone. Try
new things. Make decisions. Wrap your mind around new
concepts. Stand up for who you are and what you want. Not
to challenge you or to change you - but to explore you.
Who are you, really - behind that social mask of yours?

So disappearing on me between the bar and the hotel or
timidly saying "I want to but I'm afraid" - just say goodbye
and go annoy some other woman, please.

What is your biggest turn-off?

GIRLS GONE MILD
The newest touting of virginity by Wendy Shalit is deeply
flawed. Her basic ideas include:

1. females only have sex to get attention from males - they
only do sex to please others

2. enjoying casual sex is a sign of low self-esteem

108

3. feminists advocate a crude and public sexuality

Granted that she's a sexual pessimist but that is no reason to be uncritically embracing second-hand research, attacking those who are of another opinion as if that proves your point (which it doesn't), and generally acting as if a female's highest virtue lies between her legs and not in her heart and mind.

It is that last one that is particularly galling!

When one considers with what utter brutality the vast majority of the women in this world are treated - pushing the idea that her greatest worth is her intact hymen is criminal as well as morally corrupt. Sex is just sex and your self-esteem rests on your accomplishments and achievements on the one hand and being the best possible person you can be (given who you are) on the other.
Are you with me on this?
(opposing views welcome)

Everyone, esp ladies, should review the ENTIRE website www.seemoresideeffects.ca to see a prime example of effective marketing. Gentlemen may wish to take notes.
My daughter sent this to me!
Isn't this a kick? LOL

I am honored to be Ms. Virginia in B's Ms. Passion contest.
Thank you to the Selection Committee!

Aug 7, 2007

Miss B's Ms. Passion contest brings up the whole question of

Are you passionate?

to which I would have to answer, as evidenced by my entire life thus far

YES

It may strike you as being too much but I have always embraced life with the same fervor as I embrace men. Life is Great and I intend to Live it!

Are you passionate?

"The University of Chicago did a survey ("Sex in America," 1994) which reported that less than one-third of females always orgasm during sex, compared to three-quarters of men. The survey also found these statistics changed quite significantly when a woman's partner spent 21 minutes more on foreplay: 9/10 women always orgasmed with more foreplay."

If you really want to get the job done, fellas - begin well. BTW the mental foreplay begins as soon as the date's made.

Aug 8, 2007

Sexually speaking - you tend to get what you give. Before complaining, I suggest you try to see the issue from the other person's point of view and then make your judgments. Here are the top three complaints from the sexual advice sites:

The number one problem is a mindset that believes his/her orgasms are the other person's responsibility.

Not true! They can assist but if you're not willing to orgasm - you won't; no matter your partner does or does not do. Don't you like orgasms?

Second - a time issue. He or she takes too long or doesn't last long enough. You understand the difficulty.

Two things can be done here: don't use a racehorse to pull a plow and don't be the kind of person who needs a plow horse. Sex should be delightful fun and not a second-job for half pay and few benefits.

Adjust your sensitivity accordingly.

Finally, the last of the 3 biggest complaints involves reciprocity. One person gives and yet does not receive. Always. This is being sexually selfish.

If you get what you like, be willing to give what your partner likes. So you have to "suck it up" a bit. No big deal. You can handle this. You get yours and your partner gets theirs and both go home happy.

Humans are very variable, emotional, stress-able creatures so some leeway has to be given - even when it comes to fair play. It is not a perfect world. By becoming an "easy and generous lover" to those who meet your criteria (whatever those might be) you make the world a bit more perfect.

Fair enough?

The Aquarius Woman

Uranians need lots of fresh air, sleep and exercise, but they seldom take advantage of these remedies. They don't get much fresh air because they close their windows, pile on the blankets and still complain that they're freezing.

The safest way to enter into romance with an Aquarian female is to remember she's as paradoxical in love as she is in everything else.

This girl has all the faithfulness of the fixed signs when she's in love, but she also has the detachment and lack of emotion of the air element. It's possible to have a happy relationship with the Uranus woman if you leave her free to pursue her myriad interests and circulate among her friends. Never try to tie her to the stove or the bedpost. Ask the man who's tried.

She belongs to everyone, and yet to no one. Her love can be tender and inspired, but there will always be a vaguely elusive quality about it, like a half-remembered song. You can hum the melody, but the lyrics keep slipping away. The Aquarian girl's demand for freedom is insistent, but her allegiance to anyone who can accept romance with-in such limits is boundless.

She won't be terribly interested in your bank book. Money is never the prime consideration of the typical Aquarian woman. She won't care if you're not the richest man in town, but she'll expect you to be respected in some way for your intellectual achievements.

When you set out to catch this butterfly in your net, remember that she'll never spend her unpredictable life with a man who isn't true to himself. Her own code of ethics may be as weird as anything you've ever come across, and quite different from the accepted codes of society, but she lives up to it totally. She'll understand that your rules may also be highly individual. That's fine with her, but don't compromise those rules.

Like all Aquarians, she may have an unconscious fear that desire for one person will imprison the spirit in some way, and keep her from being true to her one great love-freedom. Freedom to experiment and investigate and freedom to give time to humanity-. Also freedom to pursue her rather kicky, off-beat fancies.

There are some pretty wild, way-out Uranian females here and there. But the average girl born under the sign of the water bearer is a social delight. She's graceful, witty, bright as a penny, and ex-tremely adaptable to all forms of society, high and low and in the middle.

Her lack of suspicion under normal circumstances is a special bonus. A traveling salesman should find his dream girl in the typical Aquarian female. If she actually catches you being unfaithful, it will cause a deep wound to her sensitive nature. You'll know it the minute you look into those strange, dreamy eyes. But she won't suspect you without cause, and she'll rarely doubt your word. The typical Uranus woman will never check up on you after you leave, phone you at the office, inspect your handker-chiefs for lipstick stains or look for blonde hairs caught in your cuff link. Deception will have to be brought forcibly to her attention; she won't go out looking for it. Before you give her too much credit, consider that her lack of passionate jealousy is due to something more than strength of character. First of all, she probably dissected your psyche under a microscope before she gave you a second glance. Besides, she has so many outside interests and so many people who turn her on to talk with, there's not much time for her to worry about what you're doing when you're out of sight.

Out of sight can often mean out of mind for Aquarians of both sexes. Absence seldom makes the Uranus heart grow fonder. She'll simply walk away. Don't try to kindle the embers, they're stone cold dead. Of course, you can still be friends. Why not? She's willing. It never embarrasses an Aquarian girl to be chummy with ex-lovers or husbands.

She's forgotten the past and wiped the slate clean of memories.

Expect her to probe into your heart until you haven't a secret left, or a dream that hasn't been analyzed. But don't try to dissect her private thoughts. That's not the way the game is played with Aquarians. She'll keep her motives hidden, and sometimes take a perverse pleasure in de-liberately confusing you. She'll usually be truthful to a fault, but remember, with an Aquarian, telling a lie is one thing. Refraining from telling the whole story is another.

Her appearance is puzzling. Most Aquarian women are lovely, with a haunting, wistful beauty. But they're change-able. They can give an impression of smooth whipped cream, then suddenly switch to salty pizza as quickly as a bright, blue, zigzag bolt of Uranian electricity. Next to Librans, Aquarian females are often the most beautiful women in the zodiac.

A conversation with her can be remarkable, to say the least. She has charming manners, and usually behaves in a timid, almost reserved way. Then comes one of those sudden Uranus urges, and out will pop a remark with absolutely no relation to what anyone is saying. Never talk down to an Aquarian female. She'll resent not being considered your equal, and an unsympathetic attitude will cause her to retreat and become unapproachable.

Even though Uranus likes to reverse the existing orders of things, before your Aquarian girl becomes a mother she has to become a wife. And before she becomes your wife, you'll have to convince her that marriage isn't synonymous with Alcatraz. She won't exactly rush into matrimony. She's in no hurry to take your name until she's weighed you, sorted you, tested you, and found out what makes you tick. The opinions of her friends and family will mean nothing, though she may ask them what they think out of curiosity. She has her own yardstick for measuring you. Assuming you pass her test, marriage to an Aquarian girl can be confusing. She'll listen pleasantly when you give her advice, but there's something in the Uranian make-up that prevents her from following directions explicitly. There's some kind of a snag in her thinking that causes her to believe just a little twist will improve any-thing. But shell smile agreeably as she goes on her own sweet way. But don't ask her why. The unique and unusual is her wave-length, that's all.

Because her nature is so impersonal, expressions of deep feeling won't come easily. Although the unique Uranus outlook leads some Aquarian girls into peculiar attachments, once they find the right mate their marriages are usually models of happiness.

The quickest ways to lose her are to show jealousy, possessiveness or prejudice; to be critical, stuffy or ultra-conservative. You'll also have to like her friends, who will come in odd, assorted sizes and shapes. She's susceptible to sudden flashes of inspiration, and her intuition is remarkable. Her judgment may not seem sound or practical at first, because she sees months and years ahead. The Aquarian girl lives in tomorrow, and you can only visit there through her. What she says will come true, perhaps after many delays and troubles, but it will come true. I suppose, after all, that's the most special thing about your February woman. She's a little bit magic.
-from EnglishWiz
Some of that's true.

Aug 9, 2007

I'm not 20 anymore and, despite never having been a "hardbody", it shows. Actually having had two kids is what did my figure in. Yeah, I have figure flaws.

Sagging, droopy, prune pussy, grey box - let's see what else have I been told or called? Usually by younger men. Any wonder why I do not care to go there? Vanity.

From older men or men my own age, I get called other things; the evidence of my past upon my body seems to remind them of their own age and its effects upon themselves. Something they're not willing to face.

It is all extremely silly! Remember that it is the person not the packaging that really matters. Physical issues can be dealt with - it's those mental ones that really wreck you.

I'll make you a deal - you forgive my figure flaws and I'll forgive yours.
Sound good to you?

Playtime with Teddybears
ROLLING
Like deep ocean swells that lift the world the orgasm kept coming and coming. 1 hour, 2 hours - it just never seemed to stop. Mix in some 'perfect storms' - yes! Wow, what a man! Just a long, slow, powerful session between two people who know, and please, each other very well. So sweet! (still purrrrring)

Aug 10, 2007
I was asked to add a post about my "special talents". This is
what I said.

My special talents involve taking a man into the deepest
wilds of unbridled, passionate sexuality by subtle, erotic,
sibylline sensualities.

This is based upon the following testimonial:
"Beware: The Kitten knows things about you, that you
don't even know yourself. That would be scary if it didn't
feel so Damn good. She will rock your universe!"

Remember, I lap-dance to the tune "Clubbed 2 Death
(Kurayamino Mix)" by Rob D.
Do you want to enjoy sex again?

Aug 11, 2007
Tis a fine art, really! How often, tell the truth now, how
often do you really, really get to totally relax? Just turn the
mind, the tension, the stress off? Not often, I'd bet.
Which is why you will currently find me in my hot tub,
sipping scotch -Laphroaig - and just letting everything fall
away!
Aaaaaaaaaaaaaaaaaaaahhh!
It is unfortunate that there aren't any teddybears here to
share this experience but sometimes life is like that.

Aug 12, 2007
Interesting by-play was witnessed. Woman 1 asked woman
2 to listen out for her. Woman 2 then said "she's going out
with someone's husband" by way of explaining it to my son
and I. My son volunteered saying he was available should
woman 1 ever want a single man while I wondered what
the problem was; esp since apparently this fellow was a

117

'serialist' - having had many gf's in the past while married. Woman 1 being gf number 4. By this time - she (the wife) should either be used to it and join in the 'swinging lifestyle' or divorce him.

Amazing what you can learn while checking out your groceries!

Halloween:
I am going as Elizabeth Bathory - The Blood Countess and wearing a most provocative dress (black) with black stilettos.

Please go and vote for me in B's Ms. Passion contest poll 8!!!. Thus far I only have two votes! One of them - mine. A very sad state of affairs, indeed!

Aug 13, 2007
What Women Want
SINCERITY - only say it if you mean it; only do it if you enjoy it; make your actions match your words.
and
COURAGE - if you say X is what you want, then stand by that when someone hands/offers you Y; esp if there are other persons involved.
The ability to "shame the devil" and dare to live the life you profess to want is very attractive.

From a 50 year old man in Alexandria, Va:

Let's be in touch to consider the possibilities!
Cheers,
D

I replied:

118

Too many "prefer not to say" in your profile.
Thank you,
EEK

He replied:

What sort of moronic response is that? What...not
having commented on my religion, or penis size, is
grounds for suspicion?
Silly woman! Hey, I wouldn't necessarily "prefer" your
saggy breasts, but I'm a bit more tolerant than that!

EEK is right! Eeeeeeek, I don't think you're my type!

D.

and he also added in a subsequent email:

You should ditch the voice intro, as you sound like a
man. Perhaps you're just a fake, or maybe it's just the
heavy smoking.
Since you're a stickler for preferences, let me make
clear that I prefer that my lady friends sound like
females!

my reply:

At least I have the courage to tell all and to put myself
out there unlike some shy, timid business man - who
undoubtedly knows how to win friends and influence
people - in a very negative fashion.

Since you 'went there' (attack mode) at the first item -
you're not MAN enough for me.

"Since you're a stickler for preferences, let me make clear that I prefer that my lady friends sound like females!" with the high "little girl" squeak and lisp too no doubt! And when she greets her friends they sound like freight train brakes clenching for dear life! I am a contralto. High and squeaky is just not going to happen.

Of course, you are god's gift to women so yeah my breasts are neither "perky" nor manufactured for masculine pleasure. But I have twin V12's under my hood - so if the chrome's not flashy enough for you - too damn bad. Unlike yourself - I'll take performance over image any day. Naturally, since you fly, you'd like the pretty little plane over anything high performance - it is soo much easier to manipulate.

The point about "prefer not to say" is that it denotes timidity. And no lady wants a timid male. Least of all - me.

Who first wrote to whom? And did DOMINATRIX escape your notice?

Of course I read his profile wherein he gave the minimal info about himself - it was all about what HE wanted. Good going, guy! That's the way to self-select yourself OUT!

Another male off my list!

And I got a reply!

Oh, my profile is quite detailed enough for me, and it is how I choose for it to be. It works just fine for me, too.

So, are we to be guided only by the boxes AFF asks one to check on our profile? Now, that's timid! And, shall I conjure up conclusions because you choose not to describe your musical tastes, or your occupation, in your profile? No, that's not my style.

Your comments were quite presumptious, and no doubt telling. I know your style...bossy and confrontational, right out of the box, since you're probably a deeply insecure lady, seeking fulfillment and worth through the guys who are willing to treat you with kid gloves!

Oh...and I note your are one of those review collectors. "She's so sexy, so smart, so classy..", blah, blah. More pitiful self esteem building on your part.

I actually have a couple of reviews on my profile, which I've activated in real time, on a couple of occasions, for several ladies to see. I consider that an optional tool, and not a public billboard.

You, however, display them like merit badges. I'm wary of those who feel the need to flash their medals! And, while I'm here for sex, too...that just looks like trailer park behavior to me!

Got some tats and piercings, too?!?

Ha...you're a hoot!

Talk about presumptuous!
(please note correct spelling)
Some men just do not take rejection well.

Aug 13, 2007

What Women Want
SINCERITY - only say it if you mean it; only do it if you
enjoy it; make your actions match your words.

and

COURAGE - if you say X is what you want, then stand by
that when someone hands/offers you Y; esp if there are
other persons involved.

The ability to "shame the devil" and dare to live the life you
profess to want is very attractive.
Are you being sincere and courageous?

Aug 14, 2007
Eyes closed, just a sensuous grazing of the lips that
stimulates and tingles the nerve endings - promising,
promising, promising - very tantalizing - a hint of moisture
perhaps from the tip of his tongue - I have no idea why I
feel COMPELLED to kiss certain men but I JUST HAVE
TO! Even if just picturing certain men in my mind I STILL
get this COMPULSION to find him, run over there and
KISS him!

Oh Hell! No teddybears immediately available! Now what I
am going to do?

Perhaps.
Maybe I'd attract more teddybears if I wore a dress like
this? Now that I have a figure, of course. Black, red, or
something more flesh-toned?
What do you think? You like? Would you be caught dead
with me when I was wearing such a dress?

122

Aug 15, 2007
Now the JRM has his own profile on AFF. So. How do I feel about that? As long as he stays away from me, I'm fine with it. Can I guarantee that he will? No, of course not. Should it come down to me paying for my pleasures - so be it. But since they (my family) already tease me about my many, many boyfriends (Yeah. Right. Hundreds!) it won't come as too much of a shock.

Well, I have to run! Thor's due at the vet's for the final part of his Kitten Package! And there's a test ride to do. And I'm going to the Richmond M&G tonight! Maybe I'll make the bed while I'm upstairs? Never know your luck! It COULD happen! Have fun A!

C Y'ALL

Aug 16, 2007

Thor Update:
The womanizing destroyer of worlds and sundry vermin (he caught and ate two spiders) THOR had his final Kitten Package vet visit today.

He now weighs in at 5 and 1/2 pounds and has outgrown his flea collar. We have almost run out of holes on his leather collar having let it out three times thus far. Thor is just 4 months old.
He doesn't have his adult fangs yet so teething should begin soon.

Then his bites will be serious!

Thor has all of his shots including the dreaded rabies. He was not pleased and for two cents would have bitten the vet who laughed and said she understood because she had wanted to bite her OB/GYN often enough.

Then he lounged in the back of the truck and pretended I was his chauffeur!

Guidance For Men
For those hopefully few men who do NOT know here is some guidance regarding corresponding with women.

1. READ the profile. If she has a blog, read a bit of that as well. You are trying to decide if she's a woman who might be a good match for you. You are also trying to find one particular thing unique to her that you can talk about in your opening email. If you do NOT meet her criteria do NOT send her any email! If she is NOT looking or is NOT available do NOT send her any email! NEVER send her a 'generic' email!

If she's not a good match for you - STOP right there and move on!

2. She's a possible match. You have that one item you'll use in your opening email. Good. Now, send her an email entitled Hello. Say your read her profile, and maybe her blogs if you did read her blogs, and you noticed she....insert that unique to her item here... and I wanted to ask you about that. Ask a short question or two. Append your profile at the end. And you're done! PLEASE use spell-check!

If she does not look at your profile and/or does not reply. Stop right there and move on.

If her auto-reply says no, or if she sends a negative Quick Reply - take the hint and move on.

If she actually sends you an email saying 'no' or 'no thank you' or just 'thank you' - it means no - move on.

3. If She reads your profile and mentions in an email to you something about your profile, good or bad, she has yet to make a determination. This is your chance to say something to capture her, to turn the bad into good, and say thank you. This is NOT the time to get huffy, to get rude, to get raunchy. This is a test.

If she sends you a negative email back, you flunked the test. Do NOT reply. Move on.

4. If she replies positively - do NOT mess it up now! Suggest three possible date/time/places where she and you might meet. Mention another item you noticed in her profile and/or blogs and ask about it. If she asked questions, answer them. End by saying you're eager to meet her in person.

If she declines to meet you at ANY of the dates/times/events AND does NOT suggest an alternative date/time/event - she is NOT suitable - send a 'sorry to have bothered you; my loss' email- and then move on.

If she declines BUT DOES suggest an alternative date/time/event - then you can decide nay or yeah from there. She is obviously an interested lady. Treat her accordingly.

This is a public service announcement made in the hopes that your emails will NOT be posted up in her blog as an example of a #%%&##&&!!!

Aug 17, 2007
BISEX
Personally not my thing, thank you, but I have noticed several "disconnections" in this area which I thought we might discuss.

1. Why okay for women but not for men?
2. If you only receive are you truly bi?

As to #1 is it just that men tend to be very homophobic? Are their egos or self-concept as a "man" that fragile whereas women aren't? Is it one of those "power" things where the alpha dog treats all other pack males as females? Naturally women are treated as females anyway so that would not apply to them. But women don't like bi-guys either - because they fear competition? Some seem to. Or it may be that they are assuaging the fears of their men? The disease factor is a wash really because you are always at risk if you're active esp if unprotected regardless of gender. It is obvious that I'm not clearly understanding something here beyond the visceral reaction. Are bi-femmes not a 'threat' whereas bi-guys are? I see no real difference myself.

In #2 above, I don't see how you can say you're bi if you only acquiesce to another's desires. To me, if you were bi you'd be after them as much as you'd be after a man - wanting to be a "couple" and so forth. And you cannot be bi if you're only doing it because some men think it is a real turn on to see to women enjoying each other. But since that tends to exclude the male - go to your room I only want her - I don't see it myself. Would I be happy to see two men

126

excluding me? I do not think I would considering I prefer coitus to masturbation any day. And if they watch and you use the guy to "finish the job" that is kind of cheating both the guy and t the bi-femme out of their due isn't it? Not exactly "full participation" of all parties.

I am not bi but I don't care if you are; I deal on a person to person basis. But bi-guys and bi-femmes SHOULD be accorded the same treatment and judged by the same standards.
In my not-so-humble opinion, the Golden Rule still applies.

Reactions/comments please!

Aug 18, 2007
Out in The Garden
It is amazing how relaxing it can be puttering around in my garden - WHACKING SHUBBERIES!!

Take that and that and that!! SNIP! SNIP! SNIP!!

Back, you ivy, you! Back, I say!

Ooops! Carefully trim the evergreens - they tend toward delicacy. Carefully give the clump of chives its haircut. Make sure the privet obscuring the hot tub, for obvious reasons, is full and big.

There! Now my yard is all neat and tidy!
But we do soooo need a decent rain, dontcha think?

Aug 19, 2007

I was at the two M&G's this week, Richmond on Wed; and Fairfax on Friday - none of you fellows who said "Yes, I'll be there" showed.
You may continue 'not showing' as far as I am concerned. Thank you.

Aug 20, 2007
The Question Was...
"There seems to be a difference in orgasms between when I masturbate and when I'm with my man - why is that?"

(question truncated and the language tidied for clarity)

my answer:

Because the stimulation is different. Btw, what you feel as "pain" is a false signal. What happens is the stimulation becomes so intense it overloads the nerve-endings and this the brain interprets as pain. If you breathe deeply and relax at this point without ending the stimulus, you will have more orgasms - massive multiples.

Next: there are three areas that will induce orgasms if properly stimulated and you permit yourself to climax: the clitoris, the G-Spot and the Posterior Fornix. Relaxing while being thoroughly aroused and stimulated should help you experience all three assuming your man is clever about it.

(Yes, I know some women do not think they can climax from all three but - usually, yes you can, if you permit yourself to do so.)

That being done - there does come a point when you become incandescent and ANYTHING at all will cause an orgasm - a breath of wind on your skin, a kiss on your elbow, anything at all! WOW - that's fun!! Relax and let the feelings run through you!

and people wonder why I LOVE sex so much!

Aug 21, 2007
Books Available
published:

Shakespeare - the short course

Introduction to Classical Music with a companion cd of the Recommended Listening List

Writing Biographies

Chat

Further Chat

Basic Cookery

my ice-cold chrome-plated steel heart

Financial Basics

Nursery Tales

The Rogue's Handbook

sex books:

beguile

The Polyamorist

Sex Education for Laypersons

Men: a primer for women

Women: a primer for men

Orgasm

Playtime with Teddybears

Notes of a Dominatrix

Working on:

Final Chat

feles mala

Designs & Scribbles

Escape Velocity

OMG! Someone bought a copy!
THANK YOU!

Aug 22, 2007
*"so all this talk about the g spot.. so many say that there is
a percentage of women unable to reach orgasm internally..
although the more people I talk to and seek out it seems as
if I'm in a very small minority.. I have been sexually active
for some time now and have had a few serious
relationships... I've been with my current partner for two
years now.. the fact that sex is unable to help me achieve*

130

orgasm troubles him to no avail.. even to the extent that he feels inadequate and almost selfish during intercourse, with the knowledge he will not get me off. I've tried masturbation, and my clitoris works just fine.. as I feel as if vie lost all hope I still hope to believe I'm missing important pieces to the puzzle.. help... I want to share this with him and for myself, I'd love to feel like a complete woman.. instead of one whose parts are dysfunctional"

"Your post is a perfect example of what worries me about the disproportionate amount of attention given to the G-spot orgasm. It gives so many women yet ANOTHER reason to feel sexually inadequate, question their femininity, and sexually "dysfunctional" to boot!

Although the G-spot and vaginal penetration without simultaneous clitoral stimulation are two ways that a minority of orgasmic women report being able to reach orgasm, research and direct observation by sexologists have demonstrated (over and over and over again) that most perfectly normal women can reach orgasm only through direct or indirect clitoral stimulation.

So orgasm achieved through stimulation of the clitoris is the most normal, most functional, and most "womanly" way to reach orgasm. That idea just doesn't sit well with men (and women) who insist that a thrusting penis must be the best way for normal women to reach the best possible orgasm. I am deeply saddened and frustrated knowing that millions of women (and their sex partners) out there believe there must be something wrong with them when these women are perfectly normal physiologically and psychologically.

Freud did women (and all of us, I suppose) a major disservice by postulating that two kinds of orgasms exist, a vaginal orgasm and a clitoral orgasm. Furthermore, he believed that vaginal orgasms can only be achieved by mature psychologically healthy women, while immature women remain stuck in some early stage of psychosexual development and can only achieve clitoral orgasms. His words have been interpreted in various ways in our culture, but ultimately, there is no credible evidence to support this widely accepted theory, and there is lots of evidence that challenges the veracity of Freud's claim.

And what is this cultural obsession with G-spots when many guys are still having trouble mastering the basics? Most women report that G-spot exploration and stimulation is physically irritating. So why do people keep trying when the pleasure button is so obvious and the G-spot so elusive?

My theory (apologies to Siggy) is that men feel threatened by the fact that his penis is less capable of producing female orgasm than her clitoris. With phallic masculinity at stake, they are GOING to find that damn spot and MAKE her come from stimulation that at least APPROXIMATES phallic penetration.

(FYI: Around the world every year about 4 million little girls have their clitoris chopped off to make absolutely certain that the clitoris can never replace the role of the phallus - keywords FGM female genital mutilation infibulation clitoridectomy.)

Yes, I know that in our culture, most women enjoy consensual vaginal penetration enormously. And yes, I know that some couples just want to explore every possible facet of their sexuality, including the G-spot. But I don't believe that either of these facts accounts for the public's continued fascination with the sacred G-spot."

What I said:

Every woman has two hands - yet some can sew and some cannot - I am one who cannot do more than reaffix buttons. Do I feel "inadequate"? No. I cannot knit either. I can cook though. Every woman has her "thing" Just know what is what and roll with what works for you.

The same applies here - just because you have all three (clitoris, G-Spot, Posterior fornix) does NOT mean that all three WILL work for you, just that they MIGHT! But if you are not aware of their existence, you are not even going to try G-Spot or Posterior fornix stimulation.

Yes, I do exactly what I say I do and all three areas work for me - does that make you feel inadequate, question your femininity, make you assume you're sexually dysfunctional? It shouldn't. I have my talents/skills and you have yours. Just the luck of the draw.

The reason why "men are still working on the basics" is because WOMEN are not demonstrating, educating, demanding a higher level of performance- witness many of the questions we're asked. "Will he respect me if I ask/tell him?" Bah! When it comes to sex, most men will enjoy whatever you care to give them. Most men are more than happy to learn as well. Some have even bought my books on these sexual subjects.

The continued fascination is due to "shiny new toy syndrome" which is not the G-Spot orgasm itself but the female ejaculation that often, but not always, accompanies such an orgasm.

There's also the "did she orgasm" question. Men do like to please their partners and often they cannot tell if they have achieved this. So a "magic button" that gives tangible, if messy, proof (the damp spot) is attractive.

"For years the only way I could have an orgasm was when I used 2 toys at once. One for penetration and one for the clitoris. I could never have an orgasm with any man that I was with. Even with that it could take me over a hour just to have a orgasm, if I had one at all.

I actually just learned how to be able to have an orgasm while having sex with my man. What I did was relaxed more. Stop tensing so much and holding my breath. Once I did that the emotions zoomed over me and I let them go. What a rush! You should try that. Loosing up when having sex. I always held my breath and tensed up b/c I thought it felt better,,, boy was I wrong.

That could be the reason why you are not having one or many. You should also try what EEK said. After all thanks to her I finally received mine (thanks again).

There is nothing wrong with you for not having one either. Just need to do some real exploring. Have him feel around inside you to find the spot, once you get that, he'll know where to go from there. Maybe even try while he's doing that (if it doesn't already get you there) to rub your clit. It might even turn him on."

You're Welcome, dear!!

Taking the time to explore, try, and communicate with your partners about sex in a relaxed and happy atmosphere results in the BEST sex.

Aug 23, 2007
Tues evening: truck died at 5:30pm while sitting in a Reston parking lot. Will not start.

Called friend A: okay nothing there
Called friend B: gave me a lift to Sears Auto to buy a battery
Friend C called: came over and put in said battery

Nothing.
It wasn't the battery.

Friend B with friend D came and gave me a lift home - took 2 hours out of their evening to help me out. Thank you!! (BIG BEAR HUGS!)

Weds: Tomcat took a half day of leave, grabbed his tools and spent the next 6 hours in and under the truck while I ran for parts, (thanks friend B for further help finding parts store) handing tools, and interpreting what it said in the repair manual.

It was not the solenoid.
It was not the ignition.
It was not the relay.

It was the starter.
(Original starter.
Truck's only 10 yrs old!
Nothing lasts anymore!)

First part was the wrong one. Go back, with the old one finally off the truck, (yes, there are 3 bolts and hand me the hammer please) and mention the significant difference to the parts guy, and then get refund for excess paid between wrong part and right part. Drive back. Fend off parking lot security and return to my interpreting job.

New starter installed.
Truck started right on up!

Kisses all around and then home, home - sweet home!
Thank you to my Friends for all of your help and support!

I didn't win Ms. Passion. I was 4th runner-Up. *chuckling*
Not that I really expected to but it was fun to try.
Thank you to all who voted for me!
and Congrats to Ms. Idaho who did win!

You know, whatever you find out later from 3rd parties may NOT be correct. However, if it bothers you THAT much - you just drop them from your circle. No muss. No fuss. No major meltdown.
But you do know - we have all either kissed cocksuckers or have been one. Bi-femmes have done both!
They must find life very frustrating.

Aug 24, 2007
Okay, time for real issues. For all of you wondering, perhaps, why little gossipy dramas are essentially uninteresting - THESE are the issues that concern me.

human trafficking,
child sex tourism,
female sexual mutilation,
honor killings.

136

For example: In Indonesia, acid is available at the drug store. Fathers are being approached by thugs who say "give us your daughter for free" not her hand in marriage but her body for free sex. When the father, as might be expected says no, these thugs throw acid into the girl's face - making her unmarriageable, or dead. Either way, no one is prosecuted.

For example: In Palestine, a brother strangled his sister with the telephone cord because she was calling her married sister and he wanted to use the telephone himself. This is not the first time this particular family has killed its female members. The mother strangled her female babies upon the orders of her husband several times. Once again - no one is prosecuted.

For example: 50 Americans were brought up upon charges of child sex tourism. 35 of them were convicted and are now in prison for 30 years each. Or didn't you read today's Washington Post?

With these sorts of horrors going on, why would I waste my time with 'who said what to whom'?
Why would you?

Under The Moon
Running under the moon
Shedding my past beneath my wheels
The ritual cleansing
Freedom again

Aug 25, 2007
I love driving, all alone on the road, by myself, Joni on the
speakers - dancing through the curves; running through the
trees; along where the water meets the evening sky.

Nirvana!

"I am as constant as the northern star.
And I said, Constantly in the darkness?
Where's that at?
If you want me I'll be in the bar."
-J. Mitchell

End of Summer
Margaritas in the Hot Tub!

What could be more delightful than a select group of
friends having a party! Labor Day Sunday noon til 6pm.

Y'all know who you are!

Aug 26, 2007
It was 29 years ago today....
...that EEK and the SRM, Tomcat, THE Teddybear of
Teddybears, got SERIOUS!

It has been an AWESOME ride!
Long may it continue!

Happy Anniversary, Darling!!

X
I know exactly what the facts are.
I know who said what to whom, when, and why.

138

I know who is "reliable" and who is not.
What you were told as fact was fiction.
Instead of doing what you'd later have to apologies for, best just to NOT do it in the first place.

Aug 27, 2007
Found this item specially interesting.

"If you (as a boy) had been taught from early childhood that your experience of sexual pleasure is acceptable only in the context of a loving committed relationship with one woman who truly respects and cares for you; if you were taught that your penis had one and only one function - to create babies; if you were taught to safeguard your virginity as a special gift to be given only to the right woman at the right time in your life; if other boys disrespected and ostracized you as a "slut" for having sex with even one girl (or many girls) just for the sheer sensual pleasure and fun of it instead of for true love; if you had the experience of being constantly leered and grabbed at by ugly horny adult women throughout your childhood and teen years; if you were afraid to go out alone after dark because you heard news reports every day that there are many women out there who want to stick a broom handle up your butt, cut off your penis, and murder you because you are a male and for no other reason; if you knew that if you were "stupid" or "slutty" enough to impregnate a girl outside of marriage, there was a 95% chance that you would be the only one responsible for taking care of that baby every night and day for many years; if all of these things were part of your sexual socialization, I bet your "hard-wiring" would go soft."

I have always found it useful, when exposing silliness, to reverse the argument and then see if it "flies". Sayer did much the same thing in her slender book Are Women Really Human? to hilarious but telling effect.

This is a device you can apply to almost any debate: for evolution, change it to gravity; for anti-gay marriage, make it anti-straight marriage as I did herein when that law was being debated here in VA.

The author of the passage above is quite right; socialization is often mistaken for biological imperatives - in this case, the idea that men are 'hard wired' to 'need sexual release'.

Paraphrasing Ravitch:
"No matter how narrow a woman's life might seem on the outside, there is in every one an internal life of fantasy and joy."
Rather nice, I thought.

Aug 28, 2007
Two M&G's and preliminary meetings with two non-bi couples. One, possibly two, parties, a photographic session, and the joy of paying bills just to keep life interesting. Anything good going on in your world this week?

Aug 29, 2007
New Profile:
Tall, lithe, blithe, polyamorous, and elegant domme' who bewitches alpha males, and only alpha males, into becoming willing cat toys as they succumb to their own desires.
My Ideal Person:
Currently not looking.
I am a soft domme and do NOT do pain, abuse or indulge in humiliation.
I want wild, rampant, skin-on-skin, multi-orgasmic, ejaculatory, full body contact sex on my terms with someone who can accept my unbridled sexuality.

"Each man is different from all other men. Just as you are an individual, so are they. Whatever the last man did has nothing to do with this man here. Your ex was not reincarnated in the man before you. Let go of whatever baggage you have with you. He was not responsible for and should not be made to pay for what your ex did, or did not, do. Not only that, this man here, does not want to hear all about your ex either. Focus upon the real life before you. Focus upon the here and now. Upon this moment hangs this relationship.

Silencing the internal monologue can be difficult but if you are ever going to sustain a relationship, you will have to learn how to do it. Think for a moment if this man has given you any reason to fear or mistrust him. If he has then you leave. Life is too short as it is. Living with an unsatisfactory man is not necessary. But if he has not, then tell your inner voice to shut up and go away. Give him his chance. Listen to him. Look at him. See him. Focus upon him, as he is right here and right now. Do not worry about next week, next month, and next year. Stop worrying altogether. Enjoy a flirtation with him. If he wants more, he will let you know. If you want more, invite his participation. Give him your number and move along."
-from The Polyamorist

Richmond M&G
What a great group this is! We began small - 3 people and then grew to take over the entire side of the bar with a few positioned as they could. Excellent people! Chattering away, mingling, flirting like mad! Such Fun!

Aug 30, 2007
No New Pix

Sorry but the painter will be here. The JRM will be here. The truck has to go into the shop for its check-up. The SRM may be here - since it is the start of the Labor Day weekend.
Y'all are just going to have to wait. I'm busy.

Calling all Cougars!
I know there are some of you out there! Come out, come out from wherever you are and participate in my latest survey.
All women who enjoy the attentions of younger men: What do you call them?
trophy-boys, toy boys, closet pets, or do you just stick with the generic arm-candy?
- me, I'm just a "teddybear collector".

Body Language

Flirtatiousness
Women who are trying to get a man's attention lean toward the man they are trying to attract and they frequently make eye contact. They laugh more often than usual and smile constantly, regardless of whether or not the guy is funny. They chew on their lips and their faces are more animated. Flirtatious women also tend to fidget more. For example, they might fiddle with their jewelry, twisting rings and tugging at necklaces. They may also play with their hair or place their hands on themselves in some small but unusual way, which is an unconscious signal that they wish the object of their desire was touching them that way.

Lust
Lust body signals are the same as flirtation signals, but they're ramped up a couple of notches. Eye contact is increased and prolonged, and dilated pupils indicate

arousal. Also, notice if she is breathing more heavily, which is indicative of desire. She may also try to touch you under any pretext.

Disinterest
If she keeps looking away while you speak to her and rarely smiles, she's probably not interested.
Other signs of disinterest may include leaning away from you or crossing her arms.

Feeling conflicted
If women are unsure of your intentions or their feelings toward you, they give off signs that they are feeling uncomfortable. they might look at you, and then abruptly turn around and look away. Maybe they'll lean in toward you, but when you move in slightly to match their actions, they'll ease back or move away. Now is the time to back off while remaining friendly. Don't be too flirtatious or overtly sexual. Give her time to warm up to you. Never touch a woman before she has touched you.

Anger
There is the icy-cold burn, which is revealed through a narrowing of the eyes and a tightly closed mouth. This can be accompanied by a head tilt and tightly clenched or closed fists. She may also cross her arms, but when she's angry, it's more pronounced. If her hands are placed on her hips, it's a very, very bad sign. It may or may not be about you. Wait for time or other people to gradually defuse her rage

Interpreting Mixed Signals
Remember that women often give out mixed signals especially if she has not yet decided what she thinks about you, or is trying to be polite but non-committal, or is

simply wishing you'd take the hint and go away. Body language speaks louder than words. Watch her moves carefully and act accordingly.
-edited from askmen

Both men and women need to "listen" to body language.

Anyone have anything to add?
One especially good comment: *Anger: Obsessively sharpening a knife while looking directly below your belt, cooking implements and crockery flung your way, looking through the closet muttering things like "Goddammit, this is a clip of 9mm. I need the 45 hollow points."*

Aug 31, 2007
"If you can make her laugh, really laugh, you're usually in with a chance. We are not speaking of a polite titter here. If you do not get her reaching for a handkerchief or a napkin, it wasn't funny enough, try again. Be light, be kind, and be witty. By all means be exasperating if you have to go that far before she asks you to stop because laughing that much makes her ribs hurt.

You might run across a woman who gets the joke but will deliberately, and usually slyly, pretend to not get it. You've met your match now, buddy. Now you're in for a round of two people deliberately and elaborately not getting each other's jokes. This game is called "Shot your Fox." The first person who actually breaks down and laughs, loses. With a sophisticated woman this can be fun and it is a good sign. A woman who is willing to play this game with you has already decided to bed you at the earliest opportunity unless you make a mistake."
-from Women: a primer for Men

Sounds like a fun time to me!

My Life in The Library
It began a long time ago when as a small child I held my
mother's hand to cross the street and went thus to the
library just there. The library by the lake just up from the
bridge over the falls where I was told a long ago cousin met
his death from drowning when he wasn't much older than
my older brother.

Back then it was Tuan defeating the evil witch and
Jabberwocky. Now it is everything, or almost, from
Atherton to Zola. From astrophysics to zoology? Perhaps
I'll get a book on zoology so I could say that.

I worked in my high school library - not very efficiently as
there was a cute male who hung out there - but I can shelve
and check out and cross-reference nonetheless.

The library at Penn State became my second home because,
being a poor student, I borrowed all of my textbooks. The
place was HUGE and it held everything an inquiring mind
would or could want including nooks where one could
dally with selected men should that be on today's agenda.

Now I have my local library which will find, and did, me
books on the Ancient Picts, the Internet, and the shelf upon
shelf of books that hold up my house.

My next, and last, home will have book shelves instead of
interior walls (with fireproofing in between and a halon
system above) since even I need a break from men.

SEPTEMBER
2007

Sep 1, 2007
On The Potomac
Beautiful weather! Great company! Had an absolute
BLAST this afternoon on the Potomac River with J , T, &
M!!!
FUN, FUN, FUN!!
What more could you ask for?

Sep 2, 2007
End of Summer Party
YEEEHAW!! WHAT FUN!!
You are the BEST people to party with!!
(No, I am not going to tell you other people what we all got
up to. You're also not going to see the pix.)

Sep 3, 2007
Today's Reading:
"and a slow but determined approach to a problem. As he
had often told me, it takes many miles to turn around an
aircraft carrier and it is better to be sure in which direction
you need to go before you start zigzagging all over the
place and showing everyone what a blithering idiot you
are."
which is both perfectly true and applicable to more than
just ship-handling.

Upcoming Events & Scheduled Items
Sept 11 - something special
Sept 27 - book signing at Horse Country
Oct 14 - 12th Hunt Country Classic Car Show
Oct 20 - Monster Mash
Polo continues until November at Chetwood and until this
weekend at Great Meadows.

The fall steeplechases and hunt races are also beginning later this month.
Sunday trail rides followed by partying is also a possibility. Let us all cross our fingers and hope so!

Free to good home = 3 very large catfish each approx 6 inches from nose to beginning of tail. Non-edible variety, silver, peaceful, fresh water; you transport - they have out-grown their tank. Inquire within.

Sep 4, 2007
Blog Awards
My nominations are:

most creative writing style(male and female).. z a
sexiest erotic writing(male and female)..W5 and s
funniest blog(male and female).. M
best news blog{male and female} S11961
most intelligent blog(male and female). zzT2
most creative blog(male and female). S
all around sexiest blogger(male and female)..bi
most artistic blog(male and female) B B B
best newcomer(male and female).. BB
most unique blog(male and female). BHL
most caring blog(male and female). C R
most all around interesting blog(male and female) - MINE! EEK
most erotic blog(male and female) W5
Most All Around Outstanding Blog Award(male and female J
sweetest blog(male and female) ckl
sexiest couple blog-.L L
silliest couple blog-.MrMrsH
grooviest couple blog-.two100
best written blog(male and female). S

If you have your OWN ideas, nominate them here:
Good luck to us all!
I wish to delegate the nominations for PICTURES to
interested parties. Inquire within.

I finally broke down and bought a distribution package
(read: ISBN) for Notes of a Dominatrix. (Sex education
beyond the basics.) Next up will be Chat.
Will let you know when you can ask Amazon for your
copy.
Welcome to Flying Finish Press!
cover photograph by Corbis

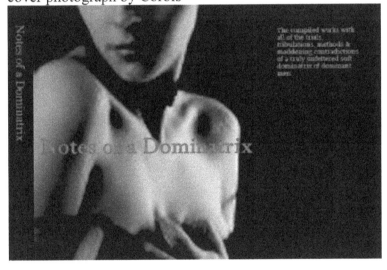

CHAT

Yeah, yeah I know. What Can I say?
Another ISBN.
So what trouble can I get into online?
cover photograph by someone special

Sep 5, 2007
That's an opportunity - on Sept 15th the End of Season 12
goal polo match will be held on the grass field at Great
Meadows. I can take 5 other persons but you'll have to ante'
up $20 and dress in "summer country casual" clothing (a
hilarious idea).
This is a champagne tailgate op.
Let me know if you would like to go.
Remember, I'm driving!

"Still, it doesn't do to murder people, however offensive
they may be."
-Lord Peter Death Bredon Wimsey
I must keep that in mind!
(best remark left by my readers: "More's the pity!")

Sep 6, 2007
It is with deep regret that I inform you that Luciano
Pavarotti, my favorite singing teddybear, has died. There is

something very attractive about living one's life with BRIO! It must also be mentioned that he donated millions to charity.
RIP

THE REGULAR FRIDAY M&G AT F&I HAS BEEN CANCELLED UNTIL FURTHER NOTICE!!!
SO DON'T SHOW UP THERE TOMORROW EXPECTING ANYONE!!

I am supposed to walk for 30 minutes every day for lunch and then do certain stretching exercises. Scotch in the hot tub is fine as long as it is scotch on the rocks and I rub my knee with the cool glass afterwards to reduce the remaining swelling. *sigh* I also have to go to physical therapy once a week for the next 4 weeks until my MRI. After that, it is off to orthopedics.
Well, the price is right. FREE!
Personally, I think it is a case of Not Enough Sex!

Sep 7, 2007
Gentlemen, do not "string me along". Either be here, in your entirety, or be gone. If we are scheduled to meet, CALL or forget the entire thing if you are going to be delayed or cannot make it. Only your death or disease (which also covers car breakdowns and sudden calls into work) excuses you from a date already made.
I want ardent, eager men NOT men who yawn, and scratch themselves as they say "Oh, it's you."
You do NOT want me to say "I have to wash my hair" DO YOU?

Sep 8, 2007
This is the absolute worst time of year for me. It is something to do with the "dying of the light" so eloquently

151

expressed by Dylan Thomas and with the passing of summer. As the end of the year approaches, it seems increasingly like the approach of the end of time.

Perhaps this accounts for this tiredness, this impatience I have been experiencing lately. There is so much I want to do, so much I must do, and so much I hope to do and yet I feel thwarted at every turn. There is no cure. One simply continues forward and moves through it.

My advice to both you and myself:

Rejoice in your accomplishments and forgive yourself your failures and your failings.

Please be aware that Fire & Ice is open for business. It is owned by B.

The M&G held there on Fridays was, D's party.

Due to the situation there (no details will be given out here), D has decided to temporarily DISCONTINUE the Friday M&Gs until she has found a suitable venue elsewhere. Please support D with us by boycotting F&I! Thank you.

So:

there is a F&I but there ISN'T any party there.

Sep 9, 2007

Boat Party!

I always enjoy a good boat party! I especially enjoy them when I can relax and let my aggressiveness come out and play as happened today! Yes, I bumped my head on the cabin ceiling a few times but WOW it was worth it!!

Such FUN people!

Thanks for inviting us!

Sep 10, 2007

"Saturday night at the corner cafe'

I had me some drinks and I'm feeling my way.

*The moon's on the rise
and it looks like a night for romance....
I'm on Easy, Easy Street"*

Yep, that's David Lee Roth belting it out and being
flamboyant to the max.
You have to admit, the man has CAJONES!
and you know how much I enjoy cajones...there's
something about a man clad only in black leather chaps and
g-string...
from the Van Halen website this morning:
"VAN HALEN IMMEDIATELY SELLS OUT
DATES, ADDITIONAL SHOWS ADDED!
Fans Across The Country Show Their Excitement for First
Van Halen/David Lee Roth Tour in More Than 22 Years.
Inducted into the Rock 'N' Roll Hall of Fame in March of
this year, Van Halen has produced a treasured body of
work that fans will admire for decades to come."

just having fun!
Sep 10, 2007
Body Worship
"You begin with him lying face down with a pillow slightly
elevating his upper chest for comfort. The idea is to both
relax and arouse him while discovering exactly what works
with his body. Start at his head and slowly kiss, nibble,
lick, suck, bite, caress with trailing tresses, lips, tongue,
hands, claws, and your body all the way down his. Slowly
means agonizingly slowly. Vary the sides, the direction of
movement, the pressure as you trace graceful arabesques
along his skin. Make a careful mental note of what he and
his body likes and dislikes in the way of touch. He is not
permitted to move during body worship. He must learn to
accept your caress. If you leave slight claw marks make a
note later of how fast they disappear.

153

Have a look at a man's anatomy. The nerves form a network that you can follow. Tracing up his spine with a slightly moist tongue tip and ending with a passionately wet and heavy kiss onto the nape of his neck while holding his shoulders tightly in your arms is most effective both from a nerve stimulating point of view but also from a psychological view, this movement being how a cat kills its prey – the bite to the back of the neck. A man is vulnerable in this position. Such small motions can have profound effects.

Also note how his muscles run and how each connects to the bone. The heaviest pressures should only be applied to areas of heavy muscle or directly onto bone. A man' shoulders and thighs are usually heavily muscled. Beware of applying any pressure onto his joints. When pressing onto bone move along the bone; for example, the femur, the large thigh bone, runs up and down and bears the weight of his body along its length. Pressure across the bone might cause damage while pressure along the bone will not. When 'Stroking the Bones', always move along the bone in the direction of their strength.

Another movement is slowly licking up the backs of his legs from the ankles to his rump. If you lave moisture behind, gently blow onto his skin. This will dry the moisture and chill that bit of skin adding more stimuli. If he has scars, they will usually be sensitive. You can use this sensitivity to great effect as well. Tickling is not desirable. Remember while you are doing this to take the time to appreciate the planes and angles of his body, the feel of his skin, the hardness of his muscles – whatever delights you since you may want to compliment him or remark on it later. Murmurs of appreciation and encouragement during body worship are optional.

Now it is time for him to roll over. Once again begin at the head; kissing the outer corners of his eyes, nibbling his

neck, kissing his throat, tracing the outline of his lips with a dry tongue-tip, etc. Gradually work your way down, do not neglect his fingers and toes either, but do NOT touch his genitals. Take your time and note nuances – learn to "listen" to his body."
-from wickedwomangroup
Explore him. Experiment upon him. Enjoy him.
sounds good to me

Sep 11, 2007
Wicked Woman Group
The idea began as an answer to masculine complaints - basically that sex was more hard work than it was worth. Part of the problem was masculine incompetence, which is addressed elsewhere, but the other part was the feminine mindset that liking sex and being good at it = SLUT. The "if I come too easily he'll think I'm easy" mindset or the "I'm not going to lose control by climaxing" mindset -thus denying a man his reward of having pleased her.
Well, no one wants to think badly about themselves so they do all sorts of mental juggling. Women themselves believe that men like sex more than women; that men need sex more than women do; and other such lies.
wickedwomangroup is MORE about "giving women permission" to ENJOY sex and to become GOOD at it than anything else. Sex does take some study and practice, you know.
Yes, I am aware that "sex isn't everything" but - when you DON'T get enough good sex, sex BECOMES everything. The lack of physical intimacy corrodes the soul.
Good women DO enjoy sex.
I encourage everyone to go to triple w wickedwomangroup dot US, read it and try it for yourselves! Very liberating!

Darling! HAPPY BIRTHDAY !!!! May you have many, many more and ALL that you desire!!!

Sep 12, 2007
Several women have asked me lately about my parties. Am I still doing them? (No, I'm not.) and Will I begin having them again? (undecided.)
I am undecided because although they were a lot of fun - for me anyway - they were also a lot of time-consuming hard work and there were always the hotel problems.
There were other issues as well but nevermind.
For now, I might attend parties given by those I know esp if held in a private home.
If I change my mind later - I'll let you know. Everyone okay with that?

Alpha Males
If you don't know what that means - you aren't one.
There is little fun in seducing submissive men into sexual subjugation. There's also no point in getting involved with "pretenders" - those guys who write things "Scared ya, huh?". PFFFT.
Both types are never "good value".
This Kitten enjoys pouncing upon big strong experienced Teddybears who know what to do as well as how to do it and who also don't give a damn what the world thinks of them for being with me. Why? Because they didn't just get laid - they got LAID!
You may expect glee, mischief, laughter, mishaps (careful, you almost fell off the bed), as well as nothing-held-back mind-blowing sex!

Sep 13, 2007
Quiverfull: "Dedicated to providing encouragement and practical help to those who are striving to raise a large and growing, godly family in today's world!"

Well there's a new movement making the rounds. It is called Quiverfull and it is based upon "that old time religion" wherein the woman subordinates herself to her husband and to God by being a stay at home home-schooling mommy of however many kids they end up having. The 'posterchild' for the movement is a lady with 17 at last count. The husband says they'll have as many children as God chooses to give them.

He sounds almost as if he, the husband, had nothing to do with it. God came down, waved his hand and "plang" up she came pregnant with another child. There's an appalling lack of accepting responsibility here.

There's also the issue of egotism - his genes are better than anyone else's so they SHOULD have as many children as they possibly can. As if this earth needs more of their kids.

I disagree with home-schooling on principle alone so we'll over-look that one for now except to say that home-schooling her kids is most likely the only mental stimulation the poor lady gets. It is also the only area in which she gets to use any of her talents/skills beyond the merely physical ones of being able to have a 'litter' which is something ANY animal can do.

Now you can live how you want to - as long as you keep it to yourself. But this movement is out there going full bore and raging against the modern world. They do not want contraception, they do not want anything other than hetero-marriage, they support the cult of virginity, they actively denigrate women as being fit for only this one role, they are firmly against the separation of church and state (see their literature). And this would make us different from the Middle East how??

Remember the Texas lady who drowned her kids in the bathtub? She was a member of Quiverfull. I do not support what she did but I also damn her husband for not caring enough about her to HELP her. She needed to be away from the kids - send them to school; nothing easier. Be there with her with the kids. He turned a blind eye to her problems. He now has a new wife and has embarked upon the same path.

There literally is no turning back the clock nor can you put the genie back into the bottle. People have tried for centuries to return to a simpler life etc. and it is all based upon fear. If we stray we'll be damned. Fear is to be faced, people. Rather than being a coward running away from life - try embracing it instead. Gird up, turn toward fear and damn its eyes while daring it to do its worst!

Beats drowning your kids in the bathtub.

Here's a tidbit from their website about contraceptives: *"Many Christians who are active in the evolving anti-birth-control arena state frankly that what links their efforts is a religious commitment to altering the moral landscape of the country. In particular, and not to put too fine a point on it, they want to change the way Americans have sex. Dr. Stanford, the F.D.A. adviser on reproductive-health drugs, proclaimed himself "fully committed to promoting an understanding of human sexuality and procreation radically at odds with the prevailing views and practices of*

*our contemporary culture." Focus on the Family posts a
kind of contraceptive warning label on its Web site:
"Modern contraceptive inventions have given many an
exaggerated sense of safety and prompted more people
than ever before to move sexual expression outside the
marriage boundary." Contraception, by this logic,
encourages sexual promiscuity, sexual deviance (like
homosexuality) and a preoccupation with sex that is
unhealthful even within marriage."*

St. Augustine of Hippo - who began all of this anti-sex
nonsense - has ALOT to answer for.

(Comment received: "I wish I could say, "sister...say it ain't
so", but I'm all too familiar with this particular evil. I didn't
know it had a name, but my oldest brother and his wife
have been practicing members forever. Six kids, and the
last one nearly killed her, all "home-schooled". The oldest
one, at 18 they married off to a man older than me and she
now has 4 children and 1 miscarriage to her credit with no
hope of ever knowing the life she could have lived. The
youngest they are getting ready to marry off to a man 20
yrs her senior, confined to a wheelchair with MS. I cry for
them often. The only one of the six who escaped is my
R...my rebellious, beautiful R. It damn near killed her, but
she found the strength and is now living HER life. As we
were never allowed to spend time with any of them, (evil
ones that we were), R found me and I cannot tell you the
joy I have had getting to know her and love her. She's a
beautiful young woman with so many questions, so many
blank spots and it does my heart good to know that she
didn't buy into the bullshit, she fought for a life of her own.
(The man they're marrying my youngest niece off to was
supposed to be R's husband...this is what finally pushed her
to run.) Long story short, I thank you for bringing things

such as this out into the open...I thank you for being the strong woman that you are...and I thank you for reminding all of us that there is much left to fight in this our "free" world.

...I'm happy to post this in the hopes that others might realize this is REAL; and I so agree with you on the women who drowned her Children. I've always thought that he too should have been brought up on charges so that the world could see HIS part in the whole sad mess.")

Sep 14, 2007
A much better group to support is: Girls, Inc.
from our local chapter's website:
"Welcome to Girls Incorporated of the Washington, DC Metropolitan Area (Girls Inc. WDCMA)!
Our mission
To inspire all girls to be Strong, Smart and Bold!
Our vision
Empowered girls and an equitable society

Girls Incorporated of the Washington, DC Metro Area is an affiliate of the national non-profit youth organization, Girls Inc., with roots dating back to 1864. Through our research–based programs and activities, we provide supportive, enriching opportunities where girls...

Develop confidence
Expand skills
Unlock talent
Broaden their vision
Become leaders
Prepare for a successful future!

Girls Inc. knows that growing up is serious business and that a strong, smart and bold girl is up to the challenge!

Girls Inc. Girls' Bill of Rights

Girls have the right to be themselves and to resist gender stereotypes.
Girls have the right to express themselves with originality and enthusiasm.
Girls have the right to take risks, to strive freely, and to take pride in success.
Girls have the right to accept and appreciate their bodies.
Girls have the right to have confidence in themselves and to be safe in the world.
Girls have the right to prepare for interesting work and economic independence.

Learn how you can GET INVOLVED!"
Please note: I support the same rights and responsibilities for boys as I do for girls.

Sep 15, 2007
The Feline Aloofness series!
Cats are not entirely as aloof as they might first appear. For example: Thor, pictured here, is intensely interested in the SRM's mowing of the lawn. Back and forth; back and forth. Cute huh?

Sep 16, 2007
Cats are not all that shy either. And here you thought it was only human males that liked 'a bit of air' around those bits or did that 'look at me' thing. Thor: The Destroyer of Worlds, clearly exhibits his 'assets' here.
Nuts anyone?

Younger cats love to wrestle, romp, stalk, and play fight.
Here, Thor, cleverly masquerading as a 'sofa leopard'
attempts to sneak up upon the tv-watching SRM.
Somehow, the mighty SRM manages to remain unafraid of
the pending assault.
Warning: Thor draws blood.
(SRM's comment "the little schnook.")

Thor has this 'thing' about water or perhaps it is plumbing.
He's always butting in and has become my 'bathing buddy'.
Very odd in a cat - a creature not generally fond of getting
wet.
Don't drink the bath water!
(Silly cat!)

Sep 17, 2007
The LeGuin Test
According to Ursula K. LeGuin, long may she reign, there
are two types of people in this world. To wit: dragons and
hamsters.
So which are you, people?!
- Totally scaly! Dragon all the way!
- Periodically scaly - only a dragon on Tuesdays and
  Thursdays.
- Morphing betwixt and between!
- Frequently furry - at least hamster three days per
  week.
- Totally furry! Now doing the Hamster Dance!

(results = 11 total votes; 5 Dragons, 1 Almost Dragon, 4
who are half and half, and 1 almost hamster. No one owned
up to being totally Hamster.)

It's Not Just in Emails!
162

There is an almost automatic sequence one can expect, at my age, to get in the chatroom from younger men.
1. Oh Wow! You're hot! I love older women! Fuck me, please!
2. No? Well, you old hag! No one wants your dried up old pussy anyway! And those saggy old breasts! You're disgusting! I won't be in here when I'm your age!
3. Send her an immediate email, once again telling her how HOT she is and reiterating the message "fuck me, please".
Yes, I'd bet their mothers are just so PROUD!
If you have slammed her in the chatroom, do NOT expect a POSITIVE response to any email.

Sep 18, 2007
Cakes
Although I am not 'the baker' of my household (that was my daughter), I can still turn out a delicious and nice-looking product.
My favorite is "Satan Cake" which is one step up from 'devil's food'. More chocolate which is never a bad thing!
For those few who are insane enough to NOT like chocolate, I also make a sprightly spice cake or a robust carrot cake. They aren't my favorites (no chocolate) but they are very tasty. For snaking, there's nothing better than my gingerbread which tends to bite you back!
I will be making a very special cake this Friday that I hope to be able to deliver Friday evening.
A small but dangerously delicious cake with hidden secrets to enjoy!
How well do you bake, baby? What is your specialty?

Daughter and granddaughters will be visiting us this October BUT if all goes well, they'll be here for 19 weeks!
Son-in-law will be enlisted, trained, and out doing whatever - finally! This is an outcome to be devoutly wished!

Some of you might face such things with some trepidation, but not this Kitten! Bring them on! I can take it! If I had ponies, I'd be teaching my granddaughters to ride! As it is, I'll teach them how to drive! LOL So they're only 1 year and a few months old- start them early!

But I betcha my daughter won't let me. She's become so very "mater familias" since she's had her babies. Stodgy, staid, sober (inset a shudder here); she must have gotten it from her father. But I have two small pink cat o' nine tails waiting for my granddaughters as symbols of their role/mission in life!

Kittens Rule!

Guys, can we talk?

Look, if I am not there waiting for you, please call. I have issues with time and getting out of the office as well as a slight problem with knitting my schedule into a cat's cradle. It really is best to double-check and make sure that I am on my way to you or that I haven't forgotten you entirely. Ten to one, I also do not have your phone number with me. Hey! I am a busy woman! So many men and so little time! The trouble is, you don't know which it is going to be beforehand and will just have to take your chances if you don't communicate.

Is you in, or is you ain't?

Sep 19, 2007
There isn't nearly enough room in helicopters. TMI??

Sep 20, 2007
No-Loads
There is this HUGE disconnect in understanding - honey, just because they don't charge a load or a 12b-1 fees, doesn't mean they pay their bills with a smile.

164

This is how it works: they take your money, invest it, get a return which they report to all and sundry, then they skim 6 to 8% of that return off the top before distributing the remainder to the account holders. So that lovely 12% return is actually a meager 4 to 6% return when it gets to you. And that's on ALL your money EVERY year.

What's really sweet is they don't have to tell you this because it is not called a "fee" or a "charge". So they get to use your money to make themselves money for FREE and they don't have to tell you they're doing it! All interest and dividends earned come from the companies the no-load fund invests in - not from the no-load fund itself.

So it is 6 to 8% per year on all your money every year in a "no-load" OR it is 5.75% (Class A) on all NEW money and at most 1.5% per year on all money thereafter. The 5.75% is only charged on money newly invested so that's done only ONCE and NOT each and every year as with a "no-load".

(pausing here so you can do the math.)

This is why actually having a financial advisor pays off! They know this stuff!

Capice, baby?

Playtime with Teddybears
WOW!!
Mmmmm caressing my rump as I lie on the bed and we discuss the grandbabies coming for a visit and how your pesky clients have been extra pesky this past month. the oil massage extends further and further as the conversation dies away and our thoughts become focused upon sex. You have got the touch, baby! Kissing breasts then lips then those other lips - you're so very good at cunnilingus! - as I caress you in return. Love your fur! Move the Kitten into position as you stand facing the side of the bed. Kissing my instep and you slide on in. I have no defenses with a man

165

who knows how to caress G-Spots and posterior fornixes. Wow! Again and again and again. Just keep rolling! Trickling on more oil. Further caresses here and there. You came twice and I've lost count. Doesn't matter! Rolling over and lying face down as my teddybear moves on and in. You love it when I come all over you. So wet. More cunnilingus. Incredibly good! Mmmmm and that vibe! Rolling into spoon and then moving on to missionary. Squeezing down on you; getting so very wet; turning you into a frenzied fucking fiend.
6 for you was it? I'll have to do better next time!

Sep 21, 2007
The cake parts are done and awaiting assembly. Everything has turned out well.
The library books are over-due by one day.
I haven't made my bed or gotten dressed yet.
Polo tonight but I have no plans afterward - yet.
And lunch - well, he called to say he's running late.
How is your Friday going?

Proofreaders Needed!
Both Chat and Notes of a Dominatrix have their ISBNs and I need proofreaders to look them over for those errors and subtle things that can go wrong.
Any volunteers?
p.s. there is recompenses

Sep 22, 2007
Too busy so you cannot have a blog post today.
Sorry, but there it is.

Sep 23, 2007
And you cannot have a blog post today either!
Because you weren't bad enough! LOL

Sep 24, 2007
I Was Tagged?
Oh dear!
1. I am a risk-taking adventuress. One glimpse of my driving record will prove it.
2. I love science and graduated from high school third in my state in science.
3. I actually did lose the top of my bikini while body surfing at the beach one summer.
4. I cook meat better than I bake although I can bake a good loaf of bread.
5. I can shoot rather well, fence pretty well, but cannot cast a fishing line correctly to save my soul.
6. A natural-born brunette. All of my brothers and my sister began as blondes but not me. I was dark from the start.
7. My two books will be out in time for you to buy them as XMas gifts for your BFFs.
8. If I don't get 15 hours of good to awesome sex each week, I get "testy".
9. I would cheerfully and without the slightest hesitation slaughter the entire population of the world to protect my children and my grandchildren.
10. I cannot whistle.
Ok. That's it!
Consider yourselves, all of you, as TAGGED!
dare ya!!

Feeding Off of the Male
It is no good trying to get away from me. Don't think you're going to control the motion either. If you try it, I'll just growl at you and press you down more firmly onto the bed. Just lie still and give it up like a man, baby!
GRRRRRRRR
Atkins approved!

Sep 25, 2007
Today I baked three types of cookies - choco chip, oatmeal raisin, and peanut butter. Baked up a dozen of each and stored the remaining dough for next time.
They were goooooooood!!!
hiding the cookies from you people

Sep 26, 2007
Darwin Awards
I'd like to nominate OJ Simpson.
Who would you like to nominate?

In my list of criteria, I state that a man must be "nearby". Thank you to all of you from Spain etc who write in. This requirement is entirely for my convenience. I have done enough traveling in my life. I do not host either.
Nearby = 60 minutes at 74 mph MAX with 30 minutes being the minimum.
Got it?

"Come over to the Dark Side! We have cookies!"
LOL
Answers posted: "I'm there! I thought you were hiding them from us.", "Do we get milk too?", "Unloved cookies is a terrible thing. How can I help?!", and "Hmmmmmmmmmmm.... Coookkkkieessss (homer simpson)".

Sep 27, 2007
"Pray tell what dark side is that, m'lady?"
"That where I tie men up and do with them what I will."
Yes, I'll give you a cookie afterwards.

"EvilKitten... how about Option #3: you wearing nothing at all standing in front of me - just in reach
ps - love how you wave your tail!"
This tail? Thank you. Option #3? That might work!

VOTE FOR ME!
If all of you 330 watchers vote for me, and the competition is tough, I might win something! Fancy that! Would be nice. Vote here sexiest look in a pic! and here BLOG THAT IS THE MOST FUN!.
Pretty please?
I can always make more cookies.

Sep 28, 2007
Well, I'm tied with a guy for "Sexiest Look" and am tied for second on "Most Fun Blog". Oh well! No win for me! Do I still have to deliver those cookies? I suppose I'll just have to console myself...somehow.

Sep 29, 2007
Please go here, BEST NEWCOMER!!!, and vote for my friend, B B! And here, MOST ALL AROUND INTERESTING BLOG!, to vote for this blog! Well, of curse mine is the 'most all-around interesting' - after all, YOU read it! Then here, funniest blog:, to vote for M! You KNOW he's hilarious! Quoting M:
"You know you're going to Hell when you have just bought your wife's 20th wedding anniversary present from the woman who just gave you a blowjob. I'm so doomed! "
Thank you!

Sep 30, 2007
Spent the day relaxing, as much as one can, with my granddaughters, daughter, and son-in-law. Lots of things to

169

do! We wrote out a list for the coming week! Tomorrow, the bank and Tuesday, the financial planner, etc., etc., etc. Cha cha cha!!!

Took some fabulous pictures which you are NOT going to see since my granddaughters are children - but they are incredibly CUTE!

Sexual Agendas

There are those who follow the concept of "few" and those who follow the concept of "many". Generally speaking those who are into "few" are female and those who are into "many" are male. At least that is the theory. One is not reproductively successful when one has children. Your children's children's children have to have children before you can say you are reproductively successful. Your existence proves that your ancestors were successful but that is no guarantee that you will be. To combat this uncertainty, those who follow the concept of "few" seek out the best partner possible, they have only a few children themselves, and then they invest a great deal of time and effort making sure those children are healthy and have healthy children of their own. they are committed to just those few. Those who follow the concept of "many" have as many children as they physically can and leave it up to chance or providence that those children will thrive and go onto reproduce in their turn since they themselves cannot possible look after that many children on their own. They are playing the odds. As a society, America has gone, for the most part, from being a nation using the concept of "many" under the idea that "many hands make light work" to being a nation that embraces the concept of "few" in which we invest everything we can.

What do you think?

While I am a distant third in all of the contests for which I have been nominated; Baby Brandy is second and M is almost dead last. Shame, shame, shame!
Please add your vote while there is still time!
Else I shall have to take 'drastic measures' *EG*

October
2007

Oct 1, 2007
Picture two cats: one a large gray ex-male tabby and one
big but not as big fully-male ginger tabby playing "OJ
Simpson Slow Car Chase" all over the house with the
occasional pounce and bursts of "express train". They're
just playing! Add in an intrepid 1 and 1/2 year old child
who loves cats. So now you know how it is around here!
PANDEMONIUM!!!
I need a drink!

No Comments, huh? Well, you asked for this!
Quote:
"You trust me, don't' you, baby" I whisper in your ear as
the blindfold goes around your head. "Yes, ma'am, I do."
You whisper back. We are standing in my home office; you
naked before me. I just adore your muscles and the fur that
lightly covers them. "Hmmmm, you look so very tasty." I
purr at you while I kiss the side of your neck. I cuff your
wrists together and slip the connecting chain over a hook in
the ceiling. You can stand easily yet your hands are out of
the way. Now I can do with you whatever I will. We
haven't been together for some time so you are already
excited. Your penis is erect and aching – begging for me.
Not yet. Not yet. I move around you caressing all but your
penis and testicles with the articles of clothing I remove
from myself ending up facing your back. "Ready, baby?"
"Yes". "What do you say?" "Please." My claws slowly
rake down your shoulders, your back, and over your rump –
deep enough to be felt but not so deep as to leave marks.
Ah! The pleasure you feel! Gently, I soothe your skin with
my hands."Shhh, baby, shhh." I whisper to you. Standing
behind you, I gently caress up the front of your thighs and
onto your hips as I press up close against your back. You
can feel me, naked from the waist up, against you. My right
cheek rests against your left shoulder as I continue to stroke

your thighs, hips and tummy. With agonizing slowness I gently lick up the back of your neck and blow a gentle stream of air across it to help the moisture evaporate. I both see and feel you quiver. So very delightful. Pre-cum has formed on the head of your penis. You begin whispering over and over again "Please, fuck me." Begging me to touch your penis. Begging me to relieve your lust. Not yet. Not yet. I kiss you gently and trace your lips with the tip of my tongue as I caress your breasts and nipples. The final bits of silk undies slide over them on their way to the floor. Then I gently claw and pinch your now hard nipples. "Do you want me, baby?" I whisper to you. "Oh, yes, please." You exhale back. I lick up the front of your neck from sternum to chin and kiss your lips again. I press my now naked body against you, your penis between us. You are sweating with the effort needed to control yourself. You have to keep from cumming for as long as is possible. You have begun to pant as I continue to circle and caress you with hands, lips, tongue and claws. "Please fuck me." You are getting louder and more insistent. "Shhh, baby, shhh." I whisper back. You must learn to relax and enjoy the attention your mistress gives you. Learn to relish the agony of your desire. Feel the lust overwhelming your brain, flooding out all thoughts. You can smell my special perfume. It only adds to your frustration. You are almost weeping at being kept waiting for so very, very long. "Now." I quietly say as I take firm hold of your penis with my right hand and your testicles in my left. Your orgasm comes crashing through you from the center of the earth it seems as you throw your head back and cry out. Your cum gushing up onto your belly. Your body shakes as your senses are overloaded. You cannot see, you cannot hear, you cannot remember your own name. Yes, baby, cum for me. I want all of it. Hang there exhausted, empty, and unable to stand, with your sperm covering your belly. So

very pretty. "What do you say, baby?" "Thank you, ma'am."
UNQUOTE.
Love those "drastic measures"!
best answer received: "You would be one night I would have to dream over and over and probably still wouldn't believe came true."

Oct 2, 2007
You all grew up speaking English, spent several years in school studying English and yet here you are posting things like this: "a poem I had wrote many, many years ago". This site even has spellcheck on it!
(now reviewing my own posts for typos)
Please have mercy upon me and understand that 'brake' and 'break' are two different and not interchangeable things; that verbs have a past tense, and that both gender and number matter!
btw: just re-arranging the lines in someone's poem does NOT make it your own work. It remains plagiarizing.
When in doubt - HIT THE SPELLCHECK BUTTON!

Oct 3, 2007
BB log Awards Update
We're all third in our respective contests except for M who is fourth in his. Please vote! Links are in previous posts below on his topic.
Thank you!
We certainly do not want me to take 'drastic measures' again, do we?
EG

A new blog game for you to play!
who am I ???
Enjoy!

Oct 4, 2007
New Pix
Every 6 months or so, I like to "freshen-up" my photographs. I have several sets taken and then I edit them. They may or may not be used - depends upon how they turn out. I try to maintain a certain look - one that separates the men from the boys.

Erotic is not explicit. Erotic suggests, hints, teases - it does not get all "see my cervix"?This is why black and white is so frequently used. for erotic photographs.
I am also working on another book and will need specialized pictures for it. Black and white photographs from one specific person are required.
Fortunately, there are lots of willing photographers out there!

"Who are you to judge me? I don't believe that you are God."
No, I am not God; but when one is an adult, one is expected to exercise good judgment about what one says and does, with whom one associates, and a host of other details such as those involving one's 401k and precisely what one said to the IRS.
So, YES, you will be judged by others! You can squawk about it all you want - to absolutely no effect. - but that squawking only makes you seem more puerile than ever.
It is true that one does not stereotype others or holds others accountable for what they cannot help being - female/male/trans; likes boys/ likes girls; black/white/red/mocha/yellow; IQ of 50; and so on.
But everything else is fair game.

Vote here <u>sexiest look in a pic!</u>, here <u>BEST NEWCOMER!!!</u>, here <u>MOST ALL AROUND INTERESTING BLOG!</u>, here <u>funniest blog:</u>, and here <u>BLOG THAT IS THE MOST FUN!.</u>
Thank you!

Oct 4, 2007
PROOFREADERS
Please get those back to me ASAP thank you!
Time to get those books out there!

Oct 5, 2007
"I'm going to jump into bed and sleep for the next two weeks!"
"Who with, dear?"
"Almost anyone, dear."
Racy, racy! A Little Night Music.
The best part of the picture was when Diana Rigg smashed the mirror. One of those 'perfect moments'!

Daughter and her family here until the 12th, then only part of her family remaining; my mother coming down as well and I have no idea where she'll sleep - guess the JRM will go into a sleeping bag. Either that or the one granddaughter will have to vacate the bed.
If they were all cats I could just sit out a big box for them to snuggle/sleep in!

Upcoming events:
Oct 6- house party
Oct 14th - trail ride followed by a party
Oct 20th - Monster Mash
Oct 27th and/or 31st - Halloween
I'm going as The Vampiress - Elisabeth Bathory.
What are you going as?

Dontcha just hate it when a good gripe session gets interrupted by someone being sensible?
"no progress w/o risks"
I had to agree with him. Galling isn't it?

October Is Breast Cancer Awareness Month!!!
Need help?
www dot heavy dot com slash video slash 1100
The guys on the sofa are a nice touch.

Oct 6, 2007
Y'all are not commenting again and you know what THAT means!!!

QUOTE:
You men are so lovely. I have both of you slowly removing my clothes as I pin up my long dark auburn hair. First my top is removed, then my bra – your hands lingering. Ah! Don't linger too long! Shoes first then remove the jeans; sliding them down over my hips and thighs. Then my thongs follow the jeans onto the floor. Such hands you two have!

You each begin slowly rubbing scented oil lightly onto my arms and legs. Work from the outside in and up. Your fingers trailing lines of fire on my skin as you so slowly and gently caress my flesh. Soon my skin glistens in the firelight. My hips begin to move. I guide one of you to my vagina and the other to my breasts. Give me what I want. Forget being gentle! Do not hold back!

Kiss me, baby. Use your hands. Ah, yes! Drink deeply now. Such fine lovers you are! Come and you lay down and you? You know where you are. I press my vagina to your lips as he enters me from behind. I am so very hungry. Hold on tight! So, so very good! Assuage this rising tidal wave of lust within me! I bend my neck to feed off of you. My mouth sucking; my lips, and tongue slide around your penis. Feed me! Leave a line of small bites down my spine; livid against my skin! Come on! Come on!

Writhing, screaming, cumming, gushing in between you; nothing matters except my overwhelming desire for everything you can give me. I want it. I want all of it. I want all of it now! My flesh, wet from your sweat, becomes deep pink as I flush. You both feel so very good! Such magnificent lovers! You rotate beneath me and move up a little on the bed. I follow you and slide down on top of your penis. Oh, yes! He follows us and slides in behind. Both of you are inside of me. My muscles wrap around you in a stranglehold.

Warm and very, very wet as you both can feel. Come for me, baby you hear whispered in your ear; my breath on the side of your neck. I move with you both in an abandoned rhythm. Let it loose, baby! I want it. Give me all that you have. Come for me. Come for me. Relentless and ruthless, I drive you both toward orgasm. Yes!

Lying there between you, your afterglow barely begun, you hear something that drives forth your fear. I say, with an unmistakable gleam in my eye, "More".
UNQUOTE
Y'all ready to behave now?

GOOD NEWS/BAD NEWS
First, the BAD news:
The Oct 14th Trail Ride has been canceled due to too many conflicts in the schedule. Sorry!

Now, the GOOD news:
Alexandra, granddaughter #1, has new socks and fancy
sneakers (Reeboks) so she can run even faster now! She's
busy showing them off to her mother and the SRM as we
speak!
Rocky, son-in-law, will be able to say while under enemy
fire "This is nothing! What's REALLY scary is driving
with my mother-in-law!" I had to point out to him several
times that there aren't any brakes on the passenger side of
my truck. The G forces and loud music was enjoyed by
Alexandra as she cheerfully waved "bye bye" to the cars we
passed.
A fun-filled day thus far and a houseparty this evening!
What could be better?

Oct 7, 2007
I do soooo enjoy a good house party! That sound you hear
is me purrrrrrrrrrrrrrrrrrring. Mmmmmmmmmmm! They had
lots of teddybears there for me to play with!
What do you think makes for a good house party?

The Wicked Woman Group
We are reformatting the group:
Adventurous persons remain invited to participate but we
require HOSTS/HOSTESSES. Therefore, couples who
swing are ENCOURAGED to join with us. We can offer
you experienced, skilled, friendly, and well mannered
group players.
If you are in the lifestyle, we'd like to hear from you!

Oct 8, 2007
FLYING PINK!
QUOTE:
"Flying the friendly skies just isn't as fun as it used to be. I
enjoy a nice pat down as much as the next single gal, but I

180

need more than 3oz. of the myriad potions that make me beautiful to survive a long weekend excursion! You feel my pain, I know.

As I was jetting to and from Atlanta recently, I was sorting through your product suggestions for fun and fabulous items that benefit breast cancer research and awareness. One darling flight attendant noticed my "pile of pink" and offered a great suggestion of her own--Delta's Flying Pink initiative! When you buy a glass of pink lemonade on board your flight, your purchase helps fund a researcher in the study of breast cancer for an entire year! FLY DELTA!"

UNQUOTE

from The Little Black Book

What are you doing to support the Pink Campaign?

BLACK LEATHER ANYONE?

I will be announcing the award for the All-Around Sexiest Blogger as soon as BBB has set the date for the Awards banquet.

I will be wearing my "domme biker-chic" outfit which got this review from the SRM:

"You can ride on the back of my bike anytime, Sweetheart! Mmmmmmmmmmmmm.

I hope this will take place after the Monster Mash since I will be w/o a computer during that event.

Oct 9, 2007

Not having a working keyboard - horrific!

Using the on-screen keyboard - tedious!

Waiting for B B to open - dull!

Not being able to just buy a wireless keyboard itself - tiresome!

One wireless keyboard and mouse - $60

Being able to type like a normal person so I can annoy you all - PRICELESS!

bwa ha ha ha haaaaaa!

If you read my profile and you do NOT meet my criteria, please do NOT email me saying things like "I know I'm not _____ but I thought I'd take a chance."

WHY?
Did you think I was:
A. Merciful?
B. Desperate?
C. Confused?
D. All of the above?
HAH! I know precisely the sort of man that revs my engines and I see no reason to 'settle' or 'experiment' with other types; not after 39 years of this sort of thing, thank you. Been there; done that - three times - just to make sure! I'm sure you're all that you proclaim yourselves to be (momentary niceness - it won't happen again) but what you are is NOT what I want.
Capice?

More bad advice:
"Combining these perspectives creates a cocky, indifferent and aloof air to your personality that will put you well on your way to communicating on a sexual level."
"Be mysterious, which might entail giving her indirect answers about your work and education. When you do these things, she'll get the feeling that you are not a guy who is intimidated by women -- and she'll LOVE you for it."
"Always send mixed signals. Be unpredictable by mixing it up and changing your patterns. Never let the line go slack; always keep some tension on it. Never act apologetic or insecure, and never try to get approval or act like you're trying to impress." - from askmen.com

Fellas look: Sorry, I know the author (a male) is trying to help but this sort of thing works in reverse with self-aware women who confidently embrace their sexuality. Any mixed signals or show of being disinterested, insincere or unenthusiastic and we'll move on - there are always plenty of willing men after all.
You don't need games; you need practice.

Have you played, who am I ???, yet?
Did you guess or did you go and look for the answers?
Get in this now while it is still HOT!

"There's just something about toile. It's quintessentially "girly." It's a shabby chic decorator's staple. It's something we ladies have squarely in our column. Want to keep your handsome but burly hubby out of your favorite chair? Upholster it in toile. When used in decorating, it is the equivalent of kryptonite to males." - from The Black Book

Aaaah, so THAT'S the secret!
If I have my car's interior done in toile - will he NOT want to borrow it?

KITTEN-ISMS
1. We are all polyamorous if only we'd acknowledge the fact. We all also want a secure and loving primary relationship. Fortunately, the two are not mutually exclusive!
2. My 'test' for anything of this sort, relationships, is two years - if it lasts beyond two years, then we're a-okay! I have such a long test because once I commit, I commit - I am NOT a half-hearted woman. Of perhaps it is just because I hate admitting my mistakes? Hmmm.

3. Whores and sluts? Face it peeps, some of us are just fun-loving guys and gals.
Add your "-isms" below:

Oct 10, 2007
I am no better and no worse than most on/in here. Better than some, worse than others - sure. Aren't we all. No, you're not going to read a post about how much I have learned/changed/felt etc since coming onto this site. If you wanted that kind of thing - wrong place, darlings! I remain the same ancient, gnarled, and gravely debilitated domme I previously was. Yes, I know a lot. Read the profile and you will see that was to be expected. My library runs from Astrophysics to Zola. New books added damn near daily! I do collect authors as well.
These glasses were earned, babies!
If I do not know it all, it isn't for lack of trying!
so: Read any good books lately?

NICKNAMES
We all have them! C reminded me of my old nickname during my military days when he called me "Legs". One cannot wear size 29 x 36 jeans and be called anything else. Even the Irish comedian who dragged me up in front of the crowd at the club one summer while TDY at Wethersfield in the UK remarked that I was mostly legs. I still am even if my jean size has risen to 34 x 36. That was mine - what's yours?

Oct 11, 2007
There are two cats side by side on the windowsill and a baby Vivian on the bench in my office. All of them are making small noises similar to "squeaking brakes". It is so cute.

The orthopedic doctor says I will live. No, really! I just
have to continue doing my exercises (walking) and all will
be well; even at "my time of life" - how I HATE it when
they say it!

The son-in-law departs at 4pm after which the daughter
will be despondent. Son-in-law signed the paper nicely so
all will be well there. Oh well! Grilled flank steak and red
wine for dinner! Other than this it has been the usual day
around here.

How has your day gone today?

THREESOMES

"A threesome is the term which describes a sexual act
involving three people, also referred to as a ménage à trois.
To clarify the roles, a threesome does not have to mean that
all three people are engaging in sexual activity specifically
with all people in the threesome, but can be one person as
the focus of attention (two men focusing on one woman,
two women focusing on one man, etc.), and the other two
engaging in sex with the same one person, but not
necessarily with each other. However, all people are
together in the same location during the experience. Some
people think that when two men are with one woman that
the men must somehow be bisexual, but this is often not the
case. Instead, they just jointly participate in the threesome,
both focusing on the same one woman.

Threesomes are of course also possible between all-same-
sex participants, ie. three men or three women. This in fact
removes one of the complications described above, as all
the participants are presumably of the same or similar
sexual orientation.

Another term for this is "The Tricycle"."

-Wikipedia

Often seen as a "beginners" step into swinging, but there are those who prefer threesomes since finding one more compatible person is easier than finding two more compatible people.

It is a common misconception that bisexuality MUST exist for a successful threesome - this is not the case. Usually, the singleton gets the attention of the other two. They gang-up on him or her. This is why I like MFMs.

Some couples tell me that finding women to join in an on-going relationship is easier. They feel that women are more socially open even if not bisexual. Then there are those couples where sex with women somehow does not "count" and they go that route to assuage the husband's territorial feelings. There are women who feel that "one cock is enough". You see this here on this site - couple seeking only females or other couples for full swaps or FMFs.

This is why threesomes are regarded, by the swing community, as a beginner's step. Most swingers do full swaps, since most are couples, without bisexuality. Although bisexual women are acceptable, bisexual men are not except in select circles. Unfair but what are you going to do?

I prefer MFMs with two comely and congenial teddybears but with an especially skilful comely teddybear I'll enjoy a non-bi FMF.

How about you? Which do you prefer, FMF or MFM, and why?

Oct 12, 2007
This morning a 27 yr old Phillipina almost killed the 52 yr old SRM at the Rte 123 interchange on 95 North. She dove for the exit right into the SRM on his big, noisy, bright red HD Ultra Classic. They were "together" long enough for the SRM to punch a hole in her car. They all stopped and

the police came. Police did not do an accident report "since there was no injury and no serious damage". Now the SRM's lower leg hurts, his hand might also hurt, and he's very angry - the bike may not be straight but it is drive-able. The JRM saw them and stopped to ask if the SRM was okay?

Guess what the woman said?
I never saw him!
Grrrrrrrrrrrrrr!

Oct 13, 2007
We have found the almost perfect party place for our weekly Friday evening M&G's!
Fireplace, sofas, dance floor, decent music, pool tables, tables and chairs that aren't bolted to the floor, smoking, reasonable prices and a $2 cover charge after 8pm, outside terrace for the summer, well located - and it is NOT crowded although it has a 300 person capacity (more or less).
Check it out for yourselves and see if our "Advance Committee" is not correct!

The first proofreader has returned his copy of Further Chat and he's found some errors!
Sorry about that! I shall try to do better- really I will! I promise!
pressing the spellcheck button

Camellia halies sinesis
Green tea leaves are treated by high temperatures and not allowed to ferment resulting in a lighter tea with a grass undertone.

The green tea plant is a perennial with a 40 year life span. It is usually planted as seedlings (raised from cuttings in a nursery) in September to October (this can be later in cooler climates) in north - south rows 1.8 meter apart. The plant spacing is 300-400 mm and usually the seedlings are pruned at planting and every year for the next 4-5 years till harvesting begins. The plants usually require a complete NPK fertilizer at planting and at regular intervals after that. Weed control is important and mulching of young trees is recommended.

The production of top quality green tea requires fairly specific climatic conditions. It needs plenty of water (1200 mm or more so irrigation is essential), deep, well-drained soils, and 8-12 weeks of cold, wet, wintry weather every year. Wind can be a damaging factor, as can be late frosts which can severely affect the first flush of the green tea leaf tips.

The crop will start to produce significant quantities in about year 5 and by year 8 will be nearly in full production. It is harvested three times a year, either by hand (which is expensive) or by machine (some of the simpler ones are relatively inexpensive). The first harvest about September produces the best quality tea and typical yields are of the order of 1400 kg dry weight/ha. The second harvest in December/January produces less (approximately 1000 kg/ha) whilst the last picking in March/ April can produce quantities of 200 - 300 dry weight (DW) kg/ha and have the lowest quality. Processing equipment is essential and this can be very expensive.

The production process consists of 4 steps: withering, steaming, rolling, and drying. % pounds of tea leaves yields 1 pound of finished tea. Withering is the initial drying of the leaves to remove surface moisture. The leaves are then steamed or roasted to stop enzyme production (oxidation). This keeps the tea light, fresh, green, and antioxidant-rich. The leaves are then rolled to break down the cell barriers which releases the flavor when the tea is finally brewed. The tea is then thoroughly dried before being packaged.

Recipes:

Simple Tea Pops

Approximately 3 cup (24 oz.) of liquid - either iced tea or hot tea will be needed to make 8 tea pops. Tea used for tea pops should be brewed double strength.
6 tea bags
3 cups hot water
Brew tea bags in hot water for 5 minutes. Add sugar as desired. Let tea cool slightly. Pour tea into tea pops mold leaving a little room at the top. Place filled molds in the freezer for at least 2 hours or until solid.

Hot Spiced Tea

2 qts. tea
2 c. water
2 c. sugar
2 large cans pineapple
1 1/2 c. lemon juice
3 c. orange juice
1 stick cinnamon
1 t. whole cloves & 1 smashed clove of nutmeg - tied in cheesecloth
Directions:
Pour 2 qt. boiling water over 8 teabags. Brew 5 minutes, remove tea bags, set aside. Boil 2 c. each water and sugar

together 10 minutes to make syrup. Add remaining ingredients. Bring to boil. Simmer 20 minutes. Remove cloves and cinnamon. Serve hot.

-recipes from Stash Tea

Health Benefits

The secret of green tea lies in the fact it is rich in catechin polyphenols, particularly epigallocatechin gallate (EGCG). EGCG is a powerful anti-oxidant: besides inhibiting the growth of cancer cells, it kills cancer cells without harming healthy tissue. It has also been effective in lowering LDL cholesterol levels, and inhibiting the abnormal formation of blood clots. The latter takes on added importance when you consider that thrombosis (the formation of abnormal blood clots) is the leading cause of heart attacks and stroke.

Now you know! A substitute for all of those bottles of water you see everywhere.
(other websites addresses removed to save them embarrassment)

Oct 14, 2007
A re-write of my previous post, Guidance for Men.
No matter who you are seeking, you should precisely define your target and then give them what they want. Make sure that your entire presentation, from profile to pix, is properly calibrated to appeal to your target.
For example: I am a dominatrix. Attitude is not only expected but desired. Unlike my whip-swinging sisters, I am a "soft" dominatrix who is into psychology not pain, humiliation, or abuse - I seduce. So the attitude is changed somewhat to reflect this more "sly" and "evil" approach to getting sex on my terms. The feline is the perfect image and

by making it a "kitten" - so harmless, fluffy, and cute - well, you see where this is going don't you.

You can do the same sort of analysis and then target your market.

This does really work! Try it!

I have my own private floor show as "The Boys", Thor and Havoc, wrestle and tumble and pounce and play 'chase the cat' all over the house. Amazingly enough they sound like a herd of elephants trampling through the jungle. 'Little cat feet', my ass! Fortunately, they are NOT hurtling insults at each other so we know that they're only playing.

Seems males of all species engage in this sort of play fighting. I remember incidents between the SRM and the JRM where my daughter and I had to pretend we didn't know them.

"If we're very smooth and quiet perhaps we can just walk away and they will not notice."

NOW ACCEPTING APPLICATIONS

Tall, lithe, blithe, polyandrous, and elegant domme' who bewitches alpha males, and only alpha males, into becoming willing cat toys as they succumb to their own desires.

My Ideal Person:

I am a soft domme and do NOT do pain, abuse or indulge in humiliation. Basically I want wild, rampant, skin-on-skin, multi-orgasmic, ejaculatory, full body contact sex on my terms with someone who can accept my unbridled sexuality. I'm tired of having to hold back.

Must be between 40 and 60 years of age, 6 foot tall, unencumbered, furry, nearby, and possess more than half a brain. Strong enough to be fun but warm enough to be my teddybear.

Bad Boys, PITAs, and those who feel the need to "be a challenge" need NOT apply.

-------------------------------- (addendum)

In truth: I am only interested in a discreet LT fwb R with a sincere and suitable man who is committed to "the lifestyle". Mildly evil, cute, witty teddybears without other commitments preferred.

My current group of teddybears is letting me down. *sigh*

I hate recalcitrant teddybears. Teddybears should always be both willing and available.

Apply via email to me here or by leaving a comment to that effect below.

Oct 15, 2007

MRI

Medical Center at 1 am, yes - really!, today. The place is a large well-lit tomb at that hour of the day. Found that I could get my truck into the parking garage but parked just anywhere and found my way into the building (up the elevator to the skyway, across then down the escalator, which wasn't running). Okay radiology is this way. Walk, walk, this is a big place, walk. Hmmm, food court with vending machines. Walk. Ah! a sign saying MRI with an arrow. Goody! Walk, walk, a pit stop, walk. Another sign. Where the hell am I going? Aah! Here we are. Fill this in. No, no pacemakers, no tattoos, no fake body parts, no piercings, etc and so forth. Damn it is COLD in here! Small room to change into a gray gown. Then off to meet the beast. Large pale beige plastic thing with green lights and aqua trim.

Lay down with my right knee in this holder thing, then stuff some wedges in to make sure it doesn't move at all. I'm

192

freezing! Aaaaw the nice man gave me ear plugs and a blankie! I wish I had worn my woolly socks. Then the bed slid into the machine. Okay, I can handle this, since my head was still out in the open air. I could watch the lights and the timer.

MRIs make two noises: errr errr and beep beep beep. The sounds are very loud and they vary between three pitches-all of which are annoying. The bed moves this way and that: meaning side to side as well as in and out. The machine also vibrates as the magnets do their thing. Rather like being concrete in one of those trucks, rumble rumble, except you're stationary while the mixer rotates around you. I recommend imagining yourself lying on a sunny beach, with light ocean breezes playing gently across your face in Greenland during December.

After half an hour of first errr errr and then beep beep (during which I had my hands over my ears), the bed slid out. I had been told to expect 40 minutes. I was all done! That was quick! So I dashed back, changed back into my jeans, forgot to ask when the doctor would get the results and skedaddled home - missing my 2am curfew by 19 minutes. Oh well! At least the drive was nice! 495 and 95 are great when you're the only one on it!

Adventures of the medical kind. Told y'all last night I had an appt!

In The Dark

In the dark, I stand next to you at first and then put my arm around you and breathe on your neck murmuring something to your earlobe. Close your eyes and imagine what sex with me would be like. My hand in your hair forces you to tilt your head back and I kiss your throat before lightly teasing your lips with the tip of my tongue-perhaps I will kiss you - very very lightly and fleetingly. A kiss from a wraith. Claws run slowly and lightly down your spine. Love biting the nape of your neck. Nothing about you is sacred. I will enjoy every inch of your body but so slowly, ever so slowly. Savoring. There in the dark.

In the dark, I crouch above your prostrate naked body feeling your warmth. Feeling the texture of your skin beneath my cheek as I caress you with my lips, the top of my knee resting snuggly up against your testicles. Lick a spot and then breathe on it. How would it feel getting this close to me? Claws run slowly and lightly up along the side of your hip. There is no escape for you now. There is no rest for you now. Each orgasm you have will only make you more vulnerable for the next. You have no limits with me. My skin sliding along your skin and fur. My hands, lips and body reveling in yours. Hard, soft, pleasure, pain it's all there; in the dark.

In the dark, I seek your total disintegration to orgasmic sensory overload. I want you to quiver in both fear and delight. Once. To lose all vestige of control from anticipation alone. Cum for me; then cum again, and again, and again. Feel me alongside of you. Twice. Feel me around you. Slow, relentless, rhythmic. Timed to the beating of your heart. Will you resist? Can you resist? My lips on yours. My juices all over you. The long slow sliding into oblivion. Thrice. Sucking your fingers, you nipples, your penis. Feeding from you. Hair thin red lines sloping around your waist gently licked. Before I leave you, in the dark.

purrrrrrrrrrrrr

194

Oct 16, 2007

BHL Blogland Girlfriend Contest: Round 1.....Part 16 I'm entered in this contest but I am not sure he's quite ready for me.

What do you think?

Voting closes at midnight tonight for the following contests. If you have not yet voted, please do so now.

Vote here [post 1063634], and here [post 1063639]. All the other contests have now closed.

And there remains the guessing game: who am I ???!

Join in the fun!

Even if you're NOT going to the Monster Mash, you can still come out and help us "warm-up" at the Pre-party this coming Friday evening after 9pm at Skinifatz in Woodbridge!

Y'all remember how important "warming-up" is dontcha? see below for directions.

Oct 17, 2007

"An apple a day will keep anyone away.......
.........if you throw it hard enough."
- Stephen Colbert.

London Times list of the Top Ten Wittiest British Men.
Stephen Fry at number 3:
"Animal testing is cruel, because they get nervous and get all the answers wrong"
The man is "brilliant"!

And then there's Stephen Fry's cohort: Hugh Laurie who you may well remember from various series including "A Little Fry & Laurie" and "Jeeves & Wooster".
Another brilliant comedian! And another man who looks better the older he gets!

Which does happen!

Speaking of That List
Here it is in full and I QUOTE

I say, I say, I say
1 Oscar Wilde "Only dull people are brilliant at breakfast"
2 Spike Milligan "All I ask is the chance to prove that money can't make me happy"
3 Stephen Fry "An original idea. That can't be too hard. The library must be full of them"
4 Jeremy Clarkson "Speed has never killed anyone, suddenly becoming stationary . . . that's what gets you"
5 Sir Winston Churchill "A politician needs the ability to foretell what is going to happen tomorrow, next week, next month, and next year. And to have the ability afterwards to explain why it didn't happen"
6 Paul Merton "I'm always amazed to hear of air crash victims so badly mutilated that they have to be identified by their dental records. If they don't know who you are, how do they know who your dentist is?"
7 Noel Coward "People are wrong when they say opera is not what it used to be. It is what it used to be. That is what's wrong with it."
8 Shakespeare "Maids want nothing but husbands, and when they have them, they want everything"
9 Brian Clough "The River Trent is lovely, I know because I have walked on it for 18 years"
10 Liam Gallagher "She [Victoria Beckham] cannot even chew gum and walk in a straight line at the same time, let alone write a book."

Love it!!

Oct 18, 2007
Skinifatz
DIRECTIONS:
Interstate 95 to exit 161;
right at the light;
immediate right, go to end of road;
hard left onto the driveway angling off behind your left shoulder;
up the drive and it is on your right.
Friday M&G's are now here!
Cover $2
Dress whatever's legal.
See you there?

Oct 19, 2007
SEX=MEANING
Whether it is Mr. Right or Mr. Right Now - there is NEVER any such thing as "meaningless sex". One should ALWAYS approach even the most one night stand of one night stands as if he was the most important person in the world - which, in a way, he is right then - because one can make friends between the sheets as easily as one can anywhere and everywhere else.....
......assuming he regains coherent thought after having AT LEAST 4 orgasms in a row.
SUCH FUN!!!

Oct 20, 2007
I was at Skinifatz and you WEREN'T. What is up with that? Don't you like to party with wicked felines?
I will be offline for the weekend - going to
Monster Mash
Will I see you there?

Oct 21, 2007
Results of the 3rd Annual BBB Blog Awards
Our own BABY BRANDY won 3rd place in Most
Wonderful Newcomer and The Feline of Darkness tied for
3rd place in Most All Around Interesting Blog.
CONGRATULATIONS, BABY BRANDY!
WILD APPLAUSE

Just returning from a 24 hour fuck-fest with costumes,
known as Monster Mash , the intimidatingly sexual Feline
of Darkness -
                            Thank you!!
Now, if you'll excuse me, I need a cat nap.
maybe two

reply from Baby Brandy "Oh wow...shocker! I certainly
didn't expect that this morning. I feel so special. My first
blog award appearance."

MONSTER MASH
Oh WOW! After a slow start, the party ROLLED, as far as
I was concerned. There was the three-some, the security
guy, the founder, the man with the clawed glove, and my
lovely bed-buddy.
To all who I saw there - hope you had a wonderful time
too!
To all the gentlemen I enjoyed - let's do it AGAIN!
yes I did two demonstrations of my techniques

Oct 22, 2007
CONDOMS
I know some of you have issues with them but it is better to
use them and live than to not and become dead or diseased.
Yes, condoms do work. They stop STDs very well, thank
you very much.

They come in various sizes and chances are the ones you're using are one size too small. Don't you guys ever check these things out?

If you have issues with latex, they are available in other materials. You have other choices as well: ribbed, flavored, spermicided, lubed, colored, with bumps, desensitizing, etc., etc., etc.

As far as being "nice" to men by not demanding they use them - excuse me? I'm taking you into my bed for one hell of a romp - how much "nicer" do you need? Jeez!

Wrap that bad boy up!

(this has been a public service announcement - your mileage may vary)

MORE 3rd Annual BBB Blog Awards
Yours truly won 4th place for Sexiest Look in a Picture. Thank you to all who voted for me!

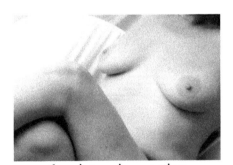

the picture in question
by Camden C. Cochran

Thor Update:
Today was the day we sent Thor to the vet ....
...............to have his testicles removed.
(I can see you guys cringing from here)

The vet just called to say "No Problems" and we can pick him up after 4pm. Thor may be a little sleepy for the next 24 hours but he came through it all very well.
"My family loves me.
They cut my balls off."

Oct 23, 2007
Suffering From PMD
POST-MASH DEPRESSION
Anyone have a cure?
reply: "kinky sex will fix you right up."

Why Some Can Share Their Men
Because they can separate LOVE the emotion from LUST the desire and because they TRUST in the bond they share. Additionally, women tend to like to please and accommodate their men's desires. Few men are as capable of sharing as women are. Then there are the bisexual women who want to be the center of attention while exploring their bisexuality.

LOVE * LUST * TRUST

Oct 24, 2007
"Le Disko"

[V1]
Hello little boys, little toys
We're the dreams you're believing
Crawling up the walls
Running down your face
Razor sharp, razor clean
Feel the weapon's sensation
On your back...

200

With loaded guns

[B-section]
Now hold onto me pretty baby
If you want to fly
I'm gonna melt the fever, sugar
Rolling back your eyes

[Chorus]
We're gonna ride the race cars
We're gonna dance on fire
We're the girls Le Disko
Supersonic overdrive

[V2]
So what's it gonna take?
Silver shadow believer....
Spock rocker with your dirty eyes
It's a chance gonna move
Gonna fuck up your ego
Silly boy, gonna make you cry

[Bridge]
If what they say is true...
You're a boy - and I'm a girl
I will never fall in love with you

[Chorus]
We're gonna ride the race cars
We're gonna dance on fire
We're the girls Le Disko
Supersonic overdrive

-by Shiny Toy Guns

Have to keep y'all up to date, ya know?

I began to smile as soon as soon as I saw him standing there; big and furry teddybear that he is. Not ruined or corrupted but new and improved and with a more extensive resume' through close association with a certain female feline. Certainly spoiled as in many ways he has me. *EG*
We talked.
But what I really wanted to do was......
Welcome back, Baby!

Met A Very Nice Man Today
He is a very nice man and I liked him. There was one minute there where he truly caught my interest too! He smiled, his face creased into a grin, and his eyes danced! WOW! I love that!
I agreed to meet him for lunch because he came into the chatroom and didn't "play dead". Hmmmm. has a sense of humor, has some courage, is decisive, not jealous or possessive, and he actually reads!!! Way cool. Ladies, I recommend j. (I also recommend nu and 11749609 but they are another story. I think. I just may be confused. Again.)
He's a bit too nice and a bit too laidback for me but I'm sure he'll suit you nice women just fine!
(I do apologize novafun4you, jcct445, and sweet 11749609 but I get so confused sometimes that I call my kids by the wrong names and end up saying "You! You know who you are, get over here!")
We'll sort out who is who later!

Reply: from n "LMAO. I can't wait to sort it out. Maybe we could all four sort it out together, mmmf-style. Then you could say, "You! You know who you are, cum in here!"

PROFILE UPDATE
Tall, lithe, blithe, polyamorous, witty, and elegant domme'
who bewitches alpha males, and only alpha males, into
becoming willing cat toys as they succumb to their own
desires.

My Ideal Person:

Currently not looking.

I am a soft domme and do NOT do pain, abuse or indulge
in humiliation. Basically I want wild, rampant, skin-on-
skin, multi-orgasmic, ejaculatory, full body contact sex on
my terms with someone who can accept my unbridled
sexuality.

Must between 40 and 60 years of age, 6 foot tall,
unencumbered, furry, nearby, and possess more than half a
brain. Strong enough to be fun but warm enough to be my
teddybear.

LTFWBR ONLY

Bad Boys, PITAs, and those who feel the need to "be a
challenge" need NOT apply.

Thank you.

Oct 25, 2007
quietude
flying down the cathedral of the night
exulting, at one with all
at one with you
-from <u>My Ice-Cold, Chrome-Plated, Steel Heart</u> by me.

This Friday, Oct 26th
Skinifatz after 9pm
HALLOWEEN PARTY
from the north:
95 South to Exit 161
at the light turn right
then immediately turn right
end of road turn hard left

from the south:
95 north to Exit 160A
go to Rte 1
turn left (going north)
cross the bridge
at the light turn left
immediately turn right
end of road turn hard left

go up the driveway and it is on your right.
See you there!

I narrowly lost, 10 votes to her 11 votes, to B with one man
abstaining since neither of us seemed right for BHL. Read
all about it here BHL Blogland Girlfriend Contest Part 16
Final!!.
Ce'st le vie!
btw it is no good voting now - they're already deep into
Round Two.

Oct 26, 2007
PERMISSION SLIP
It seems that certain humorless, thin-skinned individuals
are objecting to being included in people's blogs. Pictures,
links, games, etc. they have all been objected to.

204

Since the entire purpose of this site for us (for them it is making money - we all know that) is contacting like persons, being snarky in would seem to be counter-productive.

But they will have their way due to the site's liability concerns.

Therefore: please copy, paste, and insert your handle herein as your reply if you would like to continue OUR communication, Then sign and date.

Feel free to run this on your blog as well.

"I, _____ do hereby allow EEK1 to use a link to my main profile photo and a link to my profile with my name in it for the purpose of networking, communication, and creating fun and games on the website. To be used in blogs, email and groups. I realize that getting my name out there is a way to increase my odds of finding likeminded people I want to talk to.

Signed _____ Date ____ / ____ / ____ "

Thank you!

HAPPY 1000TH POST!!
HURRAY!!
I have made it!!
This is my one thousandth, 1000, post!!! I hope that you have found the ride interesting if not exhilarating. (Remember my driving record.)

In celebration of this auspicious event I offer you ....THIS!

"04/05/2005
'Ware! This lady has 'Control Issues'

04/07/2005
Dancing to the tune of "Clubbed to Death" from The
Matrix !! He didn't seem to mind.

04/09/2005
POLO POLO POLO - Friday and Saturday evenings are
beginning to book up! Catch us if you can!

04/14/2005
Mmmmmm life continues to be 'interesting'. The IRS, love
them!, is giving us back some money. Party time!!!

04/16/2005
"Twas brilig and the slithy toves" but appreciating the
wicked subtleties of life is truly gratifying. Chortling!!

04/17/2005
Terribly sorry to disappoint you all but you cannot rule the
world for I already do.

04/19/2005
We have met a great many wonderful people since we have
joined. Thank you all for welcoming us."

My first week's blog posts from way back then. It has been
one wild ride for me! A lot has changed since then. Some
things have been good and some bad - but such is life.
What has NOT changed, unlikely that it ever will, is the
essential JOY IN LIFE that illuminates and enriches even
my darkest days and carries me through my most savage
trials.

So, from one joyous person to another, raise your glass and let's toast the reason we're ALL here:

PARTY!!!!
(NAKED)

Oct 27, 2007
Had a GREAT time at Skinifatz! Fortunately the doctor was in the house because a little devil was there. I wore my leathers (now with more spikes!) much to everyone's amusement if not delight. We have a dancer now too! You peeps are fun! SO I DIDN'T WIN THE COSTUME CONTEST - AGAIN! LOL
Same time next week?
sorry no pix - you have to BE there!

MEN WHO SHARE
Other than being priceless, men who can 'share' have certain characteristics including the ability to separate love from lust; they can develop emotional bonds strong enough to withstand their own insecurities; the ability to not run shy and hide their activities beyond normal levels; and they tend be to a lot MORE FUN than the general run of jealous and/or possessive guys women normally have to spend so much time appeasing.
Of course one has to be fair and make sure that he does get his fair share of your attention. This is why I suggest 'hunting' together.
Come to think of it - BOTH genders should be striving for this! Dontcha think?

Reply: "Finally, someone who understands!"

Oct 28, 2007
OKAY, THAT'S ENOUGH!

It is now time to make my daughter, who has become veerrryyy stodgy and staid - I don't where she gets that from! - shake her head and think I'm being silly. Adult silliness is never so attractive as when it comes after several days of exemplary behavior!

HALLOWEEN is coming.
I have a week to use.
Let's see what adult silliness I can find!

Oct 29, 2007
NOTHING SUCCEEDS...
ardent [□a□dənt] adjective
enthusiastic; passionate, fervent; glowing;
c.1374, from O.Fr. ardant, from L. ardere
The fig. sense (of passions, desire, etc.) was earliest in Eng.; literal sense of "burning,
...LIKE ENTHUSIASM!!!

SIGH
Another year, another medical check-up. "At your time of life" - how I HATE it when they say that - I'll have to get one every year. Then it is back to orthopedics to get yelled at for smoking, physical therapy for not doing enough exercising and the lab for all of those tests!
JEEZ!
Can't I just have wild rampant sex every night instead?!?!

Mardi Gras at the Hyatt - Feb 9th, 2008
Beach Bash at the Hyatt - July 12th, 2008
Make your plans now to attend!!
You DON'T want to miss these events!

Oct 30, 2007
CHAINED DESIRES
Your one-stop-shop for all of your "lifestyle necessities",
which I find hilarious! Nevertheless, I do have to pay them
a visit because I have lost weight, not because I wanted to,
and now my "lifestyle necessity" is too large on me. I have
to go down a size. (Ladies, how often does THAT happen?)
Unfortunately, I'll have to go alone - there's a man out there
who should be kicking himself - into the wilds of central
Baltimore.

Wish me luck!

Oct 31, 2007

HAPPY HALLOWEEN

Today I wandered around Baltimore, half lost, but I not
only found the place but also found a nearby parking
space!!! With money still on the meter!!! Amazing!
My good luck continued when the lady said, Yes, it is too
big but we can have it re-fitted!!! The price was right -
about 1/3 the cost of a new one!! HURRAY!!
Seems the loss of 20 pounds due to stress this past summer
also took 4 inches off my waist. Yes, I stripped and stood
there bare-breasted while she measured me. This IS that
kind of store you know.

They were fresh out of nice red corsets and they didn't have any ankle cuffs for men immediately available so the trip only cost me gasoline and time. I think it was worthwhile. So no, the "sexual body armor" is not for sale - it is getting altered to fit me again. SORRY!
The only sad thing is I went by myself.

MEN!!!
One who loves me too much.
One who loves me too little.
One who loves me just right
but is currently out for maintenance.
Is it any wonder I am exasperated??

NOVEMBER
2007

Nov 1, 2007
The weekly M&G is Friday after 9pm at Skinifatz in
Occoquan, VA.
Tired of dress codes, no smoking signs, parking 1/2 mile
away, extortion masquerading as cover charges, and
skimpy dance floors where they don't place music you can
dance to?
Come to Skinifatz!
If it is legal, you can do it there!
They also have pool tables, a fireplace, and sofas - and not
a TV screen anywhere!

Notes of a Dominatrix and Chat both hit the shelves today!
Ask Amazon (et al) for your copy!

Nov 2, 2007
The First Dynasty c. 3400-3200 BCE
Using N. Grimal (1992) cross-referenced with
Hammerton/Barnes (1942,) one can provisionally list the
kings (Pharaohs) of Ancient Egypt during the 1st Dynasty,
the Thinite Dynasty since they came from This which was
near Abydos, as follows:

1. Aha Men (Menes) who may or may not be one and the
same person with Narmer.
(Meni and It(i) then contended for the throne but a third
ascended to it instead.)
2. Djer (Zer Atoti)
3. Djet (Za)
4. Den Semti
5. Anedjib (Enzib Merpeba)
6. Semerkhet Hui
7. Ka'a Sen

Several difficulties arise; upon their coronation they changed their names and the surviving documentation is both scanty and enigmatic.

Then there's Ip "The Scorpion" who did in fact exist. The problem lies in the relationship between Ip and Aha. If Aha was "of the blood" of Ip, then Ip should be included as the first Pharaoh. If not, then Ip should be excluded. It is this uncertainty which has led to the creation of Dynasty Zero to give Ip a place in history.

The few kings most are sure about are Aha, Den Semti, and Semerkhet Hui as the first, fourth, and sixth pharaohs respectively.

Accomplishments of the First Dynasty
1.unification of Egypt
2.introduction of the concept kings as divine
3.introduction of the census
4.establishment of trade
5.establishment of vassal states
6.introduction of the solar calendar
7.establishment of bureaucracy
8.concept of tax immunity for the religious
9.Saqqara and Abydos as religious centers
10.Memphis as capital city of unified Egypt

The final problem with Egypt is its very antiquity. By the time the ancient Greeks and Romans came around, even the Egyptians had no idea how very old their civilization actually was. It is only within the past 100 years that we have been able to make any real headway in the subject.

Nov 3, 2007
"If We Kissed"

Electricity, eye to eye.
Hey don't I know you? I can't speak.
Strip my senses on the spot,
I've never been defenseless,
I can't even make sense of this.
You speak and I don't hear a word.

What would happen if we kissed?
Would your tongue slip past my lips?
Would you run away?
Would you stay?
Or would I melt into you?
Not tonight, lust to lust,
Spontaneously combust.

The room is spinning out of control.
You act like you didn't notice, brushed my hand.
Forbidden fruit, ring on my finger.
You're such a moral mortal man.
Would you throw it away?
No question.
Will I pretend I'm innocent?

What would happen if we kissed?
Would your tongue slip past my lips?
Would you run away?
Would you stay?
Or would I melt into you?
Not tonight, lust to lust,
Spontaneously combust.
What would happen if we kissed?

214

I struggle with myself again.
Quickly the wall, I'm crawling.
Don't know if I can turn away.

What would happen if we kissed?
Would your tongue slip past my lips?
Would you run away?
Would you stay?
Or would I melt into you?
Not tonight.
If we kissed
What would happen if we kissed?
Would your tongue slip past my lips?
Would you run away?
Would you stay?
Or would I melt into you?
Not tonight.
If we kissed. If we kissed.

Artist - Fiona Apple
Album - Various Songs

Yes, I understand all too well!

CIPROFLOXACIN
No exercising.
No sun-bathing.
No breast-feeding (sorry, guys)
LOL

"Between My Legs"

(Oh my god!)
You can go out, dancing
And I'll write about you, dancing without you
And I'll shed a tear between my legs

When you were here, I missed you
Now that you're away, I'm out there without you
And I shed a tear between my legs

Though we live in the same city,
You live in another state far away from me and all of my
unfaded charms
But when the rocket ships all fall, and the bridges, they all
buckle
And everybody's packing up their station wagons
There's a number you can call, like a breast that you can
suckle
And we quietly will exit as it all is happening

Again, I'm afraid of one thing,
Will I walk away from love knowing nothing, wearing my
heart between my legs?
But when I know you're naked, lying on the bed while I'm
at the piano
All I can say is I can't fake it

When the rocket ships all fall, and the bridges, they all
buckle
And everybody's packing up their station wagons
There's a number you can call, like a breast that you can
suckle
And we quietly will exit as it all is happening again

'Cause there's a river running underground, underneath the town towards the sea,
That only I know all about
On which from this city we can flee
On which from this city we can flee

-Rufus Wainwright

I know about this too.

Nov 4, 2007
Thank you, ladies, for passing on your warnings about this man or that but please remember to whom you are speaking. Only a extraordinarily stupid, insane, otherwise mentally or emotionally disabled male would ever consider harming me.
I would kill him without compunction.
(figuratively speaking, of course)
VEG
flexing claws

Nov 5, 2007
Non-smokers go to The Firehouse Grill in old town Fairfax near the courthouse. They made it non-smoking because it is a very small and crowded place - someone's attic kind of thing. Watch those stairs.

Smokers go to Skinifatz in Occoquan just north of the bridge on Rte 1. Oddly enough - the smokers get the better dance floor. Go figure! Oh, we'll let the non-smokers come along too but they have to be FUN people.

W Know what I mean?

Nov 6, 2007

FUN PEOPLE - since I have been asked, are those whose eyes sparkle, whose lips smile, and whose humor is not malicious. They are into "wine women/men, and song". They enjoy dancing! They enjoy flirting with intent. They hold up their end of the conversation. They are into "fast horses, fast cars, and faster men/women". They are full of life and joy.

Cha cha cha!

Those Pharaohs of Ancient Egypt that everyone should know include:

Khufru (Cheops) - builder of The Great Pyramid at Giza.

Khafra (Chephren) - the pyramid next door to Cheops' and also The Great Sphinx.

Both are 4th Dynasty.

Queen Hatshepsut - under whose rule Egypt flourished exceedingly.

Tuthakhamen - who returned Egypt to itself after the dreadful Amara period.

Both of whom were 18th Dynasty.

Any Pharoah named Rames, and there were a lot of them both good and bad, was either 19th or 20th Dynasty.

Queen Cleopatra VII - yes, there were other Cleos before the famous Queen. She brought peace and prosperity to a country wracked with famine and civil war. A most able ruler. Oddly enough, her looks were only decent yet the woman had "IT" to the maximum!

The reason why you have been subjected to this series is because many of our concepts in our own government come from this time period and this civilization. Knowing where you come from is always useful - esp today when you, a common person, get to VOTE!

SO, VOTE, DAMMIT!

I was there at 7:46pm precisely. The place looked deader than a graveyard - this is a nightclub?? The doors were locked and it looked like those doors hadn't been open for the past 20 years. So, I left at 8pm.
Where were you?
erasing him from my list

You will be elated to know - I got the news today - all of my tests came back:
HEALTHY & FIT & CLEAN
YEEEHAW

Nov 7, 2007
For all of those who wish to know what they'll be getting themselves into with me, I suggest you read ALL of the Playtime With Teddybears posts herein. You will notice a pattern.
A most delicious pattern!
Care for a little experimental exploration?

Nov 8, 2007
PLAYTIME WITH TEDDYBEARS
BAY HILLS TESTRIDE
The sign on the door said "I am totally yours. Do with me what you will." He's such a brave man! French cafe' music, a bit of Laphroaig, and then we slid onto his big comfy bed where the poor man was vigorous ridden. Then I turned to him and said "Hi, how are you?" He laughed. Well, we hadn't said it beforehand. Thus began the evening of the disappearing condoms. Every time we used one, it would disappear. Hmmmm, he's good! Now that the introductions were out of the way, we settled down to some serious explorations. I caressed him all over combining massage with eroticism and left more than a few claws and teeth marks - he loved it! Up, down, around; sliding over his

219

skin. Closely examining him. The joys of a willing teddybear! We took turns on top. We rolled all over the bed. We licked the back of each other's knees. Wow! His hands and lips were all over me. I even let him mess up my hair. He is soo enthusiastic! Warm, willing, and a very good lover - could not ask for more.

Except you know I want more.

You know I want all of him.

Repeatedly.

Frequently.

Nov 9, 2007

Men need to be needed.

So when your husband or boyfriend wants to fix something - let him. He's showing you his prowess at fixing things - he's showing you that he's a competent male - he's showing you he cares by doing something for you that he knows you can do for yourself - just to do it for you so you won't have to.

Men just cannot SAY they love you - they feel they have to SHOW you they love you by fixing things or doing things for you.

If they get the impression that you think they are incompetent oafs - they will work harder and attempt things beyond their level just to prove to you that they are useful because being unable to do something means they are "less of a man" even if only in their own minds.

If they cannot immediately fix something - maybe a bolt's being stubborn or something - the problem becomes "personal". At this point it is best for you to just back off and let him run with it. Ignore anything he says until the issue has been decided since the language he will employ will not be something his mother would be proud to hear come from his lips. And he may say unkind things to

220

anyone who attempts to interfere in the struggle esp if offering to help or offering an alternative solution.
Just say "Ok, dear."

Nov 10, 2007
Sorry everyone but I have seriously injured a paw and will have to be absent from the festivities for awhile.
I have to stay off my paws. *EG*
It is not entirely a bad thing.

I had a good time at the Southern Fairfax M&G last night - met some old friends again - they have returned to the group all nicely refreshed! (nice to see you again!) We had two big tables of people all chitter-chattering away like mad. Lots of laughter! Some people even got KISSES out of the deal!
YUMMY!

Nov 11, 2007
The Resident Males are supposed to be priming the walls for paint today - yet where are they? On their computers!
Bah! I may have to chase them with a whip!
(smart-ass comment received = "how would that be any different?")
Grrrrrrrrr! Pesky males!

We all have our preferences - so what's yours, baby?
When do you MOST want SEX!
- Midnight
- Middle of the Night
- Breakfast
- Mid Morning
- Lunch
- Mid Afternoon

- Dinner
- Mid Evening
- ALL of the time!
- How about now?

Nov 12, 2007
Current Queens Regent
Beatrix (born January 31, 1938 as Beatrix Wilhelmina Armgard, Princess of the Netherlands, Princess of Orange-Nassau, Princess of Lippe-Biesterfeld) has been the Queen regnant of the Kingdom of the Netherlands since April 30, 1980.
Elizabeth II (Elizabeth Alexandra Mary;[1] born 21 April 1926) is the Queen regnant of sixteen independent states and their overseas territories and dependencies. Though she holds each crown and title separately and equally, she is resident in and most directly involved with the United Kingdom, her oldest realm, over parts of whose territories her ancestors have reigned for more than a thousand years. She ascended the thrones of seven countries in February 1952.
Margrethe II (Margrethe Alexandrine Þórhildur Ingrid) (born 16 April 1940) is the Queen regnant of Denmark.

Contested Queen Regent
Rain Queen Makobo Constance Modjadji VI (1978 - 12 June 2005) was the 6th in a line of the Balobedu tribe's Rain Queens. It is said that Makobo Modjadji had the ability to control the clouds and rivers. Makobo was crowned on 16 April 2003 at the age of 25 after the death of her predecessor and grandmother, Queen Mokope Modjadji. This made her the youngest Queen in the history of the Balobedu tribe. Because Makobo's daughter, **Princess Masalanabo**, is fathered by a commoner, the traditionalists are not likely to accept her as the rightful

222

heiress to the Rain Queen Crown. Therefore there are worries that the 400-year old Rain Queen dynasty may be coming to an end. No new Rain Queen has been chosen since Makobo died. The Modjadji or Rain Queen is the hereditary queen of Balobedu, the people of the Limpopo Province of South Africa. The succession to the position of Rain Queen is matrilineal, meaning that the Queen's eldest daughter is the heir, and that males are not entitled to inherit the throne at all. The Rain Queen is believed to have special powers, including the ability to control the clouds and rainfall.

Although there is some doubt about the rule of ancient queens, there have been approx. 135 Queens Regnant including one from Mexico, a particularly bloody-thirsty lady, several rani of India, a few Ram of Vietnam, and 18 Empresses of Japan. Queens Regnant means queens ruling in their own right as opposed to queens consort who merely married the king.
Something rather neat to know.

Nov 13, 2007
Forget that old cliché "dressing-up the women" role-play stuff. Been there, done that.
Now it is the guys' turn!
Here are some suggestions to get you started:
1. Gladiator
2. Toga
3. Motorcycle
4. Cowboy
5. Fireman/Policeman
Ladies - what would you like to see?
BARE IT, FELLAS!

"BROS BEFORE HOS"

Calling ANY woman that is grounds for lynching with malice aforethought followed by a very slow evisceration with flaying as the finale' - do I make myself perfectly clear?

It all comes down to what you want and the kind of life you want to live - 10 years from now.

Where do you see yourself 10 years from now - relationship-wise?

Where do you hope to be 10 years from now - relationship-wise?

Nov 14, 2007

When you accept a man into your life - you accept ALL of him: his past, his present, his future, his ex-es, and his children! ALL of it!

None of this half-hearted, timid stuff!

so says the tigress rolling around on the floor with her grandkittens

I'm sick. I'm sick. I'm ill. I'm sick.

So I am off to sit in the hot tub and drink scotch until this cold gives up the ghost.

A nice backrub from a teddybear would also be nice!

Tuck me up into bed, sweeties?

Nov 15, 2007

As of Nov 15th, the poll results =

17 out of 28 choose "All the Time" - 60%

"Breakfast" and "How About Now?" tied at 5 out of 28 - 17% each

and 2 out of 28 preferred "mid-afternoon". - 6%

Thank you for playing!

Nov 16, 2007

224

How to Write a Profile

This is all about marketing yourself to your target audience so carefully think and then craft your profile. Make sure that it is consistent all the way through. Coordinate your pictures and make sure you keep your pictures current and your profile up to date.

Tag line: grab her attention.

Looking For: carefully select from the options listed making sure that you do not contradict yourself in your write-up that follows

The first Section = ALL About You: You have three and only three full, complete, and correct sentences so use the language to its fullest. Lead off with your strongest suit. Sparkle! that is to say - act like you're alive and enjoying this! Remember, enthusiasm attracts. Bitterness repels. Do not repeat anything that is in your stats below.

My Ideal Person: Three and only three full, complete, and correct sentences so lead with what matters most. What must she be to even to be considered? If there is something important you may add another three sentences in another paragraph. But do NOT write an encyclopedia or put up too many barriers.

KISS OF DEATH: the following items will immediately result in you being erased from her list.
1. ghetto-speak or TM-talk as in 'yo ho' and '2' instead of to or too
2. anger, bitterness, whining, depressing language
3. 'prefer not to say' - never choose that option
4. LYING - never, ever lie

225

5. cowardice - you can edit pictures to not show your face - NOT posting a picture is NOT okay

Use spell check and grammar check before posting your profile.
Take your time and do not be afraid to edit your profile later on as needed.

Hope this helps!

Ménage à Trois
Most often confused with having a "threesome", a ménage à trois actually refers to a living arrangement - what the polyamorous call a "triad". Ménage meaning household, family, and home which suggests something a bit more permanent than a mere threesome.

I'm not sure if I could live in a ménage à trois unless I ruled. Now if it were with two delectable teddybears (my retirement plan) - there would be no problem but if with only the one teddybear and another kitten - I'm not so sure. I don't think he'd survive for very long if he had two kittens to satisfy.

So, my lovelies, would you, could you live in a ménage à trois?
btw the way - there are all the same gender ménages à trois. I am so evil.

Nov 17, 2007
That's Enough!
I have been the total 'housecat' for more than a week and I am tired of all this domesticity! Painting, chasing after the grandkittens, baking goodies for the holidays, cleaning this

and that, laundry, and all while trying to kill this cold - that's enough!
So, tomorrow, I'm going to go out and be very, very baad!

Nov 18, 2007
And I Quote
"....and let's face reality here. I mean, what kind of idiot needs to post on a message board to ask, "how do I find a dominatrix?". Well, duh, put the word in his search engine and hit "go".

...Truth be told, I wish him luck. I hope the sniveling coward does find one as he deserves a good ass kicking, and it will help cull the amount of these types out there presenting a weak, pitiful image of men, that, quite frankly, most women find detestable....beyond the dysfunctional who have a need to "hurt" men so as to solve some deep seated abuse issue from their childhood.

Notice that there is not a single female response? We green on that?"

Hey now, does he have 'issues' or does he have 'Issues". Oh the fragile male ego! This one cannot even post on a message board without getting his testicles into a twist at the thought that some men are man enough to take their testicles being twisted.
Silly boy; gonna make you cry.
LOL
Best comment Received: "For some reason, many men just feel threatened by any experience they can't share."

Nov 19, 2007
Playtime with Teddybears
THE SNEAKY KITTEN
There you were naked being slowly approached from behind by a naked Kitten. You weren't at all surprised or upset. I think you were amused. It is the bane of my existence. I try to be devastating and you only think I'm cute. True our usual foreplay is my racing you to get naked and 'last one in bed gives head!' but you could play along a bit, Sweety, when I try something new. I wouldn't want you getting bored. So I stroked your fur as we settled onto the bed. I love your scent! A bit of foreplay and then you rolled onto your back and I pounced upon you! Aaaah! I love this position! You feel so damn good! Sliding up and down. So nicely wet! Then a quick scamper over to the side to have you come in from behind. Right there! A pause - don't cum yet; another pause - don't cum yet. Now! Yes!

Of course there was more after this. I can't get enough of him. But I'm going to leave the rest up to your imagination.

It's Not Easy, Baby!
Part 1
There is a unique blend of power, surrender, responsibility, care, and trust that occurs between a domme and her submissives that many people find alien. Men are supposed to be this way and women this way.
It may come as a shock to you, but it is the submissive who holds the ultimate power in this relationship for at a word from him, the play immediately stops with no questions being asked.
It may appear otherwise but it is true.
His submission should be a joyous one to him. He should be able to take delight in his surrender and in the relationship he has with his domme. If he can't then SHE's

228

doing something very wrong. The responsibility for his joy and delight is HERS.

If HE's not having fun then it is HER fault.

Part 2

Soft dommes have it even tougher since we cannot use force to ensure compliance. The whips are just for decoration. We use seduction and his own desires to beguile him into compliance. He submits to us because he is assured that his desires will be fulfilled. In the hands of a soft domme, he will learn more about himself and his capabilities than he ever dreamed he would. A soft domme will read his mind and his body. She will learn everything about him. Then she will give him everything he desires nuanced and heightened to where the slightest bit of delight becomes earth-shatteringly intense.

In return, soft dommes get a lover whose skills almost match her own. She knows that he will do all he can to please her and will do anything she desires. She will get a lover who fears nothing, understands nuance, is confident in his abilities, and actually enjoys sex - really enjoys it! Unfortunately, she may have created a problem. Once a man's been "beguiled", he may expect the same level of sexuality and intensity with other women. He may become "spoiled". He has three choices - to teach his other lovers, to accept what he can get, or to return to the world of the domme.

This style of play is highly 'addictive'.

Part 3

Since this style of play is more than just physical, the right men for it are few and far between. He has to be a match to the domme in all areas; most importantly, he has to be mentally compatible. He definitely cannot be at all timid, weak, have any doubts about who he is, or about his masculinity. He has to be able to draw her to him like a moth to a flame just by standing there while wearing nothing but a grin.

We will go through a lot of men in our searches to find just the right one or two.

As difficult as they are to find, the real trick is keeping them. People and relationships change over time. The change is expected but how they will change is unpredictable. Some will move deeper into power play and some will move away from it. Be prepared to renegotiate as necessary.

But no matter how the relationship changes, no one should be asking "why are you still here?"

Nov 20, 2007
My readership is still falling off despite the sexual content. The helpful hints and the documentaries aren't boosting my readership either. I'm also not getting many comments - harumph! Even news about Thor does not excite your interest.

SO WHAT DO YOU PEOPLE WANT?
Answers on a postcard please to this address.

Eyes Dilated
- a medical adventure from my real life.
escorting husband back home from his eye exam

"Come along, dear." taking him firmly by the arm.

"Ouch! With you to take care of me, I'll be dead by morning."

"Yes, dear."

opening truck door and helping him inside

"Putting me in someone else's car won't get rid of me."

"It wouldn't work, dear. They'd only chase me down and force me to take you back."

"You're the meanest woman on the planet."

"Yes, dear."

"You're still my favorite wife."

"Out of your hundreds of wives? Are you sure?"

"Yes, dear."

We then argued about my driving but nevertheless made it home safely.
THE END

Nov 21, 2007
Offline Tomorrow
HAPPY THANKSGIVING!!!

Nov 23, 2007
Common Myths about Men
1. **Men Have Sex on The Brain**. Yes and no. It is their primary function but no, they think about other things as well. They aren't machines.
2. **Men Only Want One Thing**. Not any more than you do. Men want a variety of things. Mostly they want you to care about them.
3. **Men Want Virgins/Younger Women**. Some men might but most actually don't want either. Fully 80% of married men are perfectly happy in their current relationships.

4. **Older Women Have No Chance**. Not at all true! A woman of any age has a decent chance of finding a suitable man, if she remains open to the possibility.

5. **Older Men Are Creepy**. Older men have more skill, more patience, and are much more fun than younger men who still have much to learn.

6. **Men Can Have Children At Any Age**. Yes it can happen but men too have a decreasing fertility as they age. So while it is possible it becomes less likely.

7. **Jealousy is Natural**. Jealousy is based upon fear not love and is therefore only for losers.

8. **Any Man is Better Than No Man**. Also not true. If you have skills, and are sensible, you can make it on your own.

9. **You can judge the size of a man's penis by the size of his feet, or hands, etc.** Not at all true! There is absolutely NO correlation between the size of a man's appendages and the size of his penis. The average size is 5 to 8" long and 2 to 4" around.

Basically, if the sentence begins "Men are…" you can discount it. All one can say is that some men are and some men aren't.

Common Myths about Women

1. **Women do not like sex**. Entirely false. Every woman has her own appetite, of course but usually one self-aware woman can out-gun any six men you'd care to name. Just as stress, ill health, over work, and so on affect men so too do they affect women.

2. **Women are prone to mood swings**. Perhaps, but if they tend to be all that wild, it may not be just the normal hormonal stress. Medical assistance may be required. In any case, no one should have to put up with this. Be even tempered and demand the same from her.

3. **Women are emotional**. Sure and so are you but we are permitted to show our emotions, to a point. You have to decide what level of emotion suits you and deal with the issue from there.

4. **Women are irrational**. Also entirely false. We just see it differently than you do. From our point of view, you just don't understand. Effective communication is the key.

5. **Women cannot make up their minds**. Sometimes but then again you have the same problem from time to time. Some people are just more decisive than others.

6. **Women always change their minds**. Not always. As the situation changes so might the decisions. This is more situational than sexual.

7. **Women are unreliable**. Most women are doing three things, at least, at once. Multi-tasking isn't easy. If it were, men would be doing it.

Generally if the sentence begins with "women are…" you can discount it. Some women might be whatever and some aren't. Every person is a mix of delights and irritations.

Nov 24, 2007

"hey, DJ... I was just being humorous... please don't take offense. If most you mean by the majority, sure... women are naturally submissive in bed, however, there are an enormous contingency of females who like dominance, maybe not to the point of being a dominatrix, but the interest is way up there compared to years back."

Another man spouting off about something he knows nothing about! Women are 'naturally' submissive in bed?!?! I'm so sure that the past 2000 years of "masculine dominant culture" hasn't had an effect. Yeah. Right. (The misspelling is his own.)

Nov 25, 2007

It was something small yet I have been patient and still the request remains unfulfilled. I guess it is "all about you". Very well. I will stop asking.

Then the question becomes - how long before I stop Caring about you?

Let Us Review The Program

1. massage
2. necking/erotic massage
3. body worship
4. manual
5. cunnilingus/fellatio
6. cunnilingus/fellatio with manual
7. G-Spot caressing using head of penis
8. posterior fornix caressing using head of penis
9. repeat the last two alternating for as long as he can hold out

pause if required by returning to body worship

10. his climax and then cuddling
11. rest
12. repeat entire program at least three times per session.

Ideally she should have a climax at each location and with each method. That would be at 4, 5, 6, 7, 8, and 9, 9, 9, 9, 9...

Sure beats going to the gym!

Nov 26, 2007

I have finally gotten to my blog list and have perused all of those on my watch list!

Whew!

There is a lot I have missed going on lately.

To aid all of those who watch my blog:

this week's schedule:

Thurs Noon and Friday noon I have lunch appts.
Friday evening there's Wild B'Day Party, for which I need
further info, for a dear friend of mine! So no Skinifatz for
me this week.

next week's schedule:

Mon, Tues and Wed - I'm in court - let's NOT discuss it ty
I have a Scotch Tasting on the 4th and then Silk & Skin on
the 8th.

What's on your schedule?

I have compiled all of my sexual writings into one book
entitled Notes of a Dominatrix, ISBN 978-0-6151-6606-3.
Ask for it at lulu, Amazon, etc.

If you have written a book(s), send me your ISBN(s).

I now find myself in two longer distance relationships
which is not what I prefer but suitable teddybears are not
thick upon the ground. Two others are in the wings shall we
say? We will see.

And somewhere in there I have a medical appt. that I have
forgotten the specifics thereof. No doubt because I DON'T
want to do it.
Now I'm off to do my 'groups'.
Wish me luck!

to the tune of "Mary, Mary Quite Contrary" ...

Kitten, Kitten. evil and sweet,
how does your garden grow?
With hot tubs and cold Buds,
and pretty teddybears all in a row!

I am an ancient, gnarled, and gravely debilitated domme'
who enjoys wild rampant skin-on-skin full-body-contact
sex as often as I can seduce men into it which, fortunately,
is often because the above description is entirely false but
my sense of humor demands such reversals of the facts
from time to time since such reversals adds to the delight of
those men witty enough to enjoy them esp when played
with me, the queen of the run-on sentence which title you
cannot dispute, now can you?

Nov 27, 2007
You should have your "holiday" cards in the mail by
December 1st.
Your overseas packages should be in the mail by December
1st.
Your domestic packages should be in the mail by
December 7th.
Anyone here going to actually meet those deadlines?
If so, can you do mine too, please?

RANT WARNING
I have met many couples who "come on" to me until they
find out I'm straight and then it is "game over". I have been
at more than a few house parties where the guy begins with
me, then rolls off and wants to watch his wife fuck me
instead of him even when he knows I am straight, and he
insists in spite of her, and my, protests at which point I just

236

get up and stalk away wondering "what the fuck's wrong with me" and being in a less than welcoming mood thereafter.

Not all couples are like this, thank goodness. But more enough are to make this straight woman feel that 'the lifestyle', the vast majority of whom are 'couples', is VERY "single straight female unwelcome". It gets tiresome. It gets annoying. I am happy you all have found a place where you can express your bisexuality but. dammit, why can't you leave room for me too? I am in the lifestyle because I like sex and the outside vanilla world has this whole "slut" issue but that's another topic for another day.
I am not alone either. How many single women have said "I don't do couples any more"? Did you ever wonder why? They usually just say jealousy because that easiest but I'd betcha it was because they were pressured to do something they didn't desire.
If you have ever wondered why I just got up and left - that's why.

Nov 28, 2007
I was proposed to because I'm attractive, intelligent, educated, skilled and...he'd never, ever be … bored. Exasperated, elated, annoyed, dejected, amused, infuriated, beguiled and maybe even bewildered but never...bored.
I can say that I have fulfilled this prophecy.

XMAS Gift Guide
For your males: I recommend the USB Rocket Launcher for IntraOffice Warfare. Just hook it up to your cpu, dial it in, and fire soft tipped missiles at that annoying guy in the corner there. Turret rotates and makes various noises. Extensive testing by the JRM, who got one last year, has

proven it to be very reliable. Affordable & now available at thinkgeek.

For your kittens: I recommend the best small-paws friendly plush toys on the market. Microbes. Various ailments, viruses, bacteria, and pests are available. All are kitten-safe and machine washable. Each comes with a very informative tag. As an example, here's Rabies.

These also make great stocking-stuffers for older kittens. You can also use them to give helpful hints to those cats who need to clean up their act or who need to laugh at something undeniably cute.

Extremely affordable & also at thinkgeek.

For "She Who Must Be Obeyed": I recommend the neatest device the Nokia N95 8MB with the Zeiss optics. This device will require some hunting down but the effort will prove your devotion to your Magnificent Wife or Beloved Mistress. It might be available in Chicago or New York and Nokia's website lists it as "out of stock". But I know you'll find one for her, won't you?

VERY expensive & difficult to acquire. But that's rather the point.

Why Him?

"Something in the way he moves..."

I cannot tell you. But what I can tell you is that I have met men who, literally, have caught my eye and then, almost as if by magic, have lured me to their side by doing nothing at all!

"attracts me like no other lover."

Have you felt it too?

Nov 29, 2007

"Having an Affair?" A Handbook for the "Other Woman" by Sarah J. Symonds

Often reads as a divorced "because he cheated on me" woman's diatribe against cheating lying bastards. Amusing in bits and pieces but with the other woman characterized as either a golddigging leach or a foolishly in love sap the book gets tedious. Too much repetition and the book's style of presentation - like a bunch of sticky notes stuck onto a page of paper - is very poor. She does cover all of the ground and issues involved. The book is very comprehensive.

The only redeeming feature is her point that the other woman is just as injured as is the wife and that they both should save their anger for the cheating lying bastard himself, and not for each other.

As a young military member and military wife with kittens, it was mandatory that we have a designated stateside person to care for the kittens should an evacuation from overseas be necessary. A method of monetarily supporting those kittens also had to be arranged. Thus began the family savings account wherein My mother and I shared a joint account. Now that my daughter has kittens of her own and is a military wife in her own right, we have added her onto the account to ease the intrafamily transfer of funds for mutual support of each other and the grandkittens Lex and Viv.

Mom, Daughter, Lex, and I all descended upon the bank enmass (Viv was napping) and made the arrangements last Friday. I mention this because I have received the new passbook in the mail and got a kick looking at the names inscribed.

J. H. A̱.
K. A. A̱. **Z.**
K. A̱. **Z.** M

The A. and the Z. are all the same surnames carried on down the line. We do not have names, we have genealogies!

Female kittens get three names at birth while male kittens get four. Each gets a given name. Each bears the maiden name and the surname. But males also get their father's given name as their middle name. When the female cat marries, she just tacks his surname on at the end and so it continues. Some variances are permitted; for example one could choose to give a male kitten the given names of his grandfathers and a female kitten the given names of her grandmothers (which it was in my case).

So my grandkittens are:

A. **Z.** M.
V. **Z.** M.

Every family has its own way of building and keeping traditions - some good, some harmless, and some terrible - it is part of what makes them families. (Where even if they don't like you, they have to take you in.) The M.s may be dreadfully dysfunctional but it is hoped that the stubborn and relentlessly functional nature of the A.s, and the Z.s will prevail. Interestingly my daughter looks more like an H. than an A. or a Z. and the grandkittens all have H. eyes which is totally unexpected.

How's your family, baby?

Why does this always happen? You get it all set up and are all prepared - and then the schedule goes straight to hell! Today
lunch switched to tomorrow (Friday)

last night's fun switched to tonight
Friday
lawyer lunch cancelled so brought in lunch from yesterday
Wild B'Day Party still on at TPA
so no Skinifatz for me tonight
Then next week's Court dates have been cancelled
HURRAY!!
Then there's Scotch on Tuesday and
Fun appt on Wed.
Skinifatz that Friday
Then the Silk & Skin on Saturday in Baltimore.
Now, I hope there aren't any more changes!

Nov 30, 2007
The Program , which, you will remember, was previously
posted herein,
WORKS !
WHEEEEEEEEEEEEEEE!!
LOL

December
2007

Dec 1, 2007

Had a marvelous time at BB's birthday party, long may she reign, last Friday evening at The Private Affair out in god-forsaken Port Deposit which you find after that OMG left hand turn and that bit of "find the signboard" adventure they call a back road, please note - the bridge is out.

Lots more single men - which is JUST what The Kitten ordered, thank goodness! AND they had a room with restraints already laid out and attached to the bed. The Jail Room. Ooo, Baby! That is MY room!

The audience didn't seem to mind watching me do my thing with E. - hmm cute guy and tasty. He invited me to go for "a walk" with him. S damn near died laughing and told him that if I threw him down onto the bed and used him, he'd only have himself to blame! S. then gave E. a general overview of what was likely to happen to him. Then E. went and re-invited me to "take a walk".
We only walked until we came upon the Jail Room and then into the restraints he went! And onto him, I went. Wheeeeeeeeeeeeeeeeeeee!

And a good time was had by all!

Have you been there?

Met some people there - apparently they don't know me too well - they had thought I'd "chicken out" since I'd be coming up there all on my own. Sillies! The guide who showed me around, my first time there, also thought I might be a timid child. *EG* Phuleeeze!

Of course I liked the place as soon as I saw little chocolate doughnuts in the snack room!

Then I had to leave -as always - so I blasted down the interstates and swung by Skinifatz - getting there circa 12:45am Saw a cute teddybear for few minutes and then romped on home with the truck on fumes.

"She's had sugar and she's ready again!"

It was quite a night!

"Teddybear, Teddybear... turn around."
Sunday afternoon - one teddybear
Monday morning - another teddybear
Tuesday evening - another teddybear
Wednesday evening - and yet another teddybear!
Pretty teddybears all in a row!
I LOVE THIS LIFE!!!

Dec 2, 2007
Nothing to Wear!
I am going to what is called a Silk & Skin party this Saturday. This is where women wear lingerie and the men are naked. Now, I do not have anything you would even remotely consider lingerie since lingerie is not usually made out of black leather but I am hoping that this bra and thong set I have made out of leather straps and draped chains will be considered suitable. I am planning to also wear my black stiletto pumps and this year's multi-colored and jingly holiday earrings.
What do you think?

Dec 3, 2007
Today I put the F150 into the shop for repairs and got the rental car from Enterprise, a black Dodge Charger - go figure -but the insurance is paying for it. Sooo then I went to Tyson's to do some XMas shopping and I swear - I'm doing mine on-line next time!

1. salespeople who either whisper or don't know where anything is

2. people who think they know how to drive

3. stores that do not have in stock the items I want even though they are in their XMas catalogs

BAH!
Online I bought myself a slinky dress for THOSE kind of parties and renewed all sorts of professional memberships and then bought my sweety and others some prezzies.
But I did have LOTS of fun driving the rental car even if it isn't the hemi version - any car I drive drives like it has a hemi engine in it because that's how I drive.
All I want for XMas is 12 cylinders!
(sing it with me people!)
How's your shopping coming, my lovelies?

LOL
Ty but I have written books, not all of them on sexual topics - just most, and they are available at lulu under the name of Allen. You fellows will find the book Women (a primer for men) most useful. There's also, for both genders, Orgasm and Superb Sex. BTW most of my sex books are "how-to" books. There are three for women: beguile , The Polyamorist, and Men (a primer for women).
Enjoy!

Dec 4, 2007
Mmmmmmm can't you just see me in this?
And best of all - it is on sale! Bwahahahaha!
You men are toast!
Yes, those are PEARLS, darling!

Tall, lithe, blithe, polyamorous, witty, and elegant domme' who bewitches alpha males, and only alpha males, into becoming willing cat toys as they succumb to their own desires.

Currently not looking.

I am a soft domme and do NOT do pain, abuse or indulge in humiliation. Basically I want wild, rampant, skin-on-skin, multi-orgasmic, ejaculatory, full body contact sex on my terms with someone who can accept my unbridled sexuality.

Must between 40 and 60 years of age, 6 foot tall, unencumbered, furry, nearby, and possess more than half a brain. Strong enough to be fun but warm enough to be my teddybear.

LTFWBR ONLY

Bad Boys, PITAs, and those who feel the need to "be a challenge" need NOT apply.

Dec 5, 2007
I will be attending the next big Mardi Gras event and my dress came in yesterday. (You have to love free overnight

shipping.) I think it is cute. It should also be very 'effective'. My legs will be all out there.

What do you think?

Will it make men want to put their arms around me and whisper sweet nothings in my ear?
Best Comment Received: "No. It will make them want to whisper wickedly, lascivious suggestions ... and then follow-through with randy, naughty somethings! How glorious!"

FURTHER PHILOSOPHICAL DEBATE
I am here for FUN with a modest amount of AFFECTION thrown in. And because I am far too busy, I want just a few reliable men with whom I can dally whenever our schedules coordinate. Hence the LTFWBR - long term friends with benefits relationship.

This means we do not ONLY spend time together in the bedroom. But if you walk three feet away from me when we're out somewhere - that's not good. Offer me an arm, dammit; I'm wearing stilettos.

You can laugh and smile, it won't kill you. Yes, others might think you're enjoying my company but I want to think you're enjoying my company otherwise what's the point? Yes, we all know the rules of the game and the likely outcome thereof, but let's make the ride as marvelous as possible.

Stop hiding!

Do we have agreement?

SCOTCH

The Macallan held a scotch whisky tasting at the Westin, 23 and M, last night. Very nice! I enjoyed it even if it was in DC. Fortunately my escort knows DC very well and is an excellent driver. He also enjoys scotch.

We sampled the following:
10 year Fine Oak
15 year Fine Oak
17 year Fine Oak - all casked in used bourbon casks from America hence the increasing "smokiness" of the scotch as it aged.

Then we went onto the:
12 year and
18 year scotch -which had been aged in used sherry casks from Spain giving it a sweetness to the flavor and a touch of ruby to its color.

All told everyone had the equivalent of two drinks of scotch.

At home, we drink The Macallan Cask Strength scotch. My teddybear asked the presenter, "The Ambassador", about it and was told that they saved that particular variety for the "master class".

They served some very nice but standard savories with it and there was ice and water available. For each scotch, they had a video with music showing news items from that time. The cell phones from 18 years ago caught everyone's attention! So funny! Almost 200 people came out last night and it was GREAT!

248

Also there, and thank you for telling me about it, were CKL and her lover. Two very nice people who add interest and fun to any event they attend. My teddybear was not feeling his best but (he looked so good in his jacket too) I kept wanting to kiss him anyway.

We each received a gift bag containing a proper whisky glass, a booklet and a small bottle of the 18 year Macallan.

Best line from the presenter:
"Islay takes its scotch seriously. They have 7 distilleries and 2 schools."

Two of those Islay distilleries are my favorites: Laphroaig and Lagavulin.

Drink scotch however you want to - just enjoy it.
And I do!

Dec 6, 2007
I, EvilEvilKitten1, give all of the men on HERE permission to worship me or lust after me from afar as they will. The men HERE may also read, review, respond to, and peruse my profile, blog, and other postings as often as they wish unless they have previously been blocked from doing so.

I, EEK, give the men of AFF who meet my criteria as stated on my profile on HERE permission to send me emails here. I do retain the right of refusal and the right to not reply to said emails however. Please be aware that particularly inane, disgusting, or otherwise unappealing emails will be posted in various blogs as examples for other men of what not to do.

I, EvilEvilKitten1, permit my fellow bloggers of either gender to place a link to my blog on their blog after which they may quote me so long as proper citations are appended.

I, EvilEvilKitten1, do permit members of either gender to nominate me for awards, etc. as, for example, those done by BBB. In the course of which they may use my profile picture and/or provide a link to my profile and/or my blog.

Signed EvilEvilKitten1

Who definitely lives up to her handle.

MAGNICIENT DESOLATION
Yes, we went and walked on the moon.
As of 2007, twelve people have walked on the Moon. No one has walked on the Moon since 1972.

1 Neil Armstrong
2 Buzz Aldrin
3 Pete Conrad*
4 Alan Bean
5 Alan Shepard*
6 Edgar Mitchell
7 David Scott
8 James Irwin*
9 John W. Young
10 Charles Duke
11 Eugene Cernan
12 Harrison Schmitt

*Deceased

The contrast between the moon - gray boulders and dust - and the Earth - bursting with life - are striking. From Mercury to Mars, only the Earth LIVES. We are a part thereof. Long may it be so.

"O brave new world that has such people in it."
-Shakespeare

JOYFUL POLYAMORY
It can be done but it is only for those with fearless hearts; those with the courage to take on everything entailed when one brings another into your life. For you have to accept all of him - the good, the bad, the ugly, the beautiful, his past, present and future, his hopes, dreams, and obsessions. All of it. And you cannot look at this with mundane, world-weary eyes but eyes that see clearly and relish what they see. Living polyamorously takes a kind of laughing high courage; an essential inner joy at simply being alive and able to share this joy with others.

I LOVE THIS LIFE!
I wish you all could share the joy of it!

Dec 7, 2007
1942
Today lives in infamy even now.
Spare some time to remember those who have gone before and those fighting now.

FOR YOUR TREE
This year, do your tree a little differently. Here's a list of OTHER decorations for you to consider.

1. rolled up stock certificates tied with a red ribbon and a name tag

2. real coins in tinted transparent bags tied with gold thread and a name tag
3. jewelry with a name tag
4. blown glass ornaments
5. molded glass ornaments
6. shiny brass, silver, or gold metal ornaments
7. crystal ornaments

I have collected glass ornaments for a while now and now have a full pack of hounds to chase the glass fox around my tree. The horses are still made of wood but I still have hopes of finding glass horses to complete the set.

Stock certificates go over better than those computer printout confirmation slips but if you buy bonds you can use them instead.

Those with children or pets may want to stick with unbreakable ornaments such as those made out of metal. The idea is to bounce the light from inside the tree, where the lights are, to the outside. Metal ornaments can often be inscribed with names and messages making them even more special.

Merry XMas!

Dec 8, 2007
Spent the morning snuggled up in my cozy bed with the SRM. A nice lazy morning of just him and I.
This is how days SHOULD begin!

Iso Grifo

So you haven't heard of it - any 7 Liter V-8 deserves your attention.

Production 1963-1974
Body style(s) 2-door coupe
Layout FR layout
Engine(s) 5.4 l ohv-V8 (Chevrolet 327), 300/355 hp
7.0 l ohv-V8 (Chevrolet 427), 400 hp (300 kW)
7.4 l ohv-V8 (Chevrolet 454), 395 hp (295 kW)
Transmission(s) 4 or 5 speed manual transmission
3 speed automatic (on request)
Wheelbase 98.4 in (2500 mm)
Length 174.4 in (4430 mm)
Width 69.7 in (1770 mm)
Height 47.2 in (1200 mm)
Curb weight 3150-3550 lb (1430-1610 kg)

All Grifos are extremely desirable today because of their beauty and un-complicated mechanicals, so most surviving cars are either restored or in the process of being restored. A former employee of Iso, Mr. Roberto Negri runs a small Company in Clusone, Italy where Grifos from all over the world are being restored to original specifications. In the end there were 322 Series I and 78 Series II cars built for a total of 400 Grifos. 332 were Series I cars; 90 were 7 Liter, but when it comes to rarity, the Series II 5-speeds and the Big Block Targas are the rarest.

You do know I like fast cars?

Dec 9, 2007
TREE DECOR METHOD
I wrap one set of multicolored non-blinking lights around the central trunk, the smaller twinkling multicolored lights a bit further out but still inside the tree and then use metallic garland and light reflecting and refracting ornaments to bring the light from the inside to the outside

of the tree. I always put the tree in front of a window so it can be seen from outside the house and feed the lights to a wall switched outlet so no climbing under and around to turn on or off the lights.

Looks magnificent!

Dec 10, 2007
MORNING SEX
Not a huge fan of morning sex because I am not a huge fan of waking up before I absolutely have to. This has been proven over the years by various males making the attempt only to be subjected to the fury of a half-asleep woman wrapping herself even tighter in her blankets, and snarling "go away".

The only way you can get morning sex is if I haven't been asleep yet and it is 2 am to 7 am, or it is between the hours of 9 am and noon - which qualifies as morning.

Synchronize your watches!

FROM FAST CARS TO FAST HORSES
Man O' War was a large, big-boned, red-chestnut stallion full of vigor and presence standing 16.2 hands at his withers. (For non-horsepersons that's 64.8 inches, 5.4 feet, at his shoulder.)

In the Blood-Horse magazine ranking of the top 100 U.S. Thoroughbred champions of the 20th Century, Man o' War was ranked No. 1.

Man o' War, (March 29, 1917 Nursery Stud farm, Lexington, Kentucky - November 1, 1947, Faraway Farm) is considered by most to be the greatest thoroughbred racehorse of all time. During his career just after World War I, he won 20 of 21 races and $249,465 in purses.

As a sire, Man o' War was impressive as well, producing more than 64 stakes winners and 200 various champions. His line traces to Godolphin Arabian.

254

In 2006, Dorothy Ours wrote a new, extensively sourced biography entitled Man o' War: A Legend Like Lightning.

Secretariat (March 30, 1970 – October 4, 1989) was an American Thoroughbred racehorse. Secretariat won the 1973 Triple Crown, becoming the first Triple Crown winner in 25 years, and set still standing track records in two of the three races in the Series, the Kentucky Derby (1:59 2/5), and the Belmont Stakes (2:24). Secretariat was affectionately nicknamed "Big Red" by his owner because of his size and brilliant chestnut color, or, perhaps, in an attempt to draw comparisons to the great Man o' War. Altogether, Secretariat won 16 of his 21 career races and finished out of the money just once — in his debut as a 2-year-old, when he was jostled coming out of the gate and finished fourth.
His blood flows through many other notable racehorses, including 2004 Kentucky Derby and Preakness winner Smarty Jones, and he is most noted as a broodmare sire, being the broodmare sire of 1992 Horse of the Year and successful sire A.P. Indy, Secretariat's grandson through his daughter Weekend Surprise, who was sired by another Triple Crown winner, Seattle Slew. AP Indy is the sire of 2007 Belmont Stakes winner Rags to Riches, the first filly to win at Belmont since 1905. Secretariat is also the dam-sire of the great stallions Storm Cat (by Storm Bird), through his daughter Terlingua, herself an excellent racemare, and of Gone West, through his daughter Secrettame.

Forego (1970-1997) was a highly successful American thoroughbred racehorse. Born on April 30, 1970, the bay gelding was owned and bred by Mrs. Martha Farish Gerry's Lazy F Ranch. Over Forego's long years of racing, he had three trainers: first Sherrill W. Ward, then when he became ill, Frank Y. Whiteley, Jr. and his son David A. Whiteley. He had two main jockeys: Hall of Famer Bill Shoemaker and Heliodoro Gustines.

Two things kept him from making a splash in 1973's race for the Triple Crown. First, he was still awkward as a 3-year-old, still growing into his size. Second and more importantly, 1970 was also the year Secretariat was born. Forego was fourth behind Secretariat in a Kentucky Derby that saw the two fastest times ever recorded in that race (1:59 2/5 by eventual winner Secretariat, and 1:59 4/5 by runner-up Sham), and while he contended in many Grade I races that year, he proved to be a late bloomer. His size and fractiousness led to his being gelded in order to race, thus setting him up for a long career. As a gelding, he raced as a champion handicap horse long after Secretariat retired to stud.

His time in the sun began when he was a four-year-old. In 57 starts, he won 34, placed in 9, and came in third 7 times. His lifetime earnings amounted to $1,938,957. Forego won the Eclipse Award for Outstanding Sprint Horse in 1974, and Eclipse Award for Outstanding Older Male Horse for four years running—1974, 1975, 1976, and 1977. He was voted the Eclipse Award for Horse of the Year for three years straight: 1974, 1975 and 1976. His countless handicap victories made this large son of Forli a handicap champion. His versatility is clearly demonstrated by his wins from 7 furlongs to the 2 mile Jockey Club Gold Cup. Because of his wins, he was constantly asked to carry more than 130 pounds, and still he won usually with a heart pounding burst of speed in the home stretch when he would close like a rocket and win in a photo finish against horses carrying up to thirty-five pounds less weight! (It was truly heart-stopping to watch him!) His dramatic style became a crowd pleaser and the horse would draw people to the track who otherwise would not have come. Once, during a strike

256

by betting machine workers, there was no wagering. Nevertheless, Forego drew over 10,000 people on a weekday who came out just to see him run in a warm up race. Forego was truly a champion handicap horse.
In the list of the top 100 U.S. thoroughbred champions of the 20th Century by Blood-Horse magazine, Forego ranks 8th.

Love the ponies!

DAMN!
Driving to an appointment tonight (Yes, Virginia, THAT kind of appointment*EG*). Incautious move tore my knee again. Cell phone had died. Just back home now - 10 pm, and taking scotch for the pain.
Just NOT my day!
You ever have days like this too?

Dec 11, 2007
MULTIPLE ORGASMS
HOW TO HAVE

FOR HER:
Three areas will induce orgasms if properly stimulated: the clitoris, the G-Spot, and the posterior fornix. Most women are fully capable of having orgasms in each area. Most women are also fully capable of having multiple orgasms because women do not have a refractory period. In order to have multiple orgasms, she has to be both relaxed and aroused. Proper stimulation of each of the three areas above, in rotation, should do it as far as keeping her aroused. For the relaxation, she should be breathing deeply, riding through each orgasm as it comes through.

257

Inexperienced women get sensitive and call it "pain" but this is just a false signal since her brain is not accustomed to this level of stimulation. They then pull back and say that's enough. This is a mistake. Relax, breathe deeply, ride it out, and enjoy the orgasms on the other side. Never hold back an orgasm. Instead, enjoy each one as it comes and then go on to have more! Well, for as long as he holds out. Recommended techniques: cunnilingus, manual stimulation of clitoris and/or G-Spot, cunnilingus with manual stimulation of the G-Spot, caressing the G-Spot with the head of the penis, caressing the posterior fornix with the head of the penis. If two men, combine methods.

FOR HIM:
All he has to do is to separate the orgasm, the pulsing of the pc muscle, from the ejaculation. THIS CAN BE DONE. Thus avoiding the dreaded refractory period. That's why men need to take breaks - to recharge as it were. If you cum without ejaculating, breaks are not needed and you don't lose your erection, etc. Do your kegels, gentlemen. When the pc muscle pulses during orgasm, stop, and employ the Squeeze Technique to prevent ejaculation, then slowly return to what you were doing. This does take some practice. Begin with Edge Play and move on from there.

"Instructions for the squeeze technique, step 1: no sexual intercourse
The couple sit on the bed facing each other, in a comfortable position. She touches, holds, caresses or kisses his penis until he has an erection and feels sufficiently aroused. He lets her know by words or sounds that he is going to get very excited. So this is before he feels his orgasm is coming. At this moment she takes his penis between thumb and two fingers, the thumb resting against the fremulum (the little muscle under the head that attaches

258

to the (fore)skin). She then squeezes, gently but with enough force, for three or four seconds. The result is that the urge to come is repressed and the penis becomes less erect. Then for a minute or so there is mutual kissing and caressing (see Great sex without intercourse), in which he also stimulates her clitoris, and then a return to the sitting position and a repeat of the squeezing. Repeat this procedure a couple of times, until you are completely relaxed and aroused at the same time. Then stop and get up or go to sleep. Do not have sexual intercourse.

Instructions for the squeeze technique, step 2: stretch the timespan of arousal
Repeat this session at least four or five times, each time without the male ejaculating. She may have orgasms by manual or oral stimulation. The sessions may become longer and longer as he learns that his orgasm is not inevitable, that she is an active participant, and that the pleasure bond is strengthened. He can stretch the timespan of his arousal, so that his request to squeeze comes later and later.
All this changes the way you make love, especially breaking through the combination of feeling excited and being worried about coming too quickly. Also it is pleasant to try something out together, to communicate about a problem that is mutual, not just his. And every time she can be caressed to orgasm, while he is aroused but does not ejaculate.
Once you have discovered that you can have and enjoy an erection long enough to feel comfortable, you can go back to having sexual intercourse, but again, it must be different from before:

Instructions for the squeeze technique, step 3: use saliva

Again you sit on the bed. Perhaps you have warmed up with or without the squeeze technique. Now she sits across your legs, resting on her knees. She holds your erect penis, which must be sufficiently strong and wet (saliva) and puts it inside her vagina, holding it there. Do not move, but look at each other and enjoy the moment. Then she takes the penis out and can apply the squeeze technique if it is called for. After half a minute she puts the penis in again, holds it for as long as he lets her, and so on. The essential thing is that both learn that the penis can be inside the vagina without the threat of an impending ejaculation. Step by step the lovemaking can be increased, leaving the penis in longer, moving the pelvis in circles, caressing each other as it were on the inside. The next time you can start moving up and down, very gently and looking at each other, aware and going up to a certain point, when you can take out the penis and squeeze again.

But probably, by the time you got this far, you are sufficiently able to have intercourse for a long enough time."

- from triple w dot nvsh dot nl slash skills slash squeeze dot htm

Edge play is bringing the man to the point of orgasm and then backing off - not letting him climax. Repeat, repeat, repeat. Try to hold out for longer and longer periods of time.

Practice makes Perfect!
Here's to Superb Sex!!

Dec 12, 2007
OMG!!
Is it too early to start drinking?

Dec 13, 2007
PARTIES PLANNED
Friday
Skinifatz in Occoquan, VA after 9 pm
Firehouse in Fairfax, VA after 0 pm (nonsmoking)
Capital Cream

Saturday
Yakadoo's in Fredericksburg which is in the Holiday Inn
off I95 Exit 133 B on Rt 17 after 9 pm
Tribeca in Newport News at the Omni hotel after 9 pm
(upstairs section, with glow sticks, rooms on the A. f. F.
floor when checking in)

Sunday
Remember to sign up for the Mardi Gras at 8 pm

Save the Date
Jan 19th at Cancun Cantina near Baltimore
Feb 7th Meeting of the Wicked Woman Group at Skinifatz
at 9 pm
Feb 8th/9th Mardi Gras at the Hyatt near Dulles

Enjoy!

Dec 14, 2007
ADVICE
I periodically read a dating site for guys that gives them
advice on how women are and how to deal with them.
Generally the advice given is poppycock! The idea behind
it is good, but the methods given are not only ineffective
but counter-productive if the woman has any character
and/or brains.

He wants guys to mimic the behavior of arrogant jerks as in "tell her what she needs to change to have a chance with you." Excuse me? Buddy I can buy what you've got. Can you say the same without seeming completely "non-functional"? No, you can't. He then goes on to tell you to really be the best man you can be and to have integrity and really be a nice guy but to still retain the behavior of being a jerk so she doesn't run roughshod over you.

I remember my husband's way of courting me 33 years ago and it was NOTHING like this advice and I was "the girlfriend from hell". I was NOT exclusive. I was NOT all cute and fluffy and attentive and I did NOT say "I love you" first. I never called him. He bird-dogged me. I couldn't move without tripping over him. Every time I turned around - there he was with a huge grin on his face.

Why did I do all of that? Because I wanted to know that when the going got rough, as it will, he could take it. I wanted him to prove to me that he had the courage and the strength of heart to deal with the worst of me in order to enjoy the best of me.

Guys, when a woman wants to know what you're made of - SHOW her! The number one issue with women is SECURITY. A woman wants a man who will NEVER run away (abusive relationships excepted).

She wants to know that when she needs you, you will be there if only to guard her back. Are you tough enough?

Understand?

"Tuff Enuff"
by The Fabulous Thunderbirds

I would walk ten miles
On my hands and knees
Ain't no doubt about it, baby
It's you I aim to please

I'd wrestle with a lion
And a grizzly bear
It's my life, baby
But I don't care

(CHORUS)
Ain't that tough enough
Ain't that tough enough
Ain't that tough enough
Ain't that tough enough

For you, baby
I would swim the sea
Nothing I'd do for you
That's too tough for me

I'd put out a burning building
With a shovel and dirt
And not even worry
About getting hurt

(CHORUS)

I would work twenty-four hours
Seven days a week
Just so I can come home
And kiss your cheek

I love you in the morning
And I love you at noon
I love you in the night
Take you to the moon

(CHORUS)

I'd lay in a pile of burning money
That I've earned
And not even worry
About getting burned

I'd climb the Empire State
Fight Muhammed Ali
Just to have you, baby
Close to me

(CHORUS)

Obviously a man willing to step up to the plate!
Some guys think he's a wuss – catering to a woman, but
then, those are the unmarried guys.

AUTO-REPLIES
WOMEN
POLITE:

"Thank you but NO, thank you." - to be used by those who
are polite but are just here to chat with friends/blog.

"Thank you for your interest. If I like you, I'll get back in
touch with you." - to be used by those who are choosy but
looking or by women who just want to be both polite and
lazy since no reply = no.

NOT SO POLITE:

"Whatever!" - to be used by those women who do not feel up to being polite and their answer is No.

"Not interested!" "BLAH BLAH BLAH" or other variants thereof also will work.

DOWNRIGHT RUDE:

"Not even if you were the last man on earth!"

"Fuck Off and Die"

But what if you might want to say Yes? You could use the "If I like you" from above or you could go with something like:

"You sound cute. Let me look over your profile."

"I might be interested. I'll let you know if I am."

Please note that they are all short and to the point. We all know how well men read profiles - they don't - so please bear that in mind when writing your auto-replies.

Here's mine for example:

"Thank you, but I am polishing my claws and sharpening my fangs. If I like you I will get back to you just as soon as I am done with this.

If I do not, then you have your answer."

AUTO-REPLIES
MEN
Since the majority of men have some kind of hang-up with language, men are permitted to cut and paste any of the following.

POLITE:

"Thank you for your email. My number is zzz-zzz-zzzz. Please call me at your earliest convenience."

(insert your cell phone number in the space provided)

NOT SO POLITE:

"YES! Call me at xxx-xxx-zzzz. NOW!"

DOWNRIGHT RUDE:

"Hey, bitch, call xxx-xxx-zzzz and lay it down for me."

Just in case, unlikely though it may be, a man might want to say NO, here are few for those men who are hesitant or commitment-phobic.

"Thank you for your email. I'll get back to you soon."

"Thank you but I'm not meeting women just now."

"Thank you. Can we chat? My yim is -----."

Just being helpful!

Dec 15, 2007
REASON
The point of my being here is to show people that sex is
NOT bad, dirty, or something to be ashamed about. Change
your mindset and you can change your life for the better.
Be willing to think things through beforehand, be willing to
set goals and to do what is necessary to make them come
true, face up to the truth and accept reality - these are the
things I try to get people to understand and attempt. Yes,
my prowess may be legendary but I'm not here to brag but
to serve as an example of what self-awareness, self-
acceptance, and facing life with both courage and joy can
achieve.

If you would have it so.

VARIOUS REPLIES
When you send an email here, several things are possible:

1. If he/she has auto reply on, the computer will send you
his/her auto-reply. NO the person has not yet read your
email. The person may not even be on-line. It is just the
machine passing along her standard message.

2. If she/he has read it and you have paid for a notice- AFF
will tell you that it has been read. Once again - it is the
machine talking, not the person.

3. You get a "standard Quick Reply" - this is a message the
person has selected for you from the list. YES, this is a
response from the person.

4. You do not get any reply at all. Move along, people.
She/he is not interested.

5. She/he writes you back - based upon what it says, choose between "Congratulations" or "Sorry, hun".

Please learn to tell when it is the person or the computers talking before reaching any conclusions. Thank you.

Naturally the above is based upon the premise that the email system is actually working correctly, which, may not be the case.

Dec 16, 2007
PARTY!!
Going to the Mardi Gras!
And I'm on the "party floor"!
Are you?

Dec 17, 2007
Consider the efforts of the various species of bower birds.

Here you have a male, fixing up this love nest, and decorating it with care: the blue stones over here, the blue feathers over there. Getting it just right. He stands before this edifice and does his song and dance trying to entice a female to come and "pick me!".

Perhaps architecture is not your field. Very well, consider the widow bird.

Small bird living in tall grass and he has to attract attention. He's leaping above the grass while fluttering his wings and calling out "Here I am! Pick me!" in his efforts to entice a female.

Being in a 'low hover' is not for you -eh? Well then, there's always the puffin.

Something of a prosaic bird, the male puffin brings fish to his prospective mate. He places it before her and steps back a step or two. If she's not immediately interested, he'll nudge the fish a bit closer to her while making a "chainsaw" noise that means "Love you. Pick me."

Humans have different rituals but essentially it is all the same thing - we're all saying "pick me!"

But you have to admit that actually seeing a human male literally doing any of these things above would be hilarious!

POLL
I have heard, that the proper response to a woman's "I love you." should be a man saying "How much?". I wonder if this is true.
Ladies, what would be your reaction to receiving a "how much?" response to your "I love you."?
(Thus far the responses have been either negative or provisionally negative.)

TALKING TO or SPANKING?
You use BOTH, of course, as the offense warrants and the age of the child increases. Younger children have no idea what you're talking about so they get spanked. (Telling a two year old that he's grounded has no effect.) Older males should be spoken to unless he is SERIOUSLY in need of an ass-kicking (I refer you to Chris Rock's video on youtube) which is delegated to the nearest capable male

relative. Older females should be sternly counseled by the senior woman then present.

That's my view. What's yours?

HAD TO TELL YOU...

,,, about nomarriage.com. In it, he details why Modern Western women are horrible creatures and how women from other countries, Asia, Latin American Eastern Europe are simply WONDERFUL and make great wives who TRULY appreciate their American husbands.
Unfortunately, the site is NOT a joke. He means it.

Here's an excerpt:

"Traditional marriage balances different privileges and obligations for men and women. Modern woman wants all the benefits of "equality" without any of the responsibilities.
Traditional Western culture balanced special privileges for women with special obligations, and the same for men.

Equality states that no one get special privileges, and that responsibilities and rights should be equally shared.

Either system is balanced and fair. The problem with modern Western culture is that many women want only the positives from both systems:

They want special privileges from the traditional system (men paying, being "gentlemen" by using special deferential manners and language to women, being the main breadwinner, etc) but not the old-fashioned obligations (being modest and ladylike, being a housewife, etc).

They want the positives of equality (rights, equal access to work and education, etc) without the responsibilities (paying your own way financially a full 50% for life, taking risks with no safety net, and taking your lumps without complaint like men do...not expecting to be protected or sheltered from harsh reality, etc).

You can't take only the good from both systems...you have to take the bad with the good in any balance you strike. When women try to have their cake and eat it in this way, the bad doesn't disappear...it gets paid by men, and this is why the current culture is one of exploitation by selfish hypocritical women...and it's why men are tired of the inequity.

If American women chose one system or the other and took their full share of the bad with the good there would be no problem. But current American culture discourages women being looked at critically, instead projecting all blame unjustly onto men; and so the inequity is rationalized away.

This is why other cultures which haven't got this fucked up as far as gender relations go, start to look attractive. The women there expect to give as well as get."
- *from nomarriage.com*

Is it me or does he seem to be slightly "superficial"? The one man I know of, not a representative sample but you go with what you have, his marriage to an Eastern European girl – whom he had dated for 4 years by then – lasted 6 months.

Dec 18, 2007
HURRAY!

I have been selected! She has put me, at number 52, in her list of the 100 Most Fascinating Bloggers of 2007.
Black roses for everyone!!
Thank you,!!!

Dec 18, 2007

Quote:
Enduring The Incessant Whining of Single Females

So here I am at work listening to the whining of single bitches in my office piss and moan about not being able to find a nice single guy.

Having been a nice guy and now having been hooked up for a while. Honey, I have a few words for you - WAKE THE FUCK UP

If you are female, single and attractive the only reason you are single is YOU. YOU ARE THE FREAKING PROBLEM. Not the guy.

Here is a potential list of issues (you being the beast not withstanding):

1. Your standards are too high (ie. I want him to have a successful career, a nice body and NOT spend too much time at work). Hint: NOBODY IS EVER GOING TO MATCH THAT.

2. You are a closet lesbian and hate men. At least be bisexual so we can watch you get it on with your friend.

3. You are selfish and self centered.

4. You are high, high maintenance. Lots of average looking girls make themselves high maintenance. Here is a hint - unless you look like a freaking super model you need to get your attitude adjusted in a hurry. Then we will put up with your shit.

5. You have a condescending attitude toward men. You thing we are all stupid. This man bashing thing is prevalent nowadays. Here is another hint: men can always tell when women are like this. We all know that if you are like this when you are single god only knows what your fucking mouth will be like when we are married.

6. Too much emphasis on your career. Your career comes first and everything else second. Getting involved with a woman like this is like 2 corporations merging. If I wanted to be fucked up the ass every day I could just stay at work.

7. Gold digging. We all know that money is job #1 with lots of women when picking out men. Hint: if you knock most us out of the running than there are slim pickings left. Deal with the fact that we all aren't VP's at companies and have a Benz in the garage.

8. You have baggage or are bitter. Suddenly every man is responsible for the fact that YOU pick out bad men. Nobody told you to date the bad boys and then get fucked and chucked. You don't like being used and abused, well than don't date bad men. This is pretty simple. You got hurt, used, abused, whatever. Get over it and move the fuck on. Whatever you do don't take out all your hostilities on us because of something someone else did.

9. You are a freak and are into some weird shit. I am not talking about bondage, anal or anything like that (we would

273

welcome that). I am talking about that you are into witchcraft, crystals, new age bullshit, etc... Stop it and become normal.

10. You are spoiled and don't know the meaning of the word compromise. Here is a hint: you will have to compromise through most of life. Deal with it.

11. You suck in bed. The Italians have a saying "men want a whore in the bedroom and lady in the living room". This is the truth. We like women that like to fuck. Bottomline. Men are easily bored after hitting the same thing time and time again. They like variety and like to be entertained. So don't be shy about trying out things or telling us you want to do some funky shit.

Last thing, I hear lots of American women bitching about American men dating foreigners. You want to know why? Because YOU SUCK. You are a pain in the ass. Period. Foreign women are easy to deal with. Having dated Europeans and Latina's, they are infinitely easier to deal with than American women. They just accept you for being a man. I hear lots of women say foreign women are pushovers - it's the furthest thing from the truth. Particularly the Italians and the Latina's - they will fight with you and are very vocal. They just don't have all this bullshit that you carry around with you. –*from nomarriage.com*
Unquote.

Seems someone is himself inflicted with no.1 & no.3 above. Can we talk about "carrying baggage" here? He seems to have a fair amount on his back. The misspellings are his own btw.

What do you think?

Ready to jet overseas to find your perfect wife yet? I know a few women who would LOVE to have a perfect wife too. LOL

(as my husband has said "well, if you can't get an American girl to marry you...")

Dec 19, 2007

To all human males who consider themselves 'tested' by women, it could be worse. Witness, the rhino.

The rhino male must chase after the female and outlast any rivals for as long as it takes. It can take some time as she intends to make a marathon out of it. So there he is trotting after her for 30 miles on average all the while saying "pick me".

Fighting between males is well known but when she has claws of her own, a male has to exercise some diplomacy.

The tiger, for all of his ferocity, is a superb diplomat. He 'chuffs' at her, she 'chuffs' at him, and there's a lot of face-rubbing. He, well known to be a slut and confident in his prowess, awaits her decision without any fuss. His "pick me" is his presence.

Speaking of sluts, there are the bonobos, both males and females, often confused with chimps, who will fuck any other bonobo, male or female, at anytime, anywhere, and at the slightest of flirtations. And you thought you had it good.

May you all have as much fun as the average bonobo!

275

Dec 20, 2007
EXERCISING JUDGMENT vs BEING JUDGMENTAL
As an adult, you are expected to exercise judgment but you are not supposed to be judgmental. A contradiction in terms? Not quite.

Exercising judgment applies to a specific decision about a specific situation, person, or question after all the available information has been duly considered. We do this all of the time and it is right and proper.

Being judgmental usually involves a blanket application of a negative value without considering all the available information to an entire class of persons without disclaimer.

It is the difference between "she's a whore." and "all women who have sex outside of wedlock are whores."

But what are your definitions?

Dec 21, 2007
THE GRANDKITTENS!!
Us tigresses had a fun time in our bath today. I make the water a bit warmer and a bit deeper than their mom does so we can linger and have fun playing in the bathwater.

SPLASH SPLASH SPLASH

A nice red pouf, rose scented soap, and warm towels - we had fun. The grandkittens got their preliminary swimming lessons while getting all cleaned up and ready to face the day. Then we ran naked down the hallway to their room for dressing. Lots of laughs and giggling!

276

What was fun for you today?

Dec 22, 2007
NOTA BENE:
Over the next 2 weeks, I will be less available. A small bit of hibernation. You will see me out and about again later so do not worry.

Dec 23, 2007
CHRISTMAS MENU
Breakfast -until 9am

Eggs & Scrapple
Toast
Coffee, Cocoa, Juice

Lunch Buffet -noon until 3pm

Beef with Hot Mustard Sauce
Swiss Cheese
Black Forest Cake
Mince Pie with Date and Orange Comfit
Petit Fours
Christmas Cookies
Chocolates
Christmas Stollen with Shallot Butter
Eggnog, Cocoa, Coffee, Orange Juice

Dinner - 6pm

Roast Turkey with gravy
Fancy Stuffing
Peas with Mushrooms in Butter Sauce
Cranberry Sauce

Pinot Noir

Dessert with Blanc d'Noir Champagne Toast -9pm

(The dessert consists of those treats from the buffet not previously devoured. If there's pie left over then we'll add vanilla ice cream on the side.)

The it is into the kitchen for the processing of leftovers and clean-up for me. Yeehaw!

What are you having for your Christmas feast?

Dec 24, 2007
CHRISTMAS PROGRAM
Christmas
The Program

Hide & Seek Stockings
(standard rules for hiding)

Breakfast

(XMas outfit donning & carols playing & telephone calls to relatives)

Present Opening

Buffet Lunch

(cooking for adults & playing/naps/walks for kids)

XMas Feast

(bedtime for kids)

Dessert and Champagne Toast

(clean-up)

then a snuggly bedtime for all !!!

Here's hoping YOUR Christmas is also wonderful !!

Dec 25, 2007
MERRY CHRISTMAS !!

Dec 26, 2007
BOOTY
No, no, NOT that kind of booty. *wink* But booty as in "loot" received.

Something I had 'misplaced' was unexpectedly returned! Thank you.
Two flagons of J'adore perfume. (Remember the ad).
Earrings suitable for Mardi Gras.
The books Wine & War, 501 Must-Taste Cocktails, and 501 Must-Read Books. So there I'll be; a book in one hand and a cocktail in the other. Hmmm.
1 Grow-Your-Own Christmas Tree kit.
A tin of home-made cookies.
"Soiree'" from Royal Doulton (bet you didn't know I collect china ladies. I now have 15 of these lovelies gracing my china cabinet.)
5 Pimm's cups (where did she FIND them?!)
Christmas ornaments, various.
a T-shirt with the chocolate molecule displayed upon it.
gift certificates, various.
a bottle of chili peppers in oil - one of those you display on your kitchen counter.

the complete set of "Jeeves & Wooster" television programs in a boxed set of dvd's which we were up almost all night watching - too good to pass up, you know! (Wooster was played by the same man who now plays Dr. House, Hugh Laurie - he's also one of these men who improve with age. He also played in the "Blackadder" series.)

As a side note: one of the benefits of watching "Jeeves & Wooster" is you get to drool over the houses and cars. P.G. Wodehouse, the author of the original books, was a gifted comic writer - he was also very fond of American girls and the U.S. Marines - whose plots zoom along like lightning leaving you both laughing hysterically and breathless.)

Excellent company. Excellent food. Excellent wines. A reasonable amount of desired loot. A warm and snuggly bedtime.

What a WONDERFUL holiday!
What did you get and how was yours?

Please note, the picture was from an advertisement made by the makers of the perfume that had been shown on nationwide television and is available on the web from the maker's website and 'Charlie' is not adverse to it either. Kindly stop being so silly about the pix I use, thank you,

BTW I want that dress she was wearing in the ad!!

Dec 27, 2007
Just read some men's profiles. You see before you an AMAZED kitten. Guys, I have to ask.

How on earth do you expect to get women with THAT?

I am aware that men are not into language to the same degree as women. I am also aware that advertising may not be your forte'. But these profiles are so very bad that it makes one WEEP!

"Come with it if you can bring it."

"I'm not shallow, I just know what I like."

Nothing cute. Nothing funny. Nothing suggesting that he's fun to be with. It is either arrogant "penis-waving" or lists of criteria specific enough to make one think he was special-ordering a woman be made just for him to suit his fancy.

Men, please remember that there are hundreds of you chasing only just so many women on this site. If you want to actually see some positive results from your efforts here, you are going to have to put some thought into your profile.

1. It is okay to state what criteria are most important for you and it stick to your guns BUT it is not okay to DWELL on them. Limit your most important criteria to three. Keep it short and sweet. I don't need to hear you say the same thing in three paragraphs covering every aspect of why you like big breasts.

2. Being at all BITTER or ARROGANT qualifies you for the JERK award. Do NOT ever be negative. Do NOT wave your penis in our face. We do not like it and we may bite. The majority of women can easily out-gun ANY 6 men you'd care to name so do NOT go on and on about your prowess.

3. BE AMUSING. Come on, it is not that hard to make us laugh and think you're cute. Women respond positively to JOY so exhibit "Light & Laughter" Nothing malicious. You do not have to be self-deprecating. For example: for you divorced guys: "Just home from the war known as the divorce court. Please don't mind the limp."

4. DESPERATE gets you nothing. Try writing your profile just after you've been enjoyed by some, no doubt, discerning woman. The nice mellowness during afterglow will take the rough out of your profile.

That should be enough to get you started. Should you wish more individual assistance, please email my sexcretary here.

Happy Hunting!!

And Another Thing...
You really didn't think you were getting off that lightly, did you? *evil grin*

Please do NOT make all of your criteria merely physical ones especially if you're not "all that" yourself, thank you. "a world famous billionaire bikini supermodel astrophysicist" usually demands a man with similar successes and attributes.

If you forgive me my figure flaws, I'll forgive you yours. Deal?

I now return you to your regularly scheduled blog.

A Bad Example:

"L's profile is 100% about what he wants and 0% about what he can offer. I think that says it all right there..."

Truer words have never been spoken! Rather than let him get 'points' for people viewing his profile I shall quote it here: Please don your special 'safety glasses' to avoid injury.

"I'm looking for a woman that can handle me not only sexually but mentally. I get bored easy. Can you handle this. Come and try!!!!!LOL

My Ideal Person:
Aim looking for a girl that is not superficial and is on earth not mars. Have some common sense and know how to say what ya mean and mean what you say. No beating around the bush here. Maybe in the bush!!!! LOL"

Let us examine this "hunk of quivering man-meat":

He's 5' 7" and of average build
He's single
SOME college and a 'service tech'
Penis = long and thick

TRANSLATION:

Short, small, stupid, but thinks being "equipped" makes up for all of his shortcomings.

His probable response to being included in my blog as an example of what NOT to do (since he's done it before):

"Get over it bitch!!!!!!! OMG IM SOOOOOOOO SCARED THAT YOU DID THAT YOU PUT ME IN A

BLOG!!!!! I THINK IM RUIN FOR LIFE!!!!!!WAAAAAAAAAAAAAAA Just goes to show you the only thing a bitch like you are good for and that's to keep you from talking with a cock in your mouth."

Lovely, dontcha think?

Manners maketh the man?

Please feel free to copy and paste this in your blog as well. This guy certainly deserves to be given the widest possible dissemination esp to those 127 people on his Friend's list.

Dec 28, 2007
PLAYTIME WITH TEDDYBEARS
Old Friends

His name popped up on yim. This was followed with a telephone conversation and so it came to be that he and I at his place (you have moved your furniture) along with scotch, cookies (Kittens live on cookies), and candlelights, exchanged 'evidence of mutual admiration'. I had almost forgotten how superb he was in bed - almost! There are some men you just cannot stop kissing! Of course you cannot kiss him when he engaged in cunnilingus but no matter, I'll wait. Then it was onto the caressing of the posterior fornix (you know how much I enjoy that!) while he kissed my ankles. About 23 orgasms later it was his turn.
He gave me a massage (purrrrrr).
Next, I got to pounce upon him. He didn't put up much of a fight. His scamper onto the bed held an almost indecent amount of glee in it. His punishment was a bit of bodyworship followed by some fellatio (poor man!). I leapt upon his defenseless body and rode him getting him all wet

284

(and awaking his neighbors) until I was completely satisfied. His turn came and then we cuddled up. The alarm went off - 3 hours is just not enough time.

I hurt my shin on the bed rail getting up (ouch!), there was only one towel, I didn't mean to pull the towel bar out of the wall like that, where did my socks go? You could stop laughing long enough to help, hun. Yes, it probably would be safer just to keep me in bed. I have got to get onto my computer for my class. Look, they didn't tow my truck this time! Kisses, then blast off! Fortunately the police were elsewhere and yes, I made it home on time.

I think he's still laughing!

BEST XMAS ADS CONTEST:
I nominate the one from Dior for their perfume J'adore - that's the one with Charlie in it - and I also nominate the ad from Harley-Davidson - the one with the 'naughty list'.

Please nominate your favorite ads from the season in a comment herein and then we'll vote.

Once again this is from a manufacturer's nationwide ad campaign and is freely available.

Dec 29, 2007
In preparation for the New Year, I will now drag out the baggage from this year and burn it in the driveway as a votive offering to the gods.

It has been one hell of a year and NOT in a good way.

Disaster began I'd say Feb. Then we had 3 months of Hell. My second grandkitten was born in May. HURRAY! Things looked brighter but then we suffered a set-back in

August. Things went downhill from there. That's personally, the family en toto is somewhat better than previously.

Professionally things are improved but not as much as they needed to. Still this area is looking better than it had been.

Now as far as the "playtime" goes, outside pressures have taken all of my collared sluts. They caved to the pressure from you all out there who have stereotypes imprinted on your brains. "He's with her so he must be sub." You idiots! There's no fun in seducing a submissive man. Kittens require Teddybears, not Hamsters. Didn't it ever occur to you that I am demanding? He has to have brains, advanced sexual skills, and a wickedly fast sense of humor to keep my interest. Think of it rather as "He must have something because he's with her." (No, I'm not above kicking you when you're down if you deserve it. And you do.) Nevertheless the year ended slightly improved.

Two books published is a great improvement.

Now pouring on lighter fluid, and there's the match! As we watch the dancing flames, I have to ask...

What are you offering up for this past year?

Dec 30, 2007
STATS
The Year's Blog Stats.

353 watchers
Average Views per Post = 350
Average Comments per post = 3

Total Blog Stats
Number of Posts = 1116
Number of Comments = 4221
Comments per Post = 3.78

Beginning of the Year vs Ending of the Year
Average Views per Post - down from 800
Average Comments per Post - down by 2
Number of watchers = up by 290

Any ideas to boost readership?

ANNOUNCEMENT
My dear blog-friend BPB is asking for YOUR help with an
important project. Please go to: What I Wish I Knew Way
Back When and give her your input.

On this note, there was a letter to the editor that asked
"what is wrong with teaching abstinence?" I'll tell you what
is wrong with it. How it is being taught is what's wrong
with it. They are using mis-information, fear tactics, and
outright lies to motivate teens against having sex.

For example:

1. Condoms do not work 100% of the time
2. The Pill causes breast cancer.
3. Emotional trauma will follow any sexual activity before
marriage.

All of which is not the whole story or is just wrong. They
are back onto this virginity is special. Sex is bound up with
love, children, and self-worth and if you indulge in sex
before getting married to the man then you're a dirty slut
whom no one will respect. Sex is debasing while also being

something special that you should save and present to your husband as if a trophy, grand prize, or gift.

What they don't say is that by repressing her desires and teaching her to say NO, and teaching her that sex is dirty, etc - that they are setting him up for a sex-less life when they've been married for 20 years and she's done having kids. She will not permit herself to orgasm. She will not regard sex as glorious but instead as "something men have to have but ho-hum I could have had a V-8."

We can prevent almost ALL of this by telling teens the truth. This why I am asking you to support BPB in her great work.

Dec 31, 2007
BRAISED BEEF in BAROLO
Just perfect for those cold days ahead. Use top round roast or chuck roast and use a decent but not top flight Barolo wine.

Sear the beef in olive oil then set aside.
In the same pan, saute' chunks of onion, carrots and celery with some freshly smashed garlic. Add salt.

Return the meat to the pot and add rosemary, sage, black peppercorns, dried porchini mushrooms, a dash of freshly grated nutmeg.

Add just enough Barolo wine to cover and bring to a boil. Then simmer partially covered for about two hours. Internal temp of meat should be 160 degrees at least.

Serve hot on a bed of the vegetables from the pot. Figure 8 ounces of meat per person.

Actually any wine will do and as long as the beef is not the tenderest cut, say a brisket, this cooking method will be perfect.

MIDNIGHT
HAPPY NEW YEAR !!!

by corbis

January
2008

Jan 1, 2008
NEW ENGLAND CLAM CHOWDER
Another 'keep you warm' meal packed with everything you
need to sustain life.
Add white wine and a chunk of Hawaiian Sweet Bread to
make a complete meal.

Butter and olive oil in soup pot saute' lots of cubed potatoes
and lots of minced clams with white pepper and a few
minced onions (garlic optional) until fragrant and the
potatoes have a bit of color. (For those NOT dieting -
substitute 1/2 pound of bacon, chopped for the butter and
olive oil, set the bacon bits aside.)

Add enough chicken stock to cover and boil then simmer
for 1 hour then remove from the heat.
Add just as much milk as you added chicken stock and
return to the heat to warm through.

Just before serving toss in minced chives or parsley and the
bacon bits.

BTW one of my books is a cookbook.

SUBTLETIES
These moves may seem too little, but trust me, they send
powerful messages to the recipient and mark you as a
sensuous lover. I've had men friends in their 40's tell me
they are EXTREMELY effective when seducing women
they find attractive and I have been known to use them too.

Lightly yet lingeringly with just the slightest hint of tongue
tip kiss the outer corner of his eye. This is "the eye kiss"
and its highly effective. Another "not to forward" thing to
do is "the finger caress", This is where you place your hand
292

over his, with your fingers stretched out but between his and you gently slide your fingers back and forth, slowly now, along his. Every now and again move over one 'slot' and continue.

I have others if you'd care to know more.

Jan 2, 2008
Came across last years' resolutions and realized that I didn't achieve ANY of them. Sad really since they were so mild.

EEK's Resolutions for 2007
1. be nicer to the SRM
2. *****
3. @@@@@
4. #####
5. increase savings
6. $$$$$
7. no tickets at all
8. finish coursework
9. %%%%%
10. keep all of my current men happily by my side

None of them! Not one! I'll take a deep breath, turn my face toward the sun and harden my heart and then attempt to achieve last year's resolutions this year.

Do you do resolutions? If so, what are they? Can you tell me? Do you achieve them?

ON MY DOORSTEP
There was a package on my doorstep when I went out to my appointment this evening. It was the XMas gift I had sent to my BFF T.J. On the label was one word DECEASED.

It was true.

DAMN

I never got the chance to give her strength.
I never got the chance to give her hope.
I never got the chance to help her laugh.
I never got the chance to say goodbye.

Where's the scotch?

Jan 3, 2008
DE MORTUOUS
While you live, you can hope.
While you live, you can attempt.
While you live, you can reach out for help.

Keep the faith!

with the sweet comes the bitter
but
the reverse is also true

FURTHER SUBTLETIES
Now then get yourself an anatomy book and pay close
attention to the nervous system. Note the location of next -
those bundled areas where nerves join up. the nape of the
neck is one - for example. Another thing to note: areas
where there are LOTS of nerves leading to increased
sensitivity such as the lips, hands, feet, groin. These areas
can be gently yet persistently caressed in a sensuous
manner to great effect.

Learn to kiss both "wet" and "dry". One of the most erotic
kisses you can give a man on his lips is a dry, barely felt,

294

sliding across his lips kiss that promises delight to come. Should you wish, continue this along his jawline back and down toward the side of his neck. Gently, gently - then lightly wet kiss the side of his neck and breathe onto the same spot to evaporate the moisture before moving around to the nape of his neck and firmly plant a wet kiss right there. If he does NOT shudder with delight - you haven't made the contrast strong enough; moving from dry to wet and from gentle to firm. In order of progression, I'd recommend the finger caress, then the eye kiss, and then the program I just outlined above.

All he has to do is to feel.

THURSDAY
Spent the morning shopping with a teddybear - such fun! - and snagged a bottle of LAGAVULIN at 20% off!!! JACKPOT!!

Then found two pairs of Levis blue jeans - also on sale.

Then we went and bought some groceries. Total bill for which went down by almost $30 with various coupons.

Back home for lunch, grandktten-sitting (they napped) and just spending time chattering.

A nice way to spend a Thursday.

Lagavulin Rocks !!

Jan 4, 2008
blue

lying lizard-like

sweated, sand-caked
before that endless ebb
before that rising flow
on the cusp of blue oblivion

-from My Ice-Cold, Chrome-Plated Steel Heart

Jan 5, 2008
BAD ADVICE
From time to time, I read the advice on askmen, just to
keep up with the latest "advice to little boys" on how girls
are. It is like watching a train wreck.

This past Thursday's advice was horrific! They have this
purportedly female 'sexual correspondent' I. Snow. I
seriously doubt her credentials are more than of the
physical kind because she began her column, Dominate a
Dominant Woman, with the following:

"We often associate dominant women with whips, chains
and a pitiful man groveling at their feet while licking a pair
of vinyl boots. This certainly occurs with some regularity,
but you may be surprised to learn that dominance doesn't
always translate into sadism."

It seems rather clear that she's confusing some terms here
as well as missing a comma. BDSM are 4 separate items
hence the use of the 4 initials.
Right from the start, I am questioning her cognitive
abilities. Then there's the issue of the 'comic book
stereotype' of what is or is not a dominant woman.

Then she states this as her reason why men who are with
dominant women, should dominate them as:

296

"Dominant women tend to be physically aggressive in the bedroom; these are the chicks who'll throw you down on the bed and ride you like a champion. While this vision may appeal to most men, allowing this to happen on a regular basis puts you in a subservient role -- and that'll carry over into other areas of your relationship. If you want to wear the pants, you're going to have to show her you can."

The highlight is mine. Excuse me? What any person wants in bed does NOT of necessity carry over into other aspects of his/her relationship. Yet, she says that this will happen. There is no disclaimer used.

And then there's the advice which begins:

"To dominate a dominant woman, the next time she pounces, turn the tables and flip her onto her back. Keep her firmly (but not painfully) pinned to the bed and let her writhe for a bit. As she struggles to regain the upper hand, calmly let her know you're going to be in charge for the rest of the evening. Her panties will be soaked by the time you finish the sentence. Just be prepared to deliver the goods, as you're bound to have one horny woman on your hands."

Now whether or not a particular dominant woman enjoys the occasional 'night off' or not is one thing; but to suggest that ALL dominant women do is quite another.

Her advice only gets worse from then on. I'll spare you. (You're welcome.)

Granted she's writing for a particular on-line magazine with a particular style and a certain unintelligent audience with special needs - but even having said all of that - they could at least give out GOOD advice!

My advice:
Look, buddy, if you don't like tigresses, don't mess with them. If you're not a tiger, just leave the tigresses alone.

Jan 6, 2008
SUNDAY
The transmission on the clothes washer went. The heating element in the clothes dryer went. There is a half ton of wet laundry lingering. So I went to Sears for their appliance sale.

Found just the right machines and just the right price including delivery, hook-up and haul away. Perfect! This was at 1:30pm.

Then, BOTH Sears cards "bounced"? WTF? Called Customer Service and the little girl got 'snarky'. Went out to the truck and called up again, smoking a cig you see, this time Customer Service was REALLY customer service! Excellent! She told me precisely what "we" could do to get my purchase done. We did it. and Voila! My machines will be delivered tomorrow morning! By this time it was 3pm.

Customer Service people: Yes, I deal with the public myself, BUT you are there to help your company make money by issuing credit, for the sale of their goods, upon which they can charge interest. You are NOT there to 'make a point'.
'Making a point' does NOT make them money. You almost lost someone who has been a customer since 1979 for a credit account balance of ZERO dollars due.

Apparently this is what happens when you DON'T use your charge cards!

Jan 7, 2008
"The meaning of intimacy varies from relationship to relationship, and within a given relationship. Intimacy has more to do with shared moments than sexual interactions. Intimate feelings may be connected or confused with sexual arousal. Intimacy is linked with feelings of closeness, safety, trust and transparency among partners in a collaborative relationship. For intimacy to be sustainable and nourishing it also requires trust, transparency and rituals of connection. It is possible to compete over intimacy but that is likely to be self-defeating. Intimacy requires empathy - the ability to stand in the other's shoes."
-Wikipedia

We're all seeking some degree of intimacy.

Don't you think so?

Jan 8, 2008
We seem to have agreement re: intimacy. Yes, we want it, but as written earlier, and not by me personally - I just quoted, it varies in kind between relationships.

I'm here for a vacation from my ordinary life which tends to be more highly stressed than most. Yes, intimacy of a relaxed, sustainable, 'nourishing' kind is desired - hence the LTfwbR.

You support me. I support you. We're all friends here. Great sex with affection and laughter AND just hanging out - as the kids say.

Of course it could be just because I like kissing men.

THE KITTEN DIET
For all of you seeking to gain a slender figure. Be aware that this sort of thing is not endorsed by any one responsible or medically qualified in any way. Following this is AT YOUR OWN RISK.

Breakfast = 1 cup of coffee or hot chocolate or 1 Diet Coca-Cola, or 8 oz. of fruit juice. Such vitamins as you choose to take. Your meds if any.

Lunch - your meds if any, otherwise - just skip it.

Optional Afternoon Snack - find some guy and get some protein off of him.

Dinner - 8oz. of some meat, 1 Cup of some green vegetable, 1 Cup of some other vegetable, 16 oz. of 2% cow's milk. Skip dessert. Optional 1 4oz. glass of red wine. Your meds if any.

Evening - find about 5 guys and do your workout, shower, then go out dancing. Drink only Diet Coca-Cola.

Enjoy!

Jan 9, 2008
THE TAXMAN COMETH!
a poll
Results indicated that the most (by one vote) do their own taxes - the rest use accountants.

Jan 10, 2008
ELABORATE BEAUTY RITUALS

300

Most women have a ritual they do every day, twice a day to preserve the quality of their skin, hair, nails, etc - to be attractive, healthy, and feel good about themselves (therapy). Clean, tone, moisturize.

Mine tend to be elaborate, and extensive since I do my entire body, but they vary with the seasons.

1. Summer - I sunbathe so exfoliate and then pile on the unguents. If it has been a very sweaty sticky day - then use the sugar scrub or the mud beforehand to cleanse before exfoliating.

2. Winter - cold tends to suck the life out of me and my skin so now it is massaging with warmed oils and unguents. Slather it on and press it in, sweety! Mmmmmmmmmm.

This is in addition to the tooth-brushing we all do twice a day and the shaving thing.

Perfume, earrings, and a bit of lipstick and its "playtime"!

What is your Elaborate Beauty Ritual?

Jan 11, 2008
HEPATITUS C

Hepatitis C is an inflammation of the liver caused by infection with the hepatitis C virus.

Persons who may be at risk for hepatitis C are those who:
Received a blood transfusion prior to July 1992
Received blood, blood products, or solid organs from a donor who has hepatitis C

Inject street drugs or share a needle with someone who has hepatitis C
Have been on long-term kidney dialysis
Have frequent workplace contact with blood (for instance, as a healthcare worker)
Have or have had sex with multiple partners
Have or have had sex with a person who has hepatitis C
Share personal items, such as toothbrushes and razors, with someone who has hepatitis C
Were born to hepatitis C infected mother

There are approximately 4 million people in the United States who are infected with hepatitis C (about 1 in 70 to 100 people). Other hepatitis virus infections include hepatitis A and hepatitis B. Each viral hepatitis infection is caused by a different virus.

Symptoms
Many people who are infected with the hepatitis C do not have symptoms. Hepatitis C is often detected during blood tests for a routine physical or other medical procedure. If the infection has been present for many years, the liver may be permanently scarred -- a condition called cirrhosis. In many cases, there may be no symptoms of the disease until cirrhosis has developed.

The following symptoms could occur with hepatitis C infection:
Jaundice
Abdominal pain (right upper abdomen)
Fatigue
Loss of appetite
Nausea
Vomiting
Low-grade fever

Pale or clay-colored stools
Dark urine
Generalized itching
Ascites
Bleeding varices (dilated veins in the esophagus)

Exams and Tests
Hepatitis virus serology
ELISA assay to detect hepatitis C antibody
Hepatitis C PCR test
Elevated liver enzymes
Liver biopsy shows chronic inflammation
Hepatitis C genotype. Six genotypes are present around the world. Most Americans have genotype 1 infection, which is the most difficult to treat.

Treatment
There is no cure for hepatitis C.

Another thing to test for when doing your STD/STI check, people!

sigh

Jan 11, 2008
"Sex Is Not The Enemy"

No evolution
Sometimes it depresses me
The same old same
We keep repeating history
The institution curses curiosity
It's our conviction
Sex is not the enemy

A revolution
Is the solution
A revolution
Is the solution

I won't feel guilty
No matter what they're telling me
I won't feel dirty and buy into their misery
I won't be shamed cause I believe that love is free
It fuels the heart and sex is not the enemy

A revolution
Is the solution
A revolution
Is the solution

True love is like gold
There's not enough to go around
But then there's god and doesn't god love everyone?
Give me a choice
Give me a chance to turn the key and find my voice
Sex is not the enemy

A revolution
Is the solution
A revolution
Is the solution
Sex is not the enemy
A revolution

-by Garbage, from their album "Bleed Like Me" released in
2005

Jan 12, 2008

304

SHOT THROUGH THE HEART
I for one, LOVE St. Valentine's Day!

And why not?

For this is the day when men are asked to "let it all out, baby!" Grab hold of her and dance about! Come on, flex those muscles! Don't take "But I'm cooking dinner!" for an answer! Mess up the bed and her hair!

You KNOW you WANT to!

Jan 13, 2008
MY PROCESS
I do NOT meet one-on-one for the first meeting with unknown men.

The first meeting will occur at a social event such as a Meet & Greet.

Any attempt to 'jump' or to otherwise circumvent my process will meet with profoundly negative results.

Remember to whom you are speaking.

Do we have an understanding?

Best Reply: quoting a friend

"PRICELESS...

Unfortunately when WE say *play by my rules*..the following insults are thrown...

Bitch, you ain't all that, who the hell do you think YOU are?, aren't you a bit ugly to expect all that?

lol But I STILL do as you EEK...toe the line guys! My way or no way."

Fortunately, the men who speak to me tend to be much more respectful to me than they are to my friend. I wish they would be more polite to everyone.

Jan 14, 2008
I wish! Currently my collars are empty. Seems guys have this thing about hanging out with me because other men and women think they're submissive and therefore ICK! Few people seem capable of understanding that I dominate ONLY dominant men. *sigh* People can be such PITAs! They tend to ruin it for others.

Open up your minds!

Now if only I can find men who didn't give a damn what those other people thought, and could laugh about the whole thing...life would be great!

They have got to be here somewhere!

BLOG PRESIDENT
If I ran for Blog President, an election being held in another blog, who would run as my vice president, serve as my campaign manager, etc. etc. etc.

Any volunteers?

give you a cookie!

ANNOUNCEMENT
I have bribed a few people with cookies, living up to my
handle you understand so now I can announce my
candidacy for Blog President with Ms H (sweetness to
balance my bite)as my vice prez., That Damn Cowboy as
my PR person (because he's cute) and Bugsy-7 (wicked
legs) as my campaign manager!

My platform:

WILD, RAMPANT, MIND-BLOWING SEX FOR
EVERYONE!

Jan 15, 2008
OK
Which one of you people did the Snow Dance???

readying my snow shovel

EXPECTATIONS
We all have them regardless of the venture we're
contemplating but we have to manage those expectations to
avoid disappointment.

First, realize that reality rarely matches up to fantasy. Real
life is neither as good nor is it as bad as we can imagine it
will be. Accept that the outcome may not be precisely what
you had ordered.

Bearing that in mind:

Second, consider that you may not be properly seeing the
reality. "So she's not the hot babe you dreamed of - you still
got laid, didn't you? And it was great sex? So that's good,
right?"

This may require you stepping back and taking a more objective look at reality.

Just because you were not pounced upon by all of the hot hunks as you imagined you would be, does NOT mean that you didn't have a good time. (Being gender equitable here.)

Bottom line: have expectations in line with reality. I know that not all of the men will be falling at my feet in hopeful lust. That would be nice, and it makes a great fantasy, but I don't believe it will ever happen IRL.

Just because you're on this site - do not expect to have all of your expectations fulfilled. Some, but not all.

And discovering which ones are fulfilled is part of the fun!

THE CAMPAIGN
The campaign for Blog President is heating up. Anyone else care to be on my team?

I'll need a driver, a body guard, an intern, two researchers, and various Ministers. I also need a new Vice Prez.

there are cookies involved

Pick your position, please!

Jan 16, 2008
YOU KNOW...
He's/She's a "keeper" when they say, in answer to the perennial "what shall I wear?" JUST SHOW UP.

That's it! JUST SHOW UP. Then the major problem of the evening has been solved! Life and our insecurities have a way of messing up our playtime plans.

So if your date does JUST SHOW UP in spite of the various plan-wrecking pitfalls, all is right in the world!

Answering all questions and hesitations by saying JUST SHOW UP indicates a lovely confidence as well and confidence is always a 'desirable' trait in woman or man.

Remember people -

JUST SHOW UP !!

Jan 17, 2008
LAST NIGHT
Got a call around noon Wed from hysterically crying sister-in-law. Father-in-law not doing well. Acute Repertory Distress. Come quickly.
Called the Resident Males at work to relay the news.

On the road to PA at 4pm.
Got there at 8pm.
Left at 11pm
Arrived home 2am.

Daughter, who is on the road to OK, from AL after having driven from VA to AL the day before, with her father-in-law and the two grandkittens called at 3:35am with a problem Answered the problem. Went back to sleep - kinda.

Which is why you find me today...

EXHAUSTED!!

Jan 18, 2008
THE QUESTION HAS BEEN RAISED
How honest have you been regarding your presence here on this site? Have you been honest about yourself, your goals, and your reasons for being here?

Have you been honest with yourself?
Have you been honest with others?

Each of us has three questions to answer: who are you? Why are you here? What/who do you want?

If you cannot answer those questions then perhaps you should take some time for thought and THEN get back to us. We cannot read minds.

I am not speaking to the fakes, professionals, and players of either gender. We all know why they are here and what they are after. I am also not speaking to those 'wounded persons' both male and female who, like vampires, require far more than any person should be asked to give to another. I am speaking to the rest of us.

My reasons and goals for being here have not changed. All I want is 'a few good men'. This I have gotten. Oh, I've had my 'adventures' as the long-time readers of this blog can attest, but 'a few good men' for fun has always been my focus. I am honest with them as well. WYSIWYG.

How honest have you been?
Have you changed?
Has your focus changed?

310

Jan 19, 2008
SEXUAL RESUME'S
Just as an exercise, I attempted to write my sexual resume'
today. Now I could, and have, written books about what I
do and how I have gotten here but this resume' is limited to
a single page. It is tougher than you might think to write
one of these. Totally honest, of course, and limited to the
salient facts - it makes it difficult because you cannot
'tailor' it to suit a particular audience. Such a resume' has to
have a wide appeal.

To begin:

Handle(s)

Preamble describing your style.

Specific Skills

Statistics

Life Experience

Sexual Experience

.
and finally, "how it is to be with you".

It was with that last section that I hit a wall. For the life of
me, I simply cannot describe how it is to be with me.
Perhaps those who have been 'enjoyed' can weigh in and
tell me? It would be nice and appreciated!

Your responses will be kept CONFIDENTIAL.

JUST BECAUSE:

I can, my next truck might be a Ford F150 Lariat in pink with a Hello Kitty motif! That way, guys can shudder and say...

"I love that truck! I hate that truck!"

LOL
GOTCHA, GUYS!

Jan 20, 2008
NOTES
1. 20-somethings need NOT apply especially not after that rant from one in the chatroom last night. *waving a dismissive paw*

2. I have a mischievous streak a mile-wide so be prepared! *extending arms to indicate width*

3. Alcohol is NOT required to get me going. But my public demeanor will always be decorous. *knit one, purl two* Behind closed doors...is another thing entirely *very evil grin*

4. Only men, only men, and only men... all ladies MUST delegate whatever to the nearest available male(s).

5. Sexual harassment is not encouraged but will be graded on an A to F scale. *looking at you over my glasses*

You have to come to me with your mind up and running, laughter in your heart, and the fire of desire for me in your eyes.

Jan 21, 2008
HWP

312

Not to cast anyone into gloom, but the question was posed from a mechanical engineering and physics viewpoint - the 'mechanics' of coitus.

Is it easier for the average woman to fuck a non-HWP man than it is for the average man to fuck a non-HWP woman?

The average male being endowed with 6 to 8 inches mind you and the goal is for him to reach her posterior fornix.

For those who do not know, the posterior fornix is the area of her vagina that is down (below the cervix) and way in the back.

Having thought about it, I would have to say that it would depend upon the individual's 'configuration' - how their non-HWP was actually arranged and how non-HWP they were.

What do you think? Which is easier?

THE TIME IS NOW!
VOTE FOR ME!!
at
and the new president of blogsville is...

Jan 22, 2008
Only 13 Votes?!?
Come on now!
VOTE FOR ME!!
Y'all can do better than that, I know you can!

BTW
I just adore having "SEXCRETARIES" !!
(*EG*)

'paperwork' has never been so much fun!

Jan 23, 2008
My slogan:
WILD RAMPANT SEX FOR EVERYONE !!
so
VOTE FOR ME!!
you know you WANT to!

Yes, darlings, another book is out and wending its way
through the supply chain as we speak.
Joining Chat and Notes of a Dominatrix is Further Chat
with the ISBN of 978-0-6151-8655-9.
You might enjoy it.

I need a total of 100 votes to win and I currently have 18.
"Houston we have a problem."
Perhaps I should do like Thompson?

Jan 24, 2008
PORNOGRAPHY
Seems many women have "issues" when they discover their
men indulging in pornography. They wonder if he's
thinking of "those women" instead of them. They worry
that the men don't find them attractive any more. The
women seem to be taking it "personally". Then their
concerns make them feel insecure and it begins to
adversely affect their relationship their men.

STOP WORRYING!

Consider pornography as the male equivalent of those
torrid romance novels many women read. The only
difference is that usually the novels have more of a plot - an

314

actual story rather than just something easily ignored so they can get to the sex.

YOUR'RE BEAUTIFUL!

Realize that the women in those videos, etc., have a very short 'shelf-life', the average being 3 years, and are both air-brushed and 'manufactured'. Bigger breasts? No problem! In other words, they aren't real women - they are 'toys'. Suitable for fantasy only.

In the case of amateur pornography, they are real women but this is how they have their fun. Please don't take it seriously. This is just play for them. She's, or in some cases he's, 'exhibiting'.

HE WANTS YOU, AS YOU ARE - HERE AND NOW

You are real. And it isn't just all about the sex either. You and your relationship with him is about much more than that. He knows this. You know this too. Most men regard pornography as either 'escapist literature' or as 'training films' - to give them new 'ideas' to delight you with later on.

CAVEAT

I'm NOT saying that ALL pornography is good. There are some pathological types out there. So just make a note of kind he watches and if you find it disturbing - discuss it with him. "I notice you seem to like...... Tell me about it?" That sort of thing. If you notice a change in his behavior, address the behavior, leaving the pornography out of it.

MEET HIM HALFWAY

If you care to - you might want to watch with him. Shop together as it were. There are women making pornography for couples out there. There are videos made by women for women. Some experimentation may be in order.

Just please don't take it seriously. It is just fantasy after all.

Jan 25, 2008
NEWS!
LONDON - Women on the birth control pill are protected from ovarian cancer, even decades after they stop taking it, scientists said. British researchers found that women taking the pill for 15 years halved their chances of developing ovarian cancer, and that the risk remained low more than 30 years later, though protection weakened over time. The findings were published Friday in The Lancet.

"Not only does the pill prevent pregnancy, but in the long term, you actually get less cancer as well," said Valerie Beral, the study's lead author and director of the Cancer Research UK Epidemiology Unit at Oxford University. "It's a nice bonus." The study was paid for by Cancer Research UK and Britain's Medical Research Council.

Beral and colleagues analyzed data from 45 studies worldwide, covering 23,257 women with ovarian cancer, of whom 31 percent were on the pill. They also looked at 87,303 women without ovarian cancer, of whom 37 percent were on the pill.

In both groups, the women on the pill took it for about five years. The researchers found that in rich countries, women taking oral contraceptives for a decade were less likely to develop ovarian cancer. Without the pill, about 12 women per 1,000 are expected to get ovarian cancer before age 75. But that figure dropped to 8 women per 1,000 in those on the pill.

The experts estimated that use of the pill so far has prevented about 200,000 cases of ovarian cancer and 100,000 deaths from the disease. Based on current levels of oral contraceptive usage, they guessed that 30,000 cases could be avoided every year.

"To be able to save thousands of women's lives every year by using contraceptives is remarkable," said Dr. Beth Karlan, director of the Women's Cancer Research Institute at Cedars Sinai in California and an official with the American Society of Clinical Oncology. Karlan was not connected to the Lancet study.

In the West, ovarian cancer is one of the most common types of cancer in women. Older women are most at risk and survival rates are generally poor.

While the pill protects against ovarian cancer, it slightly increases the chances of breast and cervical cancer. But those risks disappear after women stop taking oral contraceptives. And the pill also provides long-term protection against endometrial cancer, which affects the lining of the uterus.

Scientists don't know why the pill increases some cancer risks while decreasing others. "It may have something to do with the hormones in the contraceptives," said Dr. Debbie Saslow, director of breast and gynecologic cancer at the American Cancer Society. "Hormones such as estrogen can be growth-promoting in some body parts and have the opposite effect in other body parts," she said.

But because there is no early test for ovarian cancer, which is often diagnosed late with a bad prognosis, doctors say that the pill's protective effects against ovarian cancer outweigh the small increased risks of breast and cervical cancer — unless women already have a history of those cancers.

"This is the first medication that we know of to cut ovarian cancer risk," Beral said. Other measures to protect against ovarian cancer are probably not things women would do unless they had more compelling reasons: having children or getting their tubes tied.

Still, most doctors do not suggest that women take the pill exclusively for its anticancer properties. The pill comes with side effects including risks of blood clots, migraines, and high blood pressure. Those risks are particularly elevated in women in their late 30s and in smokers.

In an editorial in The Lancet, experts called for better access to oral contraceptives, arguing that the drugs should now be available over the counter.

As the pill becomes more common in developing countries, experts estimate that ovarian cancer incidence will fall worldwide. In 2002, the United Nations estimated that 120 million women globally were on the pill, two-thirds of whom were in developing countries.

-from Associated Press

HURRAY!!

UPTO 21!!

And now I need 120 votes to win.
Ah me!
I'm just not 'fluffy' enough!

Jan 26, 2008
AMUSING
I found it amusing:

"I'm a polite man and never had anyone thinking otherwise......you have to realize that this is an adult site and there are many sexual acts that are intended for pure pleasure and people don't look at them as disrespect.........if you wanna judge sexual acts as if how it would appear in normal life out-side of bedroom.......then, you got a problem.....I'm not here to educate you ma'am....but it seems like you have no clue what men like or dislike...........it's obvious that we never gonna get along .....I wish you luck !!!"

All because I explained politely why I did not enjoy being spanked (or having my hair pulled or being 'broken to the saddle' through receiving anal intercourse though I left this part off). Btw: the misspellings are his own.

The point being - it does NOT matter what other women like or dislike - I do NOT enjoy such things - big surprise huh? No, I'm NOT judging various acts by "normal life", I am telling you what I like or dislike in the way of sex.

And this from a man who allegedly read and liked my profile! What part of dominatrix didn't he understand?

FOR FUTURE REFERENCE
(just in case you were wondering)
You can pet, caress, lick, scratch, grab, nibble, kiss, fondle, scritch, squeeze, and/or stroke my ass - just do not pat or spank it - nothing 'percussive'.
I'm not "good ol' dobbin" who needs to be "thanked for the ride" nor am I a "naughty girl in need of a spanking".
Just not my game, darlings.

by the authors at sex-and-relationships
My comments are in red.

Whether your sex is long lasting and romantic or fast and furious, you'll always want to enjoy the greatest satisfaction you can. These are some simple tips which will help you to make sex into a joyous occasion, whenever and wherever you make love.

1 Take time over foreplay

Most men want to roll around the bed a bit, stick it in and ejaculate as quickly as possible. An exaggeration? Perhaps, but if you're honest with yourself, not as much of an exaggeration as it might be! Men get sexually aroused more quickly than women, and often find foreplay tedious. When they are aroused, they want quick satisfaction. For men, the reward of sex is the intensity of orgasm and ejaculation. For a woman, the rewards of sex come in the form of closeness, intimacy, being with her partner - and, last of all, her orgasm. Please see The Program previously posted herein.

That's not to say women don't like orgasms, but they certainly have reported a preference for intimacy and physical affection over sexual intercourse in survey after survey during the last fifty years. It isn't JUST about penetration, fellas!

The reason for this seems to be that foreplay generally does not last long enough to get a woman properly aroused - aroused to the point where she can enjoy sex. This will vary from woman to woman.

Foreplay means anything that takes place before the act of penetration - whether that is anal, oral or vaginal. In fact I'd say foreplay is anything that happens before you reach orgasm! Kissing, fondling, caressing, stroking, mutual masturbation, and more: all these things are a kind of foreplay. For a woman the most important aspect of foreplay is to be touched, lovingly, by her partner. The first touch needs to be non-sexual, on areas of her body other than her genitals. Only as she becomes more in touch with her physical sensations and connected to her sense of arousal and her own body's response to touch, should the touch gradually transform itself into a more sexual caress, on her breasts and genitals. Doing body worship works very well!

You may think of oral sex as something like the main event at dinner, but it can be a great form of foreplay. Many woman will not reach orgasm through intercourse, but almost all women will reach orgasm through oral sex if they have had about twenty minutes of touching and caressing and kissing beforehand. This can be a great precursor to penetration for both men and women, as it does not matter if he ejaculates quickly when he enters her. Research has shown that 27 minutes is the LEAST amount of time a man should spend on foreplay.

2 Be a sensitive lover

Just taking your pleasure and ignoring her needs during intercourse is a route to disaster! A woman wants the intimacy and rewards of sex just as you do, but to get them she will need to be loved, reassured, stroked, and respected. This means many things: giving her an orgasm through oral sex before you enter her, perhaps; cuddling her after intercourse; saying how much you love her outside the bedroom as well as during your lovemaking; spending enough time on foreplay (see above); giving her the opportunity to lead and take the initiative during sex.....and so on. What represents being sensitive will be different for all women, just as it is for all men. Love the woman you're with?

One way to make sure she gets pleasure during intercourse is to learn how to control your ejaculation, so that she can get as much physical pleasure from the thrusting of your penis in her vagina as possible. Many men think they cannot control their ejaculation: the reality is that with a little motivation, it's not at all hard to learn how to treat premature ejaculation. G-Spot and posterior fornix caressing using your penis is guaranteed to make her night!

3 Reassure her about her body

She's likely to be much more sensitive about her appearance than you can imagine - even if she does have a few areas that are not perfect, as far as you're concerned, this may not matter. After all, when you're about to have sex, that's the last thing on your mind! But to her, it is incredibly important to hear that you like her body, and that you find her attractive. What's more, she'll want to hear this many times - it's no use expecting her to be reassured just because you told her she was attractive last week! A breathy "OMG you're beautiful!" works!

Such reassurance is all part of a woman's need for emotional security. She can only give herself fully, and therefore be fully into sex with you, when she is emotionally secure and happy in your relationship. Let's NOT get carried away with this idea however.

4 Be considerate and elegant during sex

Of course there are times when sex goes wrong, and these are the times when a couple who are truly relaxed with each other can laugh about it without embarrassment or shame. But for the most part, sex goes smoothly when you add a little thought to what you're doing: for example, don't leave your socks on when you undress. There are few things in life as comical as a man dressed only in his underwear and socks. When you've made love, dispose of the condom tidily, in a tissue. When you enter her during sex, don't peck around with your penis at the entrance to her vagina: if you can't find the way past her labia, ask her to guide your penis in with her hand. It's touches like these which will make sex a graceful experience. Oh - and when you've ejaculated into her, if you're not wearing a condom, have a moist towel at hand for her to mop up your semen after the flowback. Condoms are MANDATORY, dammit! Don't leap into bed without one!

5 Control your ejaculation

There is no need for a man to lose control during sex. Indeed, the mark of a good lover is that he knows exactly how near his ejaculation he is and how to stop himself ejaculating as he thrusts in his partner's vagina. If you don't have this level of control, it's worth learning to be a longer lasting lover, as it will enhance your experience of sex and it will make her respect you more. But please cum, thank you! We enjoy your orgasms too!

6 Deal with erectile dysfunction or other sexual problems

The pressure is often on men during sex to get and keep an erection, and this is not always as easy as you might think. Certainly as men get older they come to remember the proud hard erections of their youth with great fondness! The erratic erection, the low sex drive, the inability to reach orgasm: all these problems and more can be dealt with, fairly easily. If you look after your sexual health, you'll find that sex continues to be just as rewarding as it was when you were young. We take our pills, you take yours and we all roll with it, okay, dear?

7 Communicate with your partner

The answer to many sexual problems is simple: communicate with your partner and let her know what's happening for you. You don't have to reveal every detail of your sexual life (often this would not be appropriate; for example, many of men's sexual fantasies are best kept secret!), but you do need to talk about your feelings, hopes, fears, and what you want and need from your sex life. Only when you find a way to communicate about sex will you reach that relaxed and intimate place where good sex is natural.

The last is often the hardest thing to do. Women don't want to be blunt so as to not hurt his feelings so they hint and use 'femme-speak' which the men don't understand - and you see where this is going. Men say

324

something they think isn't open to interpretation only to find they have offended her.

The main points for both genders are:
1. don't think of sex as limited to just penetration
2. don't RUSH sex
3. give a damn about who you're with
4. play to your partner
5. make it JOYOUS!

That about covers it, dontcha think?

Jan 27, 2008
MISTAKES WOMEN MAKE IN BED
Yes, women make mistakes in bed too. So, in the interests of fairness, here they are!
As before, my comments are in red.

1 Expecting him to think like a woman

We've all seen loads of books with titles like "Men Are From Mars, Women Are From Venus" which highlight an unfortunate difference between the sexes. Men and women don't think the same way - and while we're not going to get into why this happens, it's important to remember that fact when you're in a relationship. In general, men are not as romantic as women, they don't see romance as a necessary prelude to sex, and they can divorce sex from their feelings in a way that perhaps most women can't. So there will be plenty of times when a man wants sex even if he isn't feeling romantic and connected to his partner.

For him, the physical pleasure of sex is a reward in itself. He doesn't need to be seduced into feeling desire (though he may appreciate it if you do seduce him!), at least most of the time, for his sex drive is a pretty constant part of his maleness. I think that's what women don't understand. They know how elusive and emotional their own sex drive is, but they don't appreciate how different it is for a man. Think of it this way: men can enjoy sex with their partner whether they are feeling loving or not; in fact they often find their feelings of love for their partner when they have sex with her. By contrast, women often say they need to feel loving before they want sex - or at least before they are prepared to give themselves heart and soul to a man. Don't get carried away here. There are romantic men and there are women with sex drives that will run men into the ground. Always allow for human variability.

2 Not showing your sexual energy

Women who were brought up to be demure "good girls" (i.e. not sexual) may find it difficult to express the essence of their feminine energy during sex. And a lot of women also have problems expressing their anger, an emotion which often adds real spice to the sexual union between men and women. This lack of sexual energy might appear as a reluctance to initiate sex, a reluctance to be the active partner, a reluctance to make noises or thrust, or simply an overall tendency to wait for the man to lead and direct what happens during sex.

Believe me, ladies, your man will really like it when you express your passion - whether that means you getting on top for woman on top sex, moving in a way that will give you the greatest pleasure, kissing him passionately, or being assertive about what you want in bed. YES! YES! YES! - let your passion run loose! MEN LOVE IT!

3 Being too gentle when you touch his penis

326

Men like a firmer touch than women, especially when it comes to our penises. If you ever have the pleasure of watching him masturbate, you'll see how much pressure he uses on his penis - especially as he nears orgasm. Ask him to tell you what you're doing right, and what he'd like done differently, and he'll really appreciate your efforts to give him pleasure. Allow for human variability however! Some men do become sensitive from time to time. ASK HIM if in doubt.

4 Not experimenting

The saying has it that men think about sex ten times an hour - or is it a hundred? Yes, of course that's an exaggeration, but it isn't much of one. While some women have a high sexual desire, it's true to say that women in general are much less sexy than men when they're not in the bedroom. Men fantasize all the time - about the things they see, what they'd like to do, how they'd like to do it, and so on. With such an active sexual imagination, it's not hard to understand why a bit of variation in the bedroom routine can keep a man sexually happy.

It doesn't have to be way out stuff like bondage, either. For example, try changing sex positions once in a while: take the initiative and get on top of him or let him enjoy rear entry for a change. Talk dirty to him if you've never tried that before; explore and play with new parts of his body such as his anus and perineum during foreplay (or even during the main event). Seduce him into a "quickie" by leaving a trail of clothes across the floor into the bedroom. Greet him at the door in sexy clothing. Phone him at work and tell him what you'd like to do to him.....well, you get the idea - use your imagination! See the site

327

5 Expecting him to read your mind

Yes, we know it's difficult to express your sexual desires directly. But men don't think like women. They don't read clues, they don't get hints. So stop communicating indirectly, and tell him what you want. And give him feedback when you get it! That way, he'll know exactly what he's supposed to be doing, how you feel about it, and whether to do it again. For example, if you like what he's doing, let him know with your moans of pleasure. No hints! Just TELL HIM!

6 Criticizing him

I think one of the reasons women can be so critical of their man is that they've never learned the art of direct communication. That's to say stating clearly and directly what you want, how you want it, and whether you got it - and how you feel about it afterwards. But men appreciate that style of talk - they know where they stand and it removes the uncertainty for them.

Criticism is an indirect way of saying that your needs are not being met - but if you read number 5 above, then maybe you've begun to understand that your man won't know what you want unless you tell him. If you're taking his ability to anticipate and meet your needs without you saying what they are as a measure of how much he loves you, well, I'm afraid you aren't likely to be very satisfied. Tell him what you like, need, desire, want, whatever - no need to be shy. He's a big boy.

7 Letting him take responsibility for your orgasm

A lot of us think that a man somehow has a responsibility to "give" a woman an orgasm during sex. After all, that's how a lot of us were brought up - that a man somehow has to look after "his" woman. And that idea extends to making sure she has an orgasm during sex.....but the truth is that women are responsible for their own orgasms. So while it might be nice for your man to help you get there, if you don't make it to orgasm through his efforts, you can always take matters into your own hands. YOUR orgasm is YOUR responsibility just as his is his. The partner only 'assists'.

8 Controlling him by withdrawing sex

One of the most unhealthy things you can do in a relationship is to use sex as a weapon. This is basically a statement that you feel powerless, and you think withholding sex is the only way you can get what you want. Rather than trying to exert some influence over your man by denying him the pleasure of your body, try communicating directly what you want and don't want. (That might even extend to simply saying you don't want sex because you don't feel emotionally close enough to your partner to want sex.) Are you 13? Daddy's Little Princess? GROW UP! Time for this nonsense to STOP!

9 Thinking he'll feel the same way about your body that you do

It just isn't so. Men don't attach the judgments to women's bodies that women do. So, for example, even if he thinks your butt really is a bit on the large side, it won't matter to him the way it matters to you. In fact, he probably quite likes it. And he certainly won't be put off making love, or want the lights off, because of it. While you waste time and emotional energy wondering if you're completely undesirable because of some aspect of your body, he'll never be giving it a second thought. It's women who judge their bodies, I think for the sake of comparison with other women, not men. **What matters is you're YOU!**

10 Not making up with sex after an argument

Well, yes, I know that a lot of couples do make up with sex when they've had an argument, but in fact many more don't. As I said above, most women think that they need to be feeling loving and close before they want sex. Yet I've met a lot of couples in my work as a sexual therapist who has found that taking the risk and jumping into bed can work really well as a way of getting close again. Even if you don't feel sexy or loving when you start, after a whole, the simple act of being physically connected in bed can make your whole outlook on each other change for the better. The old way - talking, seeking understanding, thrashing out how you feel - is fine: but once in a while try a more direct method of getting your feelings back on track - just go to bed together! **Why bother arguing? There is no need for that. You state your case. He states his and we negotiate from there until an agreement is reached. Then we CELEBRATE!**

Ladies, men are wired differently from us. They see the world and any given situation from another perspective. Give the guy some slack. Not too much slack - just enough to prevent strangulation. The reason humans even have gender at all, and therefore we have males, is for sex so of course that is the male focus. All you can really ask is for them to be damn good at it!

330

I'm joking! Men are people too. Each of us is a delightfully unique mix of the good, the bad, and the indifferent. Accentuate the good and work on conquering the bad - together!

CURRENT ELECTION STANDINGS
Votes
BBB (PRESIDENT) 130
Mz H (PRESIDENT) 27
G8V13 (PRESIDENT) 52
EEK (PRESIDENT) 27
woc(PRESIDENT) 54
LTL (PRESIDENT) 127
Total Votes 417

Come on, Friends!
Vote Now!
at
and the new president of blogsville is...

I'VE BEEN A BAD KITTEN
..and the evilness will continue until you all succumb to my rule! Bwahahahaha!...
or until we have run out of scotch..
whichever comes first.

Jan 28, 2008
IFFN YA WANNA
...get in on the b'day party...contact Smokey!

I don't know anything about it!

naturally

of course

KITTEN'S TOP 10 DON'TS
For men:

1. Don't NOT show up!
2. No spanking - ever!
3. No squeaking about my driving!
4. Leave my hair alone!
5. No silence, dammit!

For women:

1. No grabbing me with sexual intent!
2. No squeaking about my driving!
3. No being the "diva"!
4. No hogging the men!
5. No "wilting flowers"!

Nothing worse than having fun with a comely teddybear in the hot tub than having some femme come over and grab your breasts without so much as a 'by your leave'!

GRRRRRRRRRRRRR!
You interrupted my orgasms!

Jan 29, 2008
NSA
NSA meaning "no strings attached", that is, no emotional involvement, STDs and/or children made with your sex play partners. The STDS and fertility can be easily dealt with - birth control and condoms. It is the emotional issue that concerns us now.

I can understand why people use this term. You don't have the time or space for a 'relationship'. You are gun-shy or otherwise emotionally frail just now. Whatever. But I must tell you that it is not going to happen. Humans just are not made to be 'isolationists'. There is no such things as 'meaningless sex' with 'anonymous partners'. If he/she likes you well enough to enjoy sex with you, then he/she wants to see you again - just how it is.

Hey! I like you, dammit! Do you mind?

Not that we all want 'strings', but when we get naked - we take our chances.
Don't you think so?

KITTEN GAMES
I have this 'weakness' for pouncing upon nice big furry males, fucking them senseless, and then snuggling with them. I tie them down onto my bed first, of course, else they might run away. I do not ask men to submit, I only ask them to comply.
Extremely evil & mischievous grin
You game?

Jan 30, 2008
HOW DO YOU ARGUE?
Do you go at it 'hammer and tongs'? A verbal slugfest?
(You know better than to get physical I hope!)

Do you nitpick? Is an argument with you like 'death from a thousand papercuts'?

Do you berate the person or just focus upon the behavior?

Do you argue to make up?

333

I find most arguments to be a huge waste of time and energy. One need not argue to confront misbehavior. Asking "Why?" "Why do you do/say that?" is often useful. Saying things like "I feel like x when you do/say y. Is that what you want to happen?" can also be effective.

Because most arguments are caused by miscommunicating.

Yes, I know being rational when the other's emotional is often putting fuel onto their flame but someone has to cool the situation down somehow. It is worse when you care about someone esp for women. Women try so hard to NOT inflict pain that they end up being confusing to men who do NOT use nuance. Men fail to prepare a dialog and end up fumbling. Women then say "Fine!" signaling the end of the bout. But nothing has been solved. The problem remains.

"We need to talk." Every man over the age of 16 knows that this mean SHE's going to talk and HE's going to tune out after about 5 seconds. So don't say that.

"We need to have a conversation." also strikes fear in men so don't say that either. I use that with my kids and they are instantly on alert and ready to dive for cover. I never understood how such big kids could vanish so quickly and effectively! They had cockroaches beat! Poof! They're gone! Don't bother looking, you won't find them. I know - I have tried!

My coolness when under fire annoys my husband. He thinks that my NOT being upset means that I do not care. He wants me to yell and stomp around the house. (It has happened.) Ok, ok, I'll put on this show you want so badly.

There! Ya happy now? Pesky male!

I consider arguments signs that you're not saying what you really need to say to he/she who really needs to hear it in language and form that he/she understands.

I recommend mentally and emotionally stepping back, and taking time to honestly consider the issue in question. "I need time to think about this." You have your say. He/she has his say. You agree or even agree to disagree; or you break up. Always, but always keep in the fore front of your mind "what is MOST important here?"
Focusing upon that answer will prevent you from going too far wrong.

Winning at all costs may not be your best option.

Jan 31, 2008
ACCEPTANCE
Most women are still taught that sex is dirty and yet that (somehow) it is something precious that only married persons, to each other mind you, should engage in.

Most men still feel that if she doesn't orgasm, it is their (the men's) fault. Men constantly ask 'how can I make her orgasm?'.

I know this because I do on-line sex counseling.

Often the hardest thing for people have to do is to ACCEPT that they are sexual beings responsible for their own orgasms and that this is a GOOD thing.

The physical benefits of sex are due to the increased metabolic rates and the decrease in stress levels that come from participation and release. If you are an active lover these benefits are multiplied. Face it: FUN is GOOD for YOU.

Practice increases your knowledge and should also increase your skill level - both of which are benefits. Benefits you can share with subsequent lovers. Thus 'spreading the gospel'.

Ladies, most of what you have been taught about sex, men, virginity - is wrong. Just that; WRONG. A woman who truly and whole-heartedly accepts, embraces and enjoys her sexuality is the most attractive woman on earth regardless of her actual appearance especially if she personally likes and cares for each man she has sex with.

(The same applies to bi and homosexual people.)

Men: her orgasm is not your job. You assist but the responsibility is hers. For some women, orgasms are elusive and 5% do not orgasm at all, ever. However, the lack of an orgasm does not mean women, including non-orgasmic women, do not enjoy sex. Engaging in outercourse can be very satisfying.

ACCEPTANCE is therefore: a freeing of the chains that bind your mind. Wrap your mind instead around the concept that sex is GOOD, worth doing often, and worth doing well.

So, people, what are YOU doing tonight?

February
2008

Feb 1, 2008

I LOVE A GOOD HOUSE PARTY!
but
Sorry, no blog today.
I'm busy stressing!
You know how it is!

Feb 2, 2008
AFTER MIDNIGHT
There's something about being out and about after midnight
that is delicious! I always have enjoyed the darkness -
perhaps it is my inner feline. The possibilities seem more
endless beneath the moon.

The pretences fewer.
The men more alluring.
The sex more delightful.

I know you feel it too.

Feb 3, 2008
FEELING COMBATIVE
Yes, I get this way. When stressed, I get this way more
often. Some people get depressed. Some people run away.
Some people weep and wail. I get mean, irritable, and
combative.

See a problem? ATTACK IT!

Look, all I can tell you is how I feel, and why. What to do
about it - well, there are methods but if you're not sincere,
they will not work.

I only attack legit problems, mind you. There's little point
in attacking figments.

There's also little point in 'having disagreements' with someone you don't care about. The fact that I'm dragging you over the coals does mean that you do matter to me.

Odd way of showing it, true. But how many times have I hidden my fangs?

You don't do this sort of thing, do you?

(Comments permitted even if not particularly welcome.)

Yes, I know that I said that arguing is a great waste of time but this is STRESS now, not just arguing.

Feb 4, 2008
TODAY'S TOPIC
Having too much to do and too little time in which to do it.

Priorities and Procrastination!

Do you have a system? I don't. I make a note of what needs to be done. Try to tackle the closest alligator first while avoiding the others. But some things end up not getting the necessary attention.

Somehow, it seems to work out.

How organized are you?

Feb 5, 2008
PARTY! PARTY! PARTY!
"Come on take me to the Mardi Gras... where the people sing and play." Bag is packed and I'm READY!!
(Teddybears please take note and eat your Wheaties!)

SEX and LOVE
Two different things, my lovelies!

1. you can love without having sex
2. you can have sex without love

Sex = the physical expression of desire
Love = the abiding emotional bond between persons

Yes, when the two are combined it is WONDERFUL!
But let's face it: sex on it s own, when done properly, is also GREAT!
While I prefer sex with affection and friendship, I have to admit that I also do enjoy "seeing what this teddybear here can do" from time to time. Take him "out for a spin" as it were. *EG*

Well, don't you?

TO YOU WHO CAUSED THE MARDI GRAS TO BE CANCELLED

MAY YOU NEVER AGAIN KNOW THE LOVE OF ANOTHER HUMAN HEART. MAY YOU NEVER AGAIN EXPERIENCE JOY OR PEACE. MAY EVEN GOD DESERT YOU.
AND
MAY YOUR LIFE FROM THIS POINT FORWARD BE FOREVER A BARREN WASTELAND WHERE ALL

YOUR HOPES AND DREAMS LIE AS ROTTING
CORPSES.

DAMN YOU TO HELL FOR DOING HARM TO THOSE
WHO WOULD DO NONE.

Feb 6, 2008
TRAINWRECKS

We have all seen them, those people who through poor
choices made or through heavy misfortune are a walking
disaster area. Those damaged persons of both genders that
there but for the grace of God might have been us.

I also include in this category, those predators who feed
upon others. The manipulators who use another's loneliness
and/or hopes for their own gain. Face it, fellas, if she's
missing three front teeth and has needle tracks, she's NOT
Miss America or Little Bo Peep. Yes, manipulators will use
the "poor little me" approach as well - whatever works. The
"kill myself to keep to you" thing. Use your kindness
against you to get what she wants.

Ladies, if he's calling you every 15 minutes to "see how are
you are" it is not because he's concerned that you're NOT
having fun. He's making sure that you DON'T have fun
without him. Controlling is another form of jealousy and
possessiveness. Staying with such a man is exactly like
walking into prison.

"A person who has a "train wreck" for a partner is likely to
be desperate... low self-esteem allowing them to invite the
wreck into their life." Well, that's part of it. If a person
believes they cannot get anyone better, they'll take what
they think they is all they can get.

But it may also be because they enjoy running damage control behind their "train wreck" because they need to be needed - Runaway Galahad Complex. A small business owner who stays married to her heroin-addicted husband of 15 years is another example. Cannot save the world but they might be able to save their "train wreck". Thus is the joy slowly sucked out of their life as time rolls on and the 'rescue' never materializes.

People if you find yourself attracted to a "train wreck" - RUN in the opposite direction! Do NOT fall for it. Should you slip up - take every legal means to get yourself out of it as fast as you can. Leave such people to the professionals.

How to recognize a "train wreck"? By the mis-match between what is said, what is done, and the results you will know them! Is there a recurring pattern going on here? Is she behaving like at 13 year-old when she's 45? Does he miss appointments frequently because something just came up and he isn't in law enforcement, the military, or is in the medical or rescue field?
OR is it because he just couldn't get away from some guy he just met in a bar?

True love neither requires or demands self-sacrifice.

What do you think?
Do you have a story for me?

WHY IT IS JUST ME.
Because there is a serious lack of tall, long-legged, evil-minded, gorgeous brunettes in the lifestyle. That's why. You'll just have to make do. *EG*

Feb 7, 2008
SNOOPING
The latest thing, apparently, is hiring detectives or doing searches on your prospective mates and dates. In other words - snooping! This includes going through email accounts, looking through snail mail, and checking out your cell phone.

STOP IT!

1. You are debasing yourself by showing that you are an insecure loser who is unworthy of anyone's trust. You may feel you are justified but you are only deluding yourself and disgusting others.

2. If you simply cannot trust him/her then explain why you're still with him/her? Do you have any real reason for your distrust? If so - then walk. If not, then just wait - sooner or later, he'll/she'll err and you'll have all the proof you need - then you can walk.

Either you trust or you don't. You cannot love someone if you cannot trust them. It really is just that simple. This is of course assuming that you're not in some co-dependency/weird relationship where you both feed off of each other's miserableness.

Stop working so hard. You don't have to snoop.
By his/her actions, you will know them!

Don't you think so too?
Do you snoop?
Have you been subject to someone's snooping?

Feb 8, 2008

HELP!
Thor's trying to eat ALL of my chocolate!!
He pushes the box off the top of the bookshelf and then attacks it leaving gnaw marks on the chocolate and little bits of foil wrapping all over my office!
CATS!!!

Feb 9, 2008
Had a GREAT time at Skinifatz last night (ty G - such a gent!) especially when the DJ shouted out "Happy Birthday" to me and the crowd cheered. LOL
So now it is off to run errands with a grandkitten, drop her back home, and then off to a house party! Wheeeeeeeeeee!
More later!

Feb 10, 2008
PLAYTIME WITH TEDDYBEARS
HOUSE PARTY REPORT

We arrived by 8pm and began the socializing with as the other guests arrived. M & M, our hosts, have a very nice place out in the country where the entire lower floor is devoted to playing. 4 men, 4 women, 2 beds and one sofa - just what we like! All the men were nicely furred and not too skinny. The women were quite lovely, so I was told; me not being any judge.

I began with H and cunnilingus on the sofa, then moved onto M on the small bed; first me on top and then him on top. Then I took D's hand and walked him to the small bed and pounced upon him. He did not resist. Got a few female ejaculatory orgasms with C on the small bed. Then it was M, H, C, and I on the big bed - two women with two multi-tasking men! I then snuggled up with C on the small bed for several bouts then snuggle and sleep.

344

MANY ORGASMS FOR EVERYONE!

Feb 11, 2008
BEDS
I prefer a stiff box spring and a thick, firm but comfy
mattress with flannel sheets, heavy blankets and at least one
warm teddybear, maybe two if the bed is large enough.

Unfortunately, the laws of the Commonwealth do not
permit me to do that. The teddybears, I mean. They keep
saying "Only one... only one... only one."
Those 'conservatives'! They always ruin my fun!

You wouldn't mind 'sharing' now would you?

WHY "TEDDYBEAR"?
Someone warm, and cozy that a woman can take to bed
with her in complete confidence. Teddybear, of course,
referring to men not to actual stuffed animals which are
rightly called teddy bears - note the space.

Few things are more comforting than a teddy bear. But they
do tend to be somewhat ... inert. This is why large, furry,
calm, secure, skilled, confident males are called teddybears
... they are not ... inert.

Okay, so they can grumble and rumble a bit and they can
get grumpy upon occasion - we all how to cure that. *EG*
But teddybears have your back, as the expression goes, and
are usually willing participants in whatever you might have
in mind. All of which explains why I like them so verrrrrry
much!

All men should strive to become teddybears.

That's how I see it.

Feb 12, 2008
PRIMARY DAY!
So get out there and

VOTE

for the politician of your choice.

APPLICATIONS
Seems to be going around lately - women putting out dating applications. Now I do not 'date'. That implies far too much. I also do not do 'dinners'. Relaxing afterwards with an appetizer and a drink is fine but not dinner, thank you.

My application is far simpler because your involvement in my life will be limited. I am not interested in your finances, job history, morals, and whether you are good for siring excellent children. Not my thing, hun.

What I will judge you on are:
1. your manners
2. your sexual skill
3. your physical abilities
4. your mental abilities
5. your sense of humor

Here is my application for men:

1. Are you a teddybear? Yes or No.
2. Do I like you? Yes or No.
3. Do I desire you? Yes or No.

Please note that ONLY teddybears need apply therefore if you answered No to question 1 please remove yourself from my sight.

The next two questions are about me. I presume that you would NOT be filling out this application if those questions were about you since you'd hardly spend the time to complete the applications of women you neither like or desire. It is easy to tell if I like you and/or desire you because I TELL you so.

If the answer to question 2 is Yes but to question 3 is No. you are a Friend Without Benefits.

If the answer to question 2 is No but to question 3 is Yes, you are a Fuckbuddy.

If the answer to both questions is Yes, you are a Friend With Benefits.

If the answer to both questions is No, you are wasting my time. Go annoy some other woman, thank you very much.

Yes, of course this is egotistical but what did you expect? I am a dominatrix who specializes in seducing dominant men into sexual subjugation. Love the attitude or get lost.

HUGE WICKED EVIL GRIN

Feb 13, 2008
LAST CALL
for VA Beach! I will be leaving here at noon, swinging by Richmond circa 1:30pm and then running into VA Beach circa 3pm. Will be there until 10pm whereupon I have to git home.

YIM me some addresses and numbers, people!
"you don't have to go home
but you can't stay here."

Feb 14, 2008
ST. VALENTINE
To truly appreciate St. Valentine's Day, you have to have
had your heart ripped to shreds at one point, to have had
your romantic hopes fulfilled at another point; and to now
be able to enjoy both the good and the bad in life. Nothing
is so bad nor so good except those crystalline moments of
sheer JOY that bring laughter and smiles and tears to your
eyes and want to make you reach out and bear hug him/her
and say "I LOVE YOU!"

SO DO IT!!

Feb 15, 2008
SO TELL ME...
This article was posted on another "advice to men" site.
First, we have Guy A's letter in blue and then, the Advisor's
comments in Green.

"The other weekend I went out with a couple of guy
friends and we met up with some of our other guy
friends. Well, one of them has a female roommate
(friends for years) who is smoking hot. She mostly
hangs with the guys and they are very protective of her.
Anyway, right off the bat after I was introduced to her I
shot off with the "nice necklace... what, did you get that
out of a Cracker Jack box?" She had a stunned look on
her face like she just got rabbit punched. My friend, her
roommate, was all pissed at me, kept telling me to be
nice to her, not to be mean, etc. About two minutes later

I ask her if I am being mean (in hindsight I realize that was a mistake), she says no and we start talking.

I smoke when I drink and I tell her to give me a cigarette. She does. We talk a little more. I tell her to buy me a drink. She does. We start talking again and she is swinging her head, moving her hair and she grabs her breasts, you know kind of cups them with both hands. I say, "What the hell are you doing? Quit grabbing your boobs." She couldn't believe I had said that. We start talking some more and she tells me that in the all-but five minutes since I have met her, I have told her three things that no guy has ever said to her: 1) Give me a cigarette; 2) Buy me a drink; and 3) Quit grabbing your boobs. And then she proceeded to tell me, "But look who I am talking to." She was into me. I kind of went my own way afterward (didn't want to, but had to) with some other friends, but I didn't try to get her number because I knew I would see her again the next time I go over to my buddy's apartment. I had to give her the gift of missing me, ya feel me?"

My thoughts:
You're a stud. Well done.
You should have followed up when she said:

"... in all but five minutes since I have met her I have told her three things that no guy has ever said to her: 1) Give me a cigarette; 2) Buy me a drink; and 3) Quit grabbing your boobs..."

...with:

"Yea, well that's not all I'm going to tell you. Now that you're doing everything I tell you, it's time for you to decide where you're going to take me to dinner. And make it somewhere nice. I'm picky."

Before you give a woman the gift of missing you, you might want to make her like you more.
Just a thought.

My take: This guy is a LOUT pursuing an insecure DOORMAT. In such cases, of course behaving badly will get her. Of course you will not keep her. But, since she has learned that being a doormat will get her a guy, she'll continue being a doormat. Until she grows up and then she'll have "baggage" and expect all men to be assholes. Good move, guys!

But that's just me. What do you think?

Feb 16, 2008
KITTEN'S DATING ADVICE FOR MEN
For you fellows wondering how entrancing a woman with brains and character is done:

1. fix yourself up a bit - do not look like last week's dog meat. You do not have to be 'buff' but you do have to look like you are in good health and are clean and presentable.

2. decide what sort of woman you want - Does she have to be a "10"? Really? Party-girl or home-body? Do you want kids? How about if she's in the 'lifestyle'? Employed at what level?

3. hunt where she's most likely to be - home-loving women are not found at bars. Artistic types are not found a monster truck rallies.

350

4. hunt alone - leave your buddies behind. You want her focused upon you. Plus this shows courage and confidence.

5. Scope out who's there - catch her eye, hold her glance for a bit and smile. If she holds her glance and smiles back - gently move over to her and introduce yourself. After she's told you her name say "Nice to meet you,--" Then ask her something about where you're at. A question works because it gets a response. Do not ask something she can say yes or no to. You want a sentence from her. LISTEN to her responses.

6. Follow-up - develop the conversation one step more and then ask for her number by saying "I'd like to invite you to --. May I have your number?" Make whatever you invite her to generic as in "coffee" or "to this small gallery show I've heard about." Whatever fits with your previous conversation. Get her name and number and then, move on.

7. Pause - long enough to find out when and where that gallery showing is, or whatever and then call her and invite her out with you to a specific date, time, and place/event. Do NOT ask her to 'hang out' with you and your buddies. That is what children do, not what adults do. The lady wants a man so be a man.

When on this date, you want to talk of moderately personal things: likes/dislikes, hobbies, pets - that level. You want to flirt but mildly. Let her see your interest but in a way that says you are not desperate. Touch her ONLY after she has touched you. You must appear calm, confident, polite, fun, and NON-THREATENING. Smile. Laugh. Make her see that you enjoy her company - as a person too.

When walking her to her car, ask her out to another specific date. Come prepared to do this. Make it similar to what you just did but different. This time an art gallery showing, next time to an artist's studio. Do you see?

If she needs to check her schedule, tell her you'll call her tomorrow. Then call her tomorrow.

Kiss her. Yeah, yeah, yeah - nevermind all of that. Wrap those big strong arms around her, hold her firmly but gently, and caress her lips with your own and hold it for 20 seconds. Then let her go. Say "Bye, ---". and leave.

Do three dates. Talk increasingly personal one each date. If she has not yet invited you out somewhere by the end of the third date. You will have to move on to the next woman. "I have enjoyed getting to know you ---. " Kiss her as above, say goodbye and leave.

If she calls you - GREAT! If she doesn't call you, sorry, but she's not interested.

NOTE: leave the decision re: sex up to her. If she has to be coaxed or cajoled into bed - you do not want her. Let her know you would be delighted to participate in whatever she has in mind, of course, but NO PUSHING. You are a man not some desperate teenager. You want her to get the understanding that should she happen to throw herself into your arms, that not only are you more than willing to catch her, but that she may rely upon you knowing what to do with her once you have caught her and that she will thoroughly enjoy sex with you.

Good luck!

KITTEN'S DATING ADVICE FOR WOMEN
This is based upon my research *EG*...

1. fix yourself up - no, plastic surgery is not required. You want to look good but not "high maintenance". Men are visual creatures so look your best. Then forget about it.

2. scope out the room - if you catch a man's eye and you think he might be okay, then smile at him. Hold his glance and then look away - preferably, drop your glance - that is look down.

3. should he end up by your side - and introduces himself say "Hi, --- . I'm --- . It is nice to meet you." Invite him to have a seat.
Smile and wait for his opening. Respond and then ask him a question along the same conversational line.

(If he doesn't come to you, you will have to decide whether you want to go to him. The idea of dropping your glance is to entice him to you but he may not get that message.)

4. Respond and chat - but keep it limited to approximately 15 minutes. Be your fun and charming self. If he asks for your number you have three choices 1. give him your number, or 2. say "It is a bit early for me. I'll be here next ---. Why don't we meet again then." NEVER give him a bogus number. Either you are adult or you aren't. 3. Now if you DON'T like him, which can happen, just say "No. Thank you but I am not interested." and do NOT smile while you say it. No mixed signals. If you aren't sure yet, use response #2 above.

5A. Assuming you like him - then go out with him. Give the man his chance. You will want know the details about the date in advance so you will know how to dress for it.

5B. Assuming you were unsure - return as you said you would and see if you can make a decision, yes or no, this time. Then tell him what your decision is. No hints. No mixed signals.

5C. Okay you said No and he persists. The gloves may now come off. You may be a blunt as you care to be. His feelings are not your concern. Keep your poise. Call the bouncer if you wish.

6. Three dates is all you get. Make up your mind about him. Sex is your decision but whether sex is yes or no, you do have to invite him out with you on a date if you want to keep him. Yes, this time you call and you pay for everything.

When deciding upon what to ask him to, think back over your conversations and find something to do that he will enjoy. Call him and ask him out then make the arrangements.

Yes, it can be just that easy.

Feb 17, 2008
PREMIS BEHIND MY DATING ADVICE
My advice is based upon the belief that men and women are adults, interested in sex with compatible people, prefer sex with people they actually like and whose company they enjoy both in and out of bed.

354

It is also based upon the idea that when it comes to sex: Women Rule. If she says No, then it is no. She does not have to apologize for her decision. She does not have to explain her reasons for her decision. But she does have to decide. Men do not have to offer their services. They are not under any obligation. But once offered, it becomes her decision.

Please note that I never specified any gifts, etc. Nor did I say you had to go on expensive dates. Being adult means taking charge of such things yourself. Gold-diggers of either gender - get a life.

I said three dates because fair is fair and both parties have to show their interest. That is enough time for a woman to know if she likes him or not. If she does, then she should reciprocate. By asking him out to something he'd enjoy - to show she has been paying attention to him as a person and not just as a "ba-lamb" or a "bo-hunk" she'd like to drag to her lair.

One last word: We all know and understand about 'trainwrecks', The Galahad Complex, "testosterone poisoning', and so forth - there is no excuse for NOT taking charge of your life. If you find you have made a mistake, face up to it, and get out of the relationship.

Feel free to comment!

BEST QUOTE OF TODAY!
"Fumbling around for my vibrator counts as foreplay, doesn't it?"
(c) 2008 AA

Feb 18, 2008
ALERT!
There are people who firmly and fervently believe the following and are being used by groups such as Quiverful, et al, to support their philosophies.

"The premise that sex is natural must also be rejected. It depends on how it is used. Nature obviously designed the sexual apparatus to be used for procreation, not recreation. If recreation or pleasure per se were what our Creator had in mind when He designed our reproductive organs, there would be no need for all the attention, time, and tremendous sums of money spent in searching for a reliable contraceptive without harmful or undesirable side effects."

(TOTALLY WRONG. The clitoris and the G-Spot have NO OTHER FUNCTION than a woman's sexual pleasure.)

"Man is the only animal that nature allows, in his natural environment, to perform the sex act whenever he chooses to do so. All the other animals have definite mating periods when the female will accept the male organ."

(BONOBOs, small chimp-like primates, for example, mate whenever, wherever, and with whomever they wish without regard to gender or age. They put humans to shame.)

and finally:

"The human seed, of course, contains all the essential elements necessary to create another human being when it is united with the ovum. It contains forces capable of creating life. Doesn't common sense decree that such a vital fluid be carefully conserved rather than thoughtlessly squandered?"

(TOTALLY FALSE. Sperm only has his genetic material in it. Everything else required to create a human being is in the ovum.)

There's more but that's is all I can stomach.
Sometimes one has to wonder what is wrong with people!

SIGH

Feb 19, 2008
OK, I BIT.
No, is isn't the 'monster' Nokia I desired but it is neat, nifty, and has GPS so I will stop getting lost on my way to house parties.
Now if you'll excuse me, I have to do the 'woman-thing' and actually read the manual!

Feb 20, 2008
SNOW!
I am NOT a fan of snow. Yes, it can look lovely - if you do not have to go out in it and your house is well set up for the rigors of winter - but it really cuts into my sex partying time!
Bah Humbug!
So I am doing a 'no snow' dance in the hopes that this will all go away!
What say you? Snow or No Snow?

Feb 21, 2008
CONSEQUENCES
You cannot blame 'The Fates' for what has happened in your life. Once you have reached adulthood, you also cannot blame 'your parents'.

The choices one makes all come with a set of consequences; some of which you can see beforehand. The more consequences one sees, the better the decision and therefore the better the outcome.

Poor decisions generally lead to bad outcomes.

But lack of foresight has many causes: being too timid, being too bold, being too self-centered, not being self-centered enough, deliberately being blind to reality, and so on.

Cost-benefit analysis is not just for business anymore!

Consequences, both good and bad, tend to be unavoidable. One has to take them on the chin, so to speak. They are also, to the wise, educational. They also tend to predictably follow patterns of behavior. If one consistently picks one path in life, the same set of consequences, for good or ill, follow along and reoccur.

Change the behavior to change the consequences.

I will have to remember this.
How about you?

DRAT!
Had this splendid and fun week planned and...
it all came to naught.
DAMN!

Feb 22, 2008
FREEZING PRECIP
You get this when you are located in an area that is betwixt and between underneath overlapping layers in the atmosphere. Snow above that falls through a warm layer and melts then hits cold objects on the ground; or rain that falls through a cold layer but does not freeze but becomes 'super-cooled' hits cold objects on the ground - same thing happens - instant ice sheet. Your world is now a skating rink. The air temperature near the ground could be above freezing but it doesn't matter as long as the ground itself is cold.

Driving is not recommended but if you must drive go slow and steady, do not stop unless you absolutely must, and do not do anything abruptly. Think of it as ice skating on four tires. Do not so much drive as coast along. Try to stay on heavily traveled roads, rough roads, and roads that have been salted or sanded.

This was a good morning to stay home.

SEX IN CHRIST
This site was recommended to me in a comment on one of my previous posts. I checked it out.

I cannot recommend it for the following reasons.

1. it remains excessively patriarchal
2. it is excessively homo-phobic (between males only, lesbianism is okay)
3. it regards The Bible as being without error, which all scholars know to be impossible.

359

Marriage does not require a hierarchical structure but should be regarded as a team effort where the one who does a task best, does it, There is no superiority of person involved; only a superiority of a particular skill. Think of a team of horses. Both are to work together, side by side, for the good of the entire enterprise. This error is then carried forward into other areas proving that if one gets one thing wrong, one will get other things wrong as well.

If God is all knowing, then, there is no need to prohibit additional male involvement since He would know there was nothing homosexual between the men. Omission of the word lesbianism does not mean permission. There are two logical errors involved in this particular area.

Errors in translation, errors in printing, errors in transcription are all too easy to make. In one Bible, the word "not" was omitted from the Commandment "Thou shall not commit adultery". This is historical fact. One should bear the possibility of error in mind when confronting and interpreting the text, any text, including religious ones.

This site comes far but not far enough.

Feb 23, 2008
BOOZE-NESTS
An excellent idea for those who ail. The steps are simplicity itself:

1. wear your snuggliest garments
2. pile up every pillow and blanket you own
3. gather up all sundry alcoholic beverages

Snuggle into the pile of pillows, cover up with all the blankets, and then drink yourself silly.
Adding a couple of teddybears can only help.
See you tomorrow!
sequentialart no.s 362 - 364

Feb 24, 2008
HOUSE PARTIES
Have I mentioned how much I enjoy house parties? You know, where you kick the kids out and invite all your swinging friends over to get naked and have sex with whomever wherever? Yes, THOSE kind of parties. Much better than those boring old vanilla dinner parties I used to attend.

OMG they are soooo much fun! All the lovely, naked, and willing teddybears!!

I have to remember to bring a supply of chocolate donuts - we ran out far too quickly!

Happy Kitten Dance!!

THE BALKANS
Amazingly enough (yeah. right.) The Balkans are once again at each others' throats. This time, it is over the Albanian separation from Serbia. Hell, I can't blame them - the Serbians have been HUGE PITAs. So the 10% of Albania's population that are Serbian are rioting violently and blaming the US for it. "It is all your fault that I'm behaving like an spoiled child of two!" Uh-huh. That really goes a long way to establish your 'alpha-nation' status.

When 90% of the population doesn't like you, you might want to find out, oh I don't know, WHY they don't like you. In this case, it is a question of TOO MUCH HISTORY most of which is 'unpleasant'. The entire region seems to need counseling with an emphasis on anger management.

Other than dead bodies, refugees, and rubble - what have you, as a people, as a nation-state, created lately?

Having a history is nice and all but if you keep blowing each other up, you will ONLY have a history.

It isn't just individuals who have to learn to "move on".

CATCHING KITTENS

I play fast and loose with men - I always have. I enjoy men and deny them only my heart. Hey, men are great but that doesn't mean I'm going to just give them everything! Sex is one thing but hearts are quite another.

So I romp around and have times both good and bad - but there's nothing in it until he says, "stand and deliver!".

He had better be serious. Fulfilling the role of being my primary is not easy and never will be. I demand a lot from a man who wants a relationship with me not the least of which is knowing my flaws and thinking those flaws are cute as well as being able to stand up to me by demanding his fair share of my time and attention.

You have to be tough to catch this Kitten.
You have to be even tougher to keep her.

Relationships are fascinating!
Don't you think so too?

THE PRINCESS SYNDROME
This is a direct quote:

"Don't be jealous because you ain't me!"

Right. And we would want to be you...why?

Because you have that guy there? You're younger, slimmer, prettier, more desired, more fun or more whatever? Is that it?

How about I don't want to be you because you are more shallow, more fake, more stupid, more superficial, and much more doomed than I will ever be.

I say doomed because life has this way of biting people afflicted with hubris on the ass.

Those who think they are 'entitled' usually end up running themselves into trouble and then expecting everyone else to fix it for them. This being D.C. we see a lot of this all of the time.
We love watching them sputter during the interviews when they find out No, they're not all that special.

We watch and wait while 20-something becomes 40-something as The Princess becomes The Trainwreck.

Often, time is the only revenge needed.

Anyone have any stories to tell?
FOLLOW UP: further remark from the quoted 'princess':
"wasn't meant for everyone, and if I offended them, that was not my intention. but we have received some very

nasty emails because we are a cpl, and just wanted it to stop. I know many that would love to be max, and many that would love to be me. so if I hurt someone feelings, I wont apologize for it, then I guess the truth hurts."

Feb 25, 2008
LEADERLESS JIHAD
by Marc Sageman

An interesting book with a few especially interesting ideas on why "jihad fever" hasn't made the impact in America that it has in Western Europe.

1. The American Dream - in which each individual can find their own way - all things are possible to one who will try.

2. The Melting Pot - even if only a mythology- this idea remains deeply ingrained

3. Individualism - to wit:

"Americans are the most individualist people in the world." p. 97

"The relevant factor here is that individualism makes it harder for people to see their collective fate and develop a collective identity hostile to the host society." p.97

The author has done extensive research in his comparison between cultural differences, how American has the opportunity to cherry-pick those to whom it grants visas, and how America's policy of "work or starve" gives Muslim immigrants more immediate problems upon which to focus.

I recommend this book.
Care to share your thoughts?

Feb 26, 2008
PROMISCUITY
defined as: "sexual behavior of a man or woman who
engages in sexual relations with multiple partners on a
casual and/or regular basis." -Wikipedia

Some people have the idea that being promiscuous means
you are also indiscriminate. This is not necessarily the case.
She or he may just enjoy sex with a certain segment of the
population, for example. If there just happens to be a lot of
that segment around then she or he may have more
potential partners than others.

As long as everyone's being responsible and friendly about
it and are not using sex to mask other issues - I see no
harm. Others disagree for a variety of reasons.

Evolutionary biology tells us that a limited level of
promiscuity maximizes one's genetics for both men and
women. Society has not embraced this idea. Even swingers
tend to go "off-line" when procreating. Because men do not
want to raise children that are not their own biological
offspring and women want to secure the most resources for
their own biological offspring.

Procreation aside, society wants everything neat and tidy.
Even a limited level of promiscuity is seen as disruptive.
The emotional content of sex is seen as being very difficult
to manage. Social control is much easier when everyone
stays behind their white picket fences.

Religion has a difficult role in all of this. On the one hand there's the having been made by god in his image - so physically, we are as we were meant to be. And yet, the use of our bodies "of the divine" as they are is seen as being bad because it takes our thoughts and devotion away from worship of the divine.

But when one joyously loves another with light and laughter - I see only good. The sharing of intimacy, the openness, the warmth, the caring - this is all life-enhancing. I have made my choice.

Your turn!

Feb 27, 2008
"COME IN BRAIN!"
I know it is difficult for men to write coherently, language not generally being a male's forte', but sometimes one receives mail that lends credence to the idea that men find thinking difficult as well. Here are some very recent examples from my inbox here at AFF.

"Your photos got me excited. You are a goddess. MY COCK IS BUSTING OUT OF MY SHORTS. Kisses"

"I am locked in a chastity cage and instructed to please women with my mouth from my mistress. She wants me to learn how to please women with my tongue so you are to instruct me exactly how you love to be pleased. I am not allowed to have an orgasm due to my cock cage. You will help please my mistress by allowing me to service you. If interested please feel free to contact me."

"party Saturday march 1 can you cuuuuuuuuuum?"

"any way I want to tell you you do not look your age, that body looks so young and fresh, hope you start looking again"

"Will be so nice to meet you, as I said before, you are so cute and sexy, love small and nice tits you have."

Gentlemen:

Please note the kind of language used in my profile. Please attempt to be equally articulate.

I do NOT party with persons who are unknown to me.

Thank you. I am glad you find my picture exciting and attractive; especially when one considers my advanced years.

<--ancient, gnarled and gravely debilitated.

Now run along and go play outside with the other children.

How many men does it take to write an elegant and coherent sentence?

Feb 28, 2008
FINALLY! A NAP!
I wish I could just hop into my hot tub and lounge about - BUT - business calls so I must talk, talk, talk on the telephone. So between talking on the phone, send TMs, getting groceries (attended by Grandkitten #1) and going to today's BNI meeting with a client to get more clients and then swinging by the client's shop to help out employee and to set a meeting with her - I have been a very busy Kitten.

Now it is after 3pm so the office is closed and I can just relax here before assuming my other duties as a most domestic feline.

Notice how I said that with a straight face?

Tell me, how was YOUR day?

Feb 29, 2008
HAPPY LEAP DAY!
And welcome to our both clumsy and delightful way of keeping our calendar in line with the celestial progression! Clumsy because we still haven't gotten it exactly right. Delightful because, face it, perfection may be lovely but it is also boring!

The 29th of February comes round every 4 years - except it doesn't. Not exactly! This is the day that may, or then again may not, be added - think of it as a "bonus" 24 hours.

I am celebrating Leap Day by hiding from my domestic responsibilities and by going to Skinifatz tonight!

What are you doing with your bonus 24 hours?

IT HAS BEEN ASKED!
Why would a single man be in the swinging lifestyle and seeking a single female?

Lots of swingers gave their reasons but for me, the answer is simple:

because he wants to find a single swinging female to become his wife.

From his point of view, what could be better? He gets to be "number 1" with her, he has his lady, and they still get to play! Yeeehaw!

I'm wondering why they were wondering why.
Seems very simple to me!

Doesn't it seem simple to you too?

REVIVING RELATIONSHIPS
"It is generally considered normal for sex to dwindle as a relationship progresses. Familiarity with one another means there are very few surprises left, and you know exactly what the other one is going to do, when they're going to do it, precisely how it's going to be done, and what is expected of you in return. The spontaneity usually disappears and sometimes the sex stops altogether."

Sound familiar?

It doesn't have to be this way. Tell you what to do. After any medical issues have been addressed, TALK and find out what's going on in his/her head.

Does he/she think of sex as 1. dirty; 2. just for making children; 3. only for young marrieds; 4. a tool used to catch a man/women; 5. a reward for being 'good'?

Testosterone is the hormone that drives libido (the desire for sex). Women have it too. Hormone levels do change over time. Males have their maximum levels late teens and early twenties - hence their behavior. Menopausal females are at their peak testosterone levels, relative to estrogen, hence their behavior.

Unless there is a medical issue, or a serious lack of skill, there is no physical reason for not enjoying sex.

So it is all in his/her head. You have to talk openly and honestly, like adults, and try to see the issue from his/her point of view. Once the primary reason he/she is saying NO has been reached, you can both work on turning that No into a YES. If that is not possible, then you have counseling or divorce.

Many people feel that not having sex is not a reason to get divorced - "it's just sex". This is NOT TRUE. The lack of intimacy is corrosive. The relationship becomes "all work and no play".
Don't let that happen without putting up a fight.

TALK

MARCH
2008

Mar 1, 2008
LET IT BE KNOWN
That I have severed any and all ties of friendship to BHB. She has was purports to be evidence in a child abuse case and is withholding this evidence because "she doesn't want to wreck the family". She asked advice, thus transferring decision-making responsibility to stronger shoulders, to three others last night. We all told her to get it to the cops immediately. Then she hemmed and hawed and wallowed in self-pity and denial.

It is behavior like that, that gets kids killed!

Face it:
1. if the evidence is TRUE - the kid needs help NOW!
2. is the evidence is NOT TRUE - the kid needs helps - NOW
The family is already wrecked either way.

I am not the sort of woman who will condone abuse of any kind especially not if inflicted upon a child. Friends who will, either by commission or omission, immediately cease being friends. I can have NO RESPECT for anyone who puts their own comfort before another's life if they have the power to save that life, even if in only a small way.

ALL EVIL NEEDS TO THRIVE IS FOR GOOD PEOPLE TO DO NOTHING.

Mar 2, 2008
HOW TO TELL
Want to know if you're doing a good job, guys? Look for these involuntary signs...

1. flushing - if she turns pink, yes, she's orgasmed.

2. she feels hot to your touch - literally, her skin gets very warm.

3. ejaculation - yes, women do this too. She may just get very, very wet.

4. nipples harden - when you haven't been playing with them and it isn't cold.

5. dilated pupils - her pupils get really huge.

6. clenching - her vaginal muscles and her pc muscle flex and grab your hand or penis.

All are sure signs that she's enjoying having sex with you. 'Sure signs' because they cannot be faked.

What can be faked:

1. writhing - she may just be trying to move you to where she wants you to be.

2. moaning - is that pleasure or pain you're hearing?

While some men are more skillful than others, I have not yet resorted to faking it. If I'm having 'trouble' with a particular male, I just have them lie down so I can get my fun through my own efforts.

Major signs that I've orgasmed = flushing, that smile I get, ejaculating and that purrrring I do afterwards.

PLEASE READ
C_R - a heart attack at age 42 and through it all, she remains the most amazing warm and wonderful woman!

BIG BIG HUGS, C_R!!

Mar 3, 2008
GRANDKITTEN UPDATE
Alexandra remains the cutest little minx but she's learning to share. She also ate her dinner, finally! The SRM was concerned since the doctor said she was underweight at her well-baby check-up. She doesn't eat a great deal and refuses her dinner 2 times out of 3. So when she scarfed down the beef stew, everyone felt much better.

Vivian is now walking. Well, staggering, really. But she's up on her feet and putting mileage on them. Teeth, staggering, and eating baby foods off the spoon. That is a lot of change in 4 months. Unlike her sister, Vivian eats!

Very soon now they will be off on their life's adventure. This is their last 2 weeks here so we are getting in as much time with them as we can.

BOOK UPDATE
Notes of a Dominatrix is available via order from Borders. Yes, I checked their computer last Wednesday when I was in Richmond for the M&G there. I haven't yet checked the online vendors but if Borders has it, I'm sure aLibris, and Amazon have it too. Please note that it is 7 books in one; covering almost all heterosexual topics of interest.

Now finishing up the "Chat" series. Chat and Further Chat are in the works and beyond my control. The Last Chat is being written now.

Well, that's the fun stuff! Now back to my taxes.

Mar 4, 2008
PLAYTIME WITH TEDDYBEARS
REUNIONS

Your hands caressing lightly over my skin, your lips kissing me, warming my skin and relaxing me, so nice to see you again! I rolled over and you slid down for some cunnilingus. Damn you are so good at that! Then quickly, up and in. Yes! Right there! Ah! Rolling orgasms, my ankles crossed on your left shoulder, licking my ankles and moving - more orgasms! Then you're dragging me down to the end of the bed for more fun with you standing! I have missed you! MY turn now with a little something new for you. First I tie you down diagonally, one wrist and the opposite ankle - so you won't run away. Yes, you find the idea of you running away amusing. A bit of fellatio, yummmm, and I slide the vibe up to your P-Spot then pounce upon you for more orgasms! Oh my yes! You didn't last long - just long enough! Now you know how a woman's G=Spot orgasm feels. That orgasm blasted you from here to eternity. I let you up and I gleefully fell onto your bed. This time we were so together! Plain old male superior sex can be so overwhelmingly good! OMG! "You turned pink again." you said at one point! Oh hell yeah I did! WOW! We were two bits of 'plotoprasm' by time we were done. Then it was into the shower. "Another erection?!?! For me!?!?! How nice!" Thank you, Sweety!

Then a bit driving listening to the metal cd Sweety gave me to critique.

It is good to see you again! How are you, hun? We spent some time catching up and then off with the garments! You are so very, very good at massages. All the tension in my back was gone, gone, gone. Ah! I rolled over and said "no hands". I put the blindfold on you as you knelt on the bed before me and then caressed you as I got the condom ready. A caress here, a nuzzle there, with a fingertip I gently spread your pre-cum over the head of you penis, caressed your testicles as I rolled the condom on then it was inside and a perfect G-Spot massage with the head of your penis. Exquisite pleasure! I rotated my hips upward and began grasping and un-grasping your penis inside of me. You asked "What have you done?" I didn't answer, I simply continued. Rolling orgasms for me as you caressed my posterior fornix with your penis. You had to orgasm. You had no choice. "Yes! Cum for me!" I whispered. So good! The blindfold heightens your other senses. Small changes can have profound effects.

Purrrrrrrrrrrrrrr!
I am most fortunate. Such excellent teddybears!

Mar 5, 2008
ONE THING
I absolutely hate being ignored. By this I mean NOT returning phone calls. Yes, yes, I know how busy you are but, really, if I can call people...you can call people. If you say you'll call back in 10 minutes, then call back in 10 minutes. Yes, I do check my voicemail, thank you.

Oh, and btw, should I say "nevermind" - that's NOT good.

GIVE IT UP
It is THAT time of year again! Do your 1040 forms like good kids and just mail the check to those lovely people at the IRS.

grumbling while pressing calculator keys

If you need another form, just download it from their website. If not online, (how are you reading this?) just swing by your library.

taking aspirins to ward off migrane.

I really, really, REALLY, need a LOSS this year!
OH, hell! I'll just shove it all off onto the accountant and wish her the best of luck!
Grrrrrrrrrrrrr!
Anyone else having this problem?
Are teddybears tax deductable?

BEST COMMENT RECEIVED = "Yes, I do believe the latest version of the tax code added "Teddybear maintenance expenses" as a legitimate deduction. Please see your local financial advisor for complete details."

Mar 6, 2008
DATING
Dating is very simple. You go somewhere and scope out those available. You select from them and make contact. You hold a 15 minute conversation with them and get phone numbers. You set up dates and go on dates. Sex is up to her but he is always prepared. You enjoy doing the rounds until one says "stand and deliver". Then you marry that person. What's so hard about that?

What you do NOT do is date exclusively, fall in love prematurely, cling, be needy or desperate, or lie, or put on an act, or make unwarranted demands upon others.

But then, I'm not a "fluffy bunny" and I don't date.

DEMANDS WHEN DATING

Preamble: Many people start relationships by saying 'do this' or 'don't do that'. Oh, they may mask their demands with pretty words and with strokes to your ego. You may think 'this could work'. But it won't. It won't work because you two are not meeting strength to strength but weakness to weakness. To make it work, you have to be an individual, a whole person, with a life. Only then can you invite another whole person to join their life to yours.

Chapter One:

When you're dating, you have no business to demand anything. Only husbands and wives can make demands; not boyfriends, not girlfriends. Boy/girlfriends have only those rights you give them and nothing more. Those rights have to be earned and not asked for. All too often, people demand what is not rightfully theirs and if their demands are not met, they ditch the relationship claiming anything but the truth.

When you are dating, your image should be one of being an adult. You are full grown, mature, sensible, capable of humor and fun but also a person of substance. If you begin making demands, you ruin this image. You move from adult to petulant child in one step. This is true whether it is one partner or the other making demands. Contrary to popular opinion, the person making demands is not saying "I'm worth this." They are saying "I'm needy and insecure without this." What appears to be a position of strength is really a show of weakness.

When dating, you have no competition. Others are not a threat. Others do not even exist. You do not ignore their presence, you merely do not take their presence seriously. So, his or her ex is hanging about; doesn't matter. Rivals do not matter either. Your focus is only upon what is between you and the person you're dating. Is there a bond developing between you or is there not? There won't be if you go about making demands and ultimatums. Not if they're a person worth having there won't be.

Your mate for life comes to you under their own power and in their own time. They do not come because you told them to come. He or she has to come to you because they want you; all of you, the good, the bad, and the indifferent; as you are right here and right now. This is not something you can rightfully demand. The drive toward you has to come from within your partner.

Nothing less will do.

Chapter Two - next week.

LOL
Men invariably want the babes. The young babes. The younger than them by decades babes. Hey go for it! Sure. Why not? It's all good. The other guys will envy them. It is all about 'ego' stroking.

Because older women are complicated and that's not the light of adoration in their eyes. Laughter, yes; understanding, yes; sympathy, yes; perhaps even love, yes; but adoration, no.

Sorry to tell you but all you have done was trade one set of "issues" for another set of "issues". The best comedy on earth!

So I'll pin a $20 (the price of admission for this show) to your collar and wish you the best of luck!

Popcorn, anyone?

THE 2008 VIRGINIA SPRING RACE CALENDAR
Let me know if you'd like to go. I'm driving!

March 15th Warrenton
March 22nd Piedmont
March 30th Orange County
April 5th Old Dominion
April 12th Strawberry Hill
April 19th Middelburg Spring
April 20th Fairfax
April 26th Foxfield Spring
April 27th Middleburg Hunt
May 3rd Virginia Gold Cup Meet
May 4th Bull Run
May 10th Bedford County

Races begin circa noon.
Picnics and lawn chairs.
Blue jeans and boots, please.

Mar 7, 2008
THERE I WAS
listening to a song about 'estrangement' of a particular kind
and I found myself thinking, not about the man sitting next
to me, but another man and smiling.

"Used To"

You used to talk to me like
I was the only one around.
You used to lean on me like
The only other choice was falling down.
You used to walk with me like

380

We had nowhere we needed to go,
Nice and slow, to no place in particular.

We used to have this figured out;
We used to breathe without a doubt.
When nights were clear, you were the first star that I'd see.
We used to have this under control.
We never thought.
We used to know.
At least there's you, and at least there's me.
Can we get this back?
Can we get this back to how it used to be?

I used to reach for you when
I got lost along the way.
I used to listen.
You always had just the right thing to say.
I used to follow you.
Never really cared where we would go,
Fast or slow, to anywhere at all.

We used to have this figured out;
We used to breathe without a doubt.
When nights were clear, you were the first star that I'd see.
We used to have this under control.
We never thought.
We used to know.
At least there's you, and at least there's me.
Can we get this back?
Can we get this back to how it used to be?

I look around me,
And I want you to be there
'Cause I miss the things that we shared.
Look around you.

It's empty, and you're sad
'Cause you miss the love that we had.

You used to talk to me like
I was the only one around,
The only one around.

We used to have this figured out;
We used to breathe without a doubt.
When nights were clear, you were the first star that I'd see.
We used to have this under control.
We never thought.
We used to know.
At least there's you, and at least there's me.
Can we get this back?
Can we get this back to how it used to be? Yeah.
To how it used to be.
To how it used to be, yeah.
To how it used to be.
To how it used to be.
-by Daughtry

It is nice to know I don't really have to ask "can we get this back, to how it used to be."

Mar 8, 2008
BUZZ KILLERS
Please tell me YOU don't have/do any of these!

1. Bitterness - everything that has gone wrong before is your partner of the moment's fault; everything right here and right now doesn't somehow measure up to your expectations; everyone always lets you down or screws you over. All everyone ever hears from you is the dripping

venom of complaint after complaint after complaint. It sucks all the joy out of life of anyone within earshot.

2. Jealousy - yes, I know people say that if "he/she is NOT jealous, then they really don't love you" but that's utter rot! Being jealous or possessive is a huge red flag signaling weakness. The jealous person does not trust you, does not trust him or herself, and certainly does not trust the strength of your love. If you cannot trust, you cannot love. That's all there is too it. Being with a jealous/possessive person is like being in prison constantly watching your own back because your nearest and dearest always has that knife ready.

3. Leeching - This goes beyond being needy, clingy, and desperate. Leeching is literally not having any mind or life of your own so you have to get your existence through another person. These people are looking for a meal ticket and so much more. They are never satisfied. As each box is checked, there's always another one. There's also a quid pro quo variation where if you want x then you have to give y to get it.

Now, people will not come right out and say "I'm a bitter, jealous, leech.". You have to watch for the red flags and be prepared to walk away should a red flag fly.

Red Flags =

The Quiz. Where did you go? Who did you see? What did they say? What did you say? Question upon question not from a sincere wish to know but because they're searching for any hint of infidelity.

Bait & Switch. A bit of sex "you'll get more when we get there." You get there and then instead of the sex, you get a lecture about your fear of commitment.

Being Off Their Meds. It doesn't really matter what the meds are for because this is truly scary. In this case, trust your instinct that something's NOT right and run away.

Avoidance. Always answering a question with a question, or not answering it at all, or just brushing questions off as being not important. Also under this heading comes those who are never there when you need them and those who avoid accepting any responsibility.

Complaints. That is all you get from them. They have a view of the world that begins and ends with them.

Bullying. Then there are those who constantly push you to do something you do NOT want to do proving they do not listen to you and do not consider you or your wishes to be important.

If you are inflicted - please run. If you are he/she who inflicts - STOP IT!

Anyone have any examples they'd care to tell?

Mar 9, 2008
OKAY
so what's with the "no comment" that's been going on around here? Come on, you cannot expect me to believe you all are THAT shy!
Cat got your tongue?

Mar 10, 2008
PREPARATION FOR DATING
Chapter Two

Dating involves presenting yourself as a desirable partner. You do this by recognizing your best and worst attributes. Then you move one step beyond a simple cataloging to recognition of any discontinuities in your life. These discontinuities are what will ruin your chances with ever finding a life-long mate. Some examples include the 40 year old virgin, the 'failed to launch' person, the Master degreed who flips burgers for a marginal living, and the public person who privately lives the exact opposite of what they publicly support.

Remember that you have to be a whole person with a life of your own before you can ask anyone else to join you. If you are not a whole person - fix it. If your life is not what you want it to be - fix it. Yes, I know it may be almost impossible to do but if you think about your options, you may just come up with an effective plan. If the process of discovery requires cost-benefit analysis, do it. Rule one is 'no lying', not even to yourself. If you require medications, take them and get on with your life.

Next, check your baggage and your attitude. You are a decent person planning on meeting decent people. There is no need to tell others everything nor is there any reason to make this woman/man pay for what any other women/men may have or may not have done earlier. You are not a Prince/Princess and you are not Mr. or Ms. NoGood so While respect has to be earned, civility is expected. If in doubt about the quality of your manners, kindly read Miss Manners for guidance.

Please be aware that 'full disclosure' does not happen until marriage is being discussed/proposed. Before then, keep it to yourself. When fully disclosing, do not attempt to gloss over anything. This is when the truth is the only thing that will work. No one wants to be surprised and remember that you want to be accepted for all of you and not just for the good bits. Few things are worse than getting married and only then finding out that you have made a dreadful mistake.

Preparation is about the major issues in your life that would kill any chance of you having the relationship you desire. The aim is to make as it easy and as enjoyable as possible for your life-mate to join with you. See what you can do to make that possible.

Next week - Chapter 3

Mar 11, 2008
INFORMALLY SEEKING AN ANSWER
MEN, I have heard that there's a "guy thing" out there entitled "I'd do her if no one even found out." Meaning, I'm supposing here, that he desires sex but in the absence of a more acceptable/hot/whatever partner, she'd do but he would be damaging his reputation if his buddies knew it.

Is this true? What are the signs that this is the basis of your date that a woman would recognize? Anyone have any stories they'd dare to tell?

COMMENT RECEIVED ="It is true. The way to find out is to ask to meet some of his friends or family. Or ask to go somewhere very public where there is a good chance of bumping into someone he knows."

HAPPY KITTEN
A teddybear is back from maintenance! We have an appt!
All is right with the world!
HURRAY!
You see me dancing with delight!!

Mar 12, 2008
THE POSTERIOR FORNIX
I know I have mentioned the posterior fornix before but I
never told you much about it. It is one of the regions that
will induce orgasms when properly stimulated in most, but
not all, women.

The posterior fornix is that area of a woman's vagina below
the cervix, in the back, and down. Think of it as the floor of
the back room.

Properly stimulating this area begins with making sure she
is not only aroused but is also post-orgasmic. This way, her
vagina is fully lubricated and has grown to tis fullest extent
making access more comfortable for her.

In the male superior position, lean forward over her put
your legs further back and think downward. Gently, at first,
caress the posterior fornix with the head of your penis
gradually increasing speed and pressure as her orgasm
approaches. Modify your "approach" for other positions.

This is especially useful when going for multiple orgasms.
You can move from the clitoris to the G-Spot to the
posterior fornix, in rotation, moving to a new area after
each orgasm for as long as you can maintain. This will
prevent one area from becoming hyper-sensitive.

Have fun practicing!

ELLIOT SPITZER

Wall Street greets the resignation of Eliot Spitzer.
Republicans are gleeful at Spitzer's downfall, but if you
want to witness real ecstasy, visit Wall Street. As New
York's attorney general, Spitzer made his political career on
attention-grabbing settlements with banks, insurance
companies, and mutual funds, positioning himself as the
only man willing to clean up Wall Street's mess. To Wall
Streeters, however, he was a bully and a boor, less a legal
eagle than a rogue prosecutor and one-man Star Chamber.

Many of the abuses he attacked were real. He went after the
tendency of equity research to serve investment-banking
clients, rather than the retail investors who were reading it.
And his inquiry into mutual funds who were letting big
clients profit by trading shares after market close ended a
scandalous practice.

But his methods were deeply troubling.

Spitzer rarely made his case in court. This may be because
it wasn't clear many of the practices he prosecuted were
illegal, even if they were allegedly immoral. (He'd be a
better bishop than attorney general.) The rare cases he did
try disappointed: minor figures, embarrassing acquittals,
notably a stunning loss against a Bank of America broker
named Theodore Sihpol.

Unwilling to bring his crusades cases to trial, Spitzer used
two dubious tactics to secure quick settlements from high-
profile targets. Most of his cases were tried in the court of
public opinion, often based on misleadingly trimmed
quotes that sent stock prices plunging. His orchestrated
campaigns of press releases and anonymous leaks forced

executives to settle, to halt the damage to their credit and their share prices. It's not clear that this tactic distinguishes between the guilty and the innocent.

His most infamous technique was the state's Martin Act, which gives the AG frighteningly sweeping powers, like blanket subpoena power, and the ability to interrogate potential defendants stripped of their lawyers and their right against self-incrimination. Because these sweeping powers tended to provide ample fodder for geometrically multiplying class-action suits, executives had to come to the negotiating table with hats in hand. Even then, this wasn't always enough -- frustrated by an impasse in negotiations with Merrill Lynch, he filed a Martin Act suit that nearly forced the company to shut down its entire money management business until a judge stayed the order. Needless to say, this would not have been a boon to Merrill's retail clients.

Lately, his crusades have shaded into the blatantly illegal. As governor, he has been demanding that bond insurers split themselves into two companies: a sound one to insure the state's municipal bonds, and a virtually bankrupt one that would leave holders of subprime debt exposed. One assumes that Spitzer came across the notion of a fraudulent conveyance sometime in law school.

But perhaps the worst aspect Spitzer's reign was how little it profited actual investors. By pushing for masses of quick settlements, Spitzer both netted the potentially innocent, and shielded the potentially guilty from lawsuits. The settlement money went not to the investors who had allegedly been defrauded, but into state coffers. And the penalties he offered were often ludicrously unrelated to the alleged offense -- in the mutual fund case, Spitzer demanded that the funds lower their fees, which weren't illegal, and had nothing to do with the late trading practices that had harmed investors. The suits were extremely good at netting the headlines he needed to climb towards the presidency. But it left very few other than Eliot Spitzer better off. — Megan McArdle

Hoist with his own petard?

Mar 13, 2008
STD DATA NO SURPRISE
In today's Washington Post area teens tested for 4 non-lethal STDs and here are the stats:

838 girls tested
ages 14 through 19
rate: 2 out of 5 were infected
50% of African American girls were infected
20% of Whites and Latinas were infected

Why?

Because neither school nor their parents told them the truth about sex or interpersonal relationships.

In an effort to "protect" their daughters from getting emotionally hurt, parents sugar-coat and fall back on the traditional teachings re: sex ranging from "wait until you're married" to "only if you really love him." Seems once the girl's got on BCPs, they forgot all about demanding condom usage.

Instead of calling it "family life" etc., schools should call it "sex education" and be forthright. The course should be taught by someone who has been active and not Ms Polly Primrose.

The girl's also lied by falling back on the old and trite "peer pressure" and "it's on tv" answers.

The truth is that they do not want to have to accept responsibility for being sexual because then they'd be a "skank" or a "slut" or even worse "a wuss" who can't say no to a guy and make it stick. Teens also do this "hearts & flowers" routine of "we're sooo in love!" They get lost in the daydream.

And what of the guys? Do we let these non-condom-wearing louts get away scott-free? Congrats buddy, you're infected if she's infected!

The message should be
CONDOMS AND BCPs OR NO SEX

TOLD LAST NIGHT
A very nice lady told me last night that my blog was too advanced for AFF people. I'm not sure I agree with her so I thought I'd ask you people!

Is my blog too advanced?

(I was told that yes, but they enjoyed it being that way.)

PLAYTIME WITH TEDDYBEARS
MISCOMMUNICATION

His email read 3 to 5pm. It is very, very nice to see you again! A quick scamper back to the truck for the playbag. Then it is off with the clothes while we catch up on each other's news with you displaying your scars and explaining that you're a man with more than a few skills. After selecting an oil, I gleefully join you on the bed. Mmmmm so nice to nuzzle into your fur again! And then the slow foreplay begins with a kiss. The spreading of oil, licking, nibbling, caressing. Purr. Since kneeling is out of the question just now, you slide my all the way up the bed before licking my clitoris. Oh my! G-Spot massage and the orgasms begin rolling. You're up and in and bearing your weight on one knee. I add my movements to yours. So good! You have to get off your knees so it is onto your side and we'll spoon. A shoulder massage as we rejoin the movement. Then it is an amazing ride; me still having rolling orgasms and you climbing toward yours. Yes! WOW! That was one great orgasm you had! "And it's another teddybear down," you said. I'm snuggling under the covers smoking then I rejoin you trying to avoid the wet spot; yes, I know, that was me. And then I found out that the 3 to 5pm wasn't the entire appointment time, just the arrival window. Argh! I had scheduled another appointment (biz this time) for afterwards.

Damn, damn, and double damnation! I could have had more teddybear!

Such a foolish Kitten!

Mar 14, 2008
PEOPLE WATCHING
I'm not at that good at consciously decoding people's body language but I do know a few things.

The number one signal is physical tension or the lack thereof. Fight or flight responses are bad. Fidgeting is bad. Relaxed attitudes are good.

The number two signal is mental attention or the lack thereof. Zoning out, looking around at everything and everyone except the speaker is bad. Latching on like a laser target acquisitioning system is good.

Where am I going with this? I am thinking that perhaps I should pay more attention to those around me especially since I spend most of my time alone doing solitary things - like work.

What do you think? Should I get out more?

JOY
I have recently recommended the book <u>Exuberance: The Passion for Life</u> by Kay Redfield Jamison. Actually, we all could use a bit of exuberance in our lives.

This can be difficult to achieve if all we do is focus upon our troubles, concerns, or what is lacking in our lives.

After all is said and done - you're still breathing, aren't you?

For today: everything is good! Nothing is a problem. People are uniformly wonderful if quirky. All good things are possible!

Go forth and exult!

MY ISBN
Yes, it is cheaper to download them (lots are - I'm getting checks) but, hey, there's nothing like an actual book, baby! Put them on your nightstand! LOL

<u>Chat</u> 978-0-6151-6356-7

Further Chat 978-0-6151-8655-9

Notes of a Dominatrix 978-0-6151-6606-3

Please, don't fall out of bed!

Mar 15, 2008
DREAM ON, KITTEN!
I love Italian sportscars! This is no big secret. I often visit the manufacturers' websites and build cars just for fun - just on the off chance that I'll win the lottery and have enough money to say "build it, baby!"

But all websites are NOT the same.

ferrariusa -frankly, this website is EXREMELY poor. With their money, they could be doing so much better. They might as well be selling insurance for all the excitement this site generates.

maserati - a very nice website, good videos, graphics, and a nice configurator in which you can even specify the stitching of the upholstery.

lamborghini - this site kicks ass if only for the music! No configurator but you kind of forget that because the videos, long to load, are so good. I want one of these!!!

bugatti - after going to lamborghini, this site seems so mild but it does have a good configurator - beware as they seem to prefer a patchwork exterior.

Website Winner: Lamborghini - there's no contest.

Price to Value winner: Maserati - with prices for an excellent vehicle beginning at $114k.

So you have to sell the house!

MANAGING EXPECTATIONS
Chapter Three

We all have this vision in our heads about who we want. Are you chances of getting him/her realistic? Maybe not and you can continue to try, of course, but where's the joy in that? Continual rejection is highly corrosive. A better plan is to match your expectations with your reality.

This might seem depressing, but the entire point of dating is find someone you give a damn about for all of the right reasons who will give a damn about you for all of the right reasons. Correct? That person may not be that "dreamgirl/guy" you have in your head.

How many people have you passed by today? It is one thing to have a suitable selection criteria and it is quite another to ignore your reality and shoot for some mythical creature to make your life complete. We all want to feel good about our choices. But you cannot let your ego blind you.

Remember that it isn't the packaging that matters so much since the packaging is mutable. What you need to seriously consider is the person inside of the packaging. You need to seek those "right reasons" and not be content with mere eye-candy.

Life mates are not chosen for today, they are chosen for tomorrow, and tomorrow, and for all the years after today.

They are chosen so someone will still think you're wonderful and want to cuddle with you when you're 85.

You have to be objective about yourself and accept yourself as you are before you date. Set your sights accordingly. You might be pleasantly surprised to find that the life mate for you has been right next to you all along.

Next week - Chapter Four.

THREESOMES

The 3-some that works best for me is the active non-bi MFM. This is because of my high interest and high energy levels. This also makes it easier on the men because then their skills do not have to as highly developed as they have to be during a non-bi FMF. They still have to have good manners and I still have to like both of them individually but the bar isn't set as high as it would be if he were the only male.

An active non-bi FMF is where he kisses and does manual G-Spot on the one lady while penetrating and caressing the other lady. And then reversing. For as long as he can hold out and changing condoms as we go. This requires a great deal of skill as neither lady should be left feeling unfulfilled. If he cannot multi-task effectively, then I am not the additional woman for you two. While watching is nice, doing is much more fun.

I know you are wondering about what I mean by "active" 3-some. An active 3-some is where the odd gender out remains untethered and free to actively participate, move around, and have some input in what is done.

396

I have done more than few passive non-bi FMFs and they are always fun. Few men really mind being tied down, blindfolded, and enjoyed by two women all over him. Some men have been to known to leap onto the bed at the slightest hint. Anyone desiring a passive MFM with me - no. Thank you, but - no. That's far too dangerous - for them. Even I have my limits.

Successful 3-somes are kept light and fun. We're all adults, we're all friends, and we're all just here for sex. Something to drink and something light to nibble on - wine and cheese for example - would be nice. A shower is always welcome. Just lying around naked and chatting - it is all good.

Mar 16, 2008
ST. PATRICK'S DAY
The person who was to become St. Patrick, the patron saint of Ireland, was born in Wales about AD 385. His given name was Maewyn, he was born in Wales about AD 385, and he almost didn't get the job of bishop of Ireland because he lacked the required scholarship. Even then, the 'sheepskin' counted.

The next item is the wearing of the orange (Protestant) or the green (Catholic). To be ecumenical about it, an orange and green striped tie or scarf is best. Although the Celts love a good fight, I ask that you refrain and instead go with that other great Celtic love - a mighty party with drink, laughter, and dancing.

Much more fun and it saves the furniture.

"I am still of opinion that only two topics can be of the least interest to a serious and studious mood - sex, and the dead."

W.B. Yeats (1865 - 1939)
The Letters of W .B. Yeats

Mar 17, 2008
SPREADING THE JOY
Yesterday Demon Spawn #1, aka the eldest grandkitten,
and I went out to Chetwood to meet the horses. This was
her first time but the few videos we had at the house riveted
her so I thought it was time. Horse fever does bite girls
early. In this case, DS #1 is not yet 2 years old.

We pulled up at the polo barns and there were a few horses
still in their winter coats relaxing. Little Miss Brand New
White Sneakers was all eagerness to get right on in there
with them, but I convinced her that avoiding the mud was a
good idea. She was very good about that.

She was also busy cooing at and petting the horses. She
giggled at the nibblers as they checked out her pockets
looking for sugar but soon I had to carry her so she could
get up close and personal with them.

The girl is definitely BIT!
Soon, she'll be bugging her parents for a pony!

CELEBRATE!
HAPPY ST. PATRICK'S DAY!!
have some green beer for me

"LET'S TALK ABOUT SEX, BABY"
I am trying to get a consistent 4 hour 'interlude' three times
per week.
Should be easier than this.
Dontcha think?

398

Mar 18, 2008
APOLOGIZING
A friend of mine is such a kind hearted person that she tends to accept other's defects and make them her fault. "I'm to blame for him feeling/being this way." As a corollary to this, she then closes the door on seeking her dream because she thinks she can't do it pointing to the other's defect being her fault - "if she were any good at this he wouldn't be that way" as evidence. She ends up endlessly apologizing and trying to "make it up to him".

Stop. Just, stop.

Permitting yourself to be an "emotional hostage" does not a healthy relationship make. If you have made an error, get specifics and apologize for those specifics - ONCE. After that, it is out of your hands and no longer your responsibility.

It must be that way because if not, your life will be a constant "walking through a mine field" experience with your partner seemingly an armed nuclear weapon just about to blow. You'll end up coming in after her/him and apologizing to people for her behavior.

Who needs that?

Plus the constant "I'm no good at it" message revolving around in your head is highly corrosive and you find yourself limiting your life until you're in a small box quaking with fear of making a mistake to the point where you cannot find the courage to lift the lid.

I grew up with just such a person. Watching my back was my life until age 14 when I lost my temper, having been knocked to the ground one too many times, and with violent hatred told him to "stop it and never do it again or I'll disown you".

If you're wondering where my confidence comes from - I am my father's daughter.

Do not permit your kindness to make yourself someone else's slave. You cannot change anyone.
You cannot rescue anyone. Only they can do that.

If you are the 'atomic bomb' - stop it and grow up. You and you alone are responsible for your emotions and your behavior. Be adult or be gone.

If you are the "hostage" - stop apologizing. Stand up and quietly, or loudly, demand that he/she become an adult. Find the courage to act. Do what you know you must. It isn't you - it is her/him.

No more hostages!

Mar 19, 2008
WEDNESDAY
Friend L - The correct order is Job, House, and THEN the Man/Men. Borrow the repair fee, get the car and get on with building your life. Stop expecting others to 'rescue' you. Thank you.

Acquaintance D - pack her stuff up, put it on the front porch out of the weather. Write it all off as the price for getting rid of her.

My fee for babysitting for a 24 hour period is one carton of cigarettes. Thank you.

400

Let's see... what else. Hmmmmmmm.

I need to refresh my wardrobe. No that's not it. I know there was something else...

Oh well, I'll let you know what it was later!
Have fun!

Mar 20, 2008
ARTICLE
"Clueless Guys Can't Read Women" By Jeanna Bryner,
LiveScience Staff Writer

Research finds that guys have trouble reading non-verbal cues and often mistake a friendly smile to mean sexual interest.

Research finds that guys have trouble reading non-verbal cues and often mistake a friendly smile to mean sexual interest. Credit: Stock.xchng. More often than not, guys interpret even friendly cues, such as a subtle smile from a gal, as a sexual come-on, and a new study discovers why: Guys are clueless.

More precisely, they are somewhat oblivious to the emotional subtleties of non-verbal cues, according to a new study of college students.

"Young men just find it difficult to tell the difference between women who are being friendly and women who are interested in something more," said lead researcher Coreen Farris of Indiana University's Department of Psychological and Brain Sciences.

This "lost in translation" phenomenon plays out in the real world, with about 70 percent of college women reporting an experience in which a guy mistook her friendliness for a sexual come-on, Farris said.

Some might think the results come down to "boys being boys," and so even the slightest female interest sparks sexual fantasy. But the study, to be detailed in the April issue of the journal Psychological Science, also found that it goes both ways for guys — they mistake females' sexual signals as friendly ones. The researchers suggest guys have trouble noticing and interpreting the subtleties of non-verbal cues, in either direction.

The study's funding came from the National Institutes of Mental Health and the National Institute on Alcohol Abuse and Alcoholism.

Flirting or not?

To unravel it all, Farris and her colleagues examined non-verbal communication in a group of 280 undergraduates, both men and women with an average age of 20 years old.

The students viewed images of women on a computer screen and had to categorize each as friendly, sexually interested, sad or rejecting. Each student reported on 280 photographs, which had been sorted previously into one of the categories based on surveys completed by different groups of students.

Overall, women categorized more images correctly than men did. When it came to friendly gestures, men were more likely than women to interpret these to mean sexual interest.

402

More surprising, the researchers found guys were also confused by sexual cues. When images of gals meant to show allure flashed onto the screen, male students mistook the allure as amicable signals.

So ladies trying to brush off a guy at work or the gym may need to be, uh, more direct. Men in the study also had more trouble than women distinguishing between sadness and rejection.

Programmed for sex

The results help to tease out the underlying causes of guys' flirt-or-not mistakes. One common explanation for reports of men taking a friendly gesture as "she wants me," is based on men's inherent interest in sex, which is thought to result from their biology as well as their upbringing.

Following this idea, men and women would be aware of the same behavioral cues, but men would have a lower threshold for what qualifies as sexual interest. In contrast, women would wait for compelling evidence before labeling a behavior as sexual interest.

However, Farris and her colleagues didn't find this to be the case. Rather than seeing the world through sex-colored glasses, men seemed just to have blurry vision of sorts, overall. For instance, the college guys sometimes mistook sexual advances as pal-like gestures.

"I would say that there are many factors that could relate to men demonstrating insensitivity to women's subtle non-verbal cues," said Pamela McAuslan, associate professor of psychology at the University of Michigan-Dearborn, who was not involved in the current study. These factors would include socialization, gender roles and gender stereotypes, she said.

For instance, "women are supposed to be the communicators, concerned with relationships and others ... men are supposed to be less concerned with communication and to be constantly alert for sexual opportunities," McAuslan said. "This could mean that men in general may be less sensitive to subtle non-verbal behavior than women."

That doesn't mean such men can't learn to read cues or that all men are clueless decoders of women's gestures.

"These are average differences. Some men are very skilled at reading affective cues," Farris told LiveScience, "and some women find the task challenging." "

Before you go on about "male-bashing" or whatever, consider these two comments:

"If you are sending a message in such a way that 70% of your target never receives the message or receives the opposite message - clearly the sender is at fault. What's next; an article on archery entitled "Clueless targets can't catch arrows"?"

and

"The problem with the whole idea of women being more direct is that to be more direct about sexual clues is to be classed as a whore and therefore not acceptable as a long term mate by men. Men don't want women who directly ask for sex for mates. They just want to use

404

them for the night. That's not exactly in our best interests."

The real issue is that societal norms are forcing women to be increasingly subtle to the point where 70% of signals are not being properly received resulting in what can only be called The Exasperation of The Sexes.

Don't you agree?

Mar 21, 2008
THOUGHTS FOR FRIDAY
This Saturday is the first-ever **World Pillow Fight Day**! Finally! This should be almost as fun as **World Orgasm Day**! Pillows and orgasms. Hmmmm = wonder what I'm thinking?

Chocolate rabbits should be eaten ears, tail, and then the rest of it. I made a set of fancily decorated wooden eggs years ago for hiding out doors. My kids are accomplished egg finders. I'm going to have to make another set now. Do I still have my wood burner kit?

Soduko - do you do them? I do. They have a calming effect - don't you think?

Began another book. What can I say? Yes, the teddybears are hibernating. Other than sending out letters, business is slow right now. If others aren't keeping me busy - I'll keep myself busy.

Lots of people's idea of partying involves the copious consumption of alcohol and the gratuitous public display of body parts. Mine involves the mild consumption of alcohol and the uninhibited private repeated delivery of rampant

405

sex. Because doing is much more fun than watching or talking.

I have no idea how my taxes are going to work out. I just gathered up the papers, did the biz accounts, and then threw it all to the CPA along with a check. Refund please!!

This is a house weekend. Also we get started doing the lawn so we can, once again, win the Lawn Wars, Amateur Division. Well, it gives the SRM something to do.

Went on a "date" a couple of weeks ago. I'm getting sooo "vanilla"!! Horrible! ICK, ICK, ICK! Now I have to go and wash my paws!

C Y'ALL

RESEARCH
Quoted from the man's site:

"I am in my 40s, successful in business, live in a nice condo, drive a great auto, I'm in great physical shape, and I am considered handsome. The moral to this story is that none of these things matter! "Getting it" is the key that unlocked the door to my success with women.

I have your e-book, CD series and, of course, the collection of weekly newsletters. I have become a student of "getting it" and creating attraction in women. I am currently dating a 9.5 on a scale where 10 is drop-dead gorgeous, extremely intelligent, witty, sexually creative, etc. I constantly tease her, push her away, insist on her treating me on dates, give her the gift of missing me, thus driving her crazy to the point where she can't help but call me!

406

I have kicked her out of my condo for acting bratty on two occasions, and picked on her for minor flaws (that she pointed out initially). For example: She asked, "Do you think my ass needs some more toning? I need to focus on those exercises in the gym." Well, I have taken full advantage of this to bust her balls!

Here's the kicker: She will look me in the eyes with a sultry look and say to me, "No man has ever treated me so good and made me feel so complete as a woman like you do."

Now, let me qualify this for the "getting it" challenged: I am never cruel and I never ridicule her, nor do I openly embarrass her in public. I am always a gentleman, treat her like the princess that she is, but I am the new me -- extremely confident, Cocky & Funny, romantic, and powerful. I assume I am in control in every situation."

He was complimented thusly:

"Yeah, this is one of the most ironic and interesting things about learning how to be successful with women.

Never in my life have I had so many women give me so many compliments as when I tease and bust on them like there's no tomorrow.

Why is this? Because when you're doing these things, the woman gets the deeper message: that you're the kind of man she's been looking for all her life.

The kinds of things you're doing are triggering and satisfying drives and urges that have been wired into her mental, physical and emotional systems for millions of years.

You're activating powerful sexual drives and female emotions that most men will never trigger inside of her, and she's grateful to you for it.

Even though an outsider might look at an evening that you spend with her and say, "He didn't treat her very well. He was difficult, very challenging and not complimentary at all. I don't think he's going to get very far with her."

Meanwhile, at the end of the evening, the woman you're with will go home with a deep, profound feeling of inner satisfaction that she won't be able to describe. Yes, you do "get it." Congratulations."

My take: According to this site women are naturally submissive, this "hard wired for millions of years" thing (ignoring science), and this is why his "system" works. So exactly how does being cocky, funny & busting her balls - makes her feel like a princess? This sort of thing reminds me of women showing off their bruises and broken bones to each other bragging that their man beats her so he must love her; only here it isn't bruises she's showing. This "my man is more man than your man" and "I've got a REAL man" thing.

"Complete as a woman?!?!" - how very juvenile to be sure.

Please tell me you do not do/accept this stuff!!

Mar 22, 2008
HAPPENINGS OF NOTE
1. The two cats, Thor and Havoc, were let into the garage by Grandkitten #1, who now knows how to operate

doorknobs. The garage is so packed full of cars, tools, and stuff that there is no room to even swing one cat so the two cats had to make do somehow. The SRM went into the garage for a drill and saw the two cats sitting side by side in the MGB. They were peering at him through the windshield as if caught in the act of escaping. "We're outta here!" Unfortunately for the cats, the SRM had previously removed the battery. No escape was possible.

2. There is a mourning dove nesting, with her two tiny little live babies, on my potting bench out beneath the deck out back. The various RMs were busy doing yardwork and they did not want to disturb her so other than a quick check to make sure she was still on her nest, they left her alone and stayed well away. I can see her if I look out of my office window, the one on the right.

3. Every stopped everything and came out to the dining room to watch the hilarious, to them, spectacle of me hanging drapes. I'm not very good at it. They find this very amusing. I can tell you that the job would be easier without comments "they're not even!" from "down a little more on the left" the gallery. Yes, yes, very funny, now go find something useful to do!

4. Also today I had the "joy" of being assisted in my housecleaning and laundry efforts by Grandkitten #1 who is not yet 2 years of age. From feeding the clothes washing machine to handing things to me; you have to constantly keep her attention focused else she's running off to play with something she shouldn't. IT is a good thing that I can outrun her!

5. Today we also must mourn the passing of my very fancy leaded glass star - the one that hung in one of my living

room windows. The SRM, bless his heart, removed it so he could clean it, and it broke. With the best will in the world, all the solder and no flux could not fix the piece, so we have laid it aside until we can find a suitable glass artisan to fix it and not charge us the earth. Either that or the SRM takes up the art himself.

6. It was also said today that "we" need to go through MY closet and clear out the old, etc., clothing in it. I calmly said that since summer was coming that I wouldn't mind going around naked but that others might object. The subject was dropped. I thought it might be.

We then settled down to watch DVDs and eat pizza for dinner.

How was your day, today?

Mar 23, 2008
CHOCOLATE RABBITS FOR EVERYONE!!
HAPPY EASTER !!
may you also have a rebirth of
life, love
and
laughter!

Mar 24, 2008
MARKETING
Chapter Four

You want to present a certain image of yourself. You want to be a person of worth and substance, and I am not only speaking of material things. If your religion is important to you, project the image of being a religious person. If you're a decent hard-working person who is as steady as a rock, project that. The point is to go with what is important to you and your good points.

The image you project is not just a facade. It must be real and it must encompass your entire life. Dressing well while living in a hovel is not going to be effective. A few good items works better than lots of not terribly good items. Keep your marketing clean, simple, and true.

Never, ever lie; not even by omission. You can decline to answer a question. If you are asked what kind of relationship you want, please tell. If you want marriage and your date does not, it is best to know this immediately. Not to say that while seeking Mr./Ms. Right you cannot dally with Mr./Ms. Wrong but it does take time away from your main objective. Yet, time spent "just for fun" can help clear your mind if certain potential partners are confusing you. This is especially useful for men as it prevents them from falling prey to what is called, in the vernacular, testosterone poisoning.

Your image cannot change from one date to the next. It must be a consistent and coherent whole. And it must appeal to the kind of partner you want. Someone seeking a religious person will not be impressed by a player. This is because people do not feel comfortable if the gap between them and their partner is too large. You want your potential partners to feel at ease with you right from the start.

Do not be perfect. Perfection makes demands of its own and this can be scary. Potential partners may feel they can never 'measure up'. A flaw or two makes you seem more human as long as those flaws are minor and somewhat endearing.

Next week: Chapter Five.

Mar 25, 2008
BEING KITTEN FRIENDLY
Skinifatz, my "local", is the most "kitten-friendly" place I know but there are still a few flaws - things I would like to change. Number one is THE MUSIC.

Why is it that almost all the bars, etc., play such horrible music? Nothing from the top of the charts artists. No Clapton, for example. Only one song from AC/DC. No Rammstein. Only one song from NIN. It is all 'hip-hop' or CW (ick!) or that idiot "one stomp this time" song where they all line up.

Unlike the last several places, I don't have to go out into my truck for a musical intermission - cranking up "Freak on a Leash" or "Black No.1". But I am still feeling compelled to give the dj a cd of decent music along with orders to play it or die.

Hey, I am a "rock n roll" woman with leanings toward lyrical heavy metal. If you're not shaking the foundations, you're not trying hard enough! I want music that exults, that races, that picks you up and carries you along with it!

"Gigging frogs" just doesn't cut it.

What music gets you rolling, babies?

"DAMAGED GOODS"
The concept of the sexually active person, whether male or female, being "damaged goods" has got to go because promiscuity is in the eye of the beholder. But there are other reasons as well.

412

It is sad, really, that we still have issues with sexual experience and that we feel threatened by it. I say we, because some women are beginning to apply this same concept to men.
Fear is something that should be abolished not fed.

The value of a person does not lie between their legs. Enjoying sex does not make anyone a bad person. Yes, you can trust a slut, male or female.

One can commit to another regardless of the number who have 'been there before'. Sex does not equal love and love does not equal sex.

"Easy" does not of necessity mean not selective. He/she just might like you. Just because he/she likes you does not mean he/she will like someone else.

It is true that men decline to marry highly experienced women but more fool them. They sacrifice all that may be possible out of fear.

Consider one little thing:

a virgin is good at saying NO
a slut is good at saying YES

and 20 to 30 years down the road of married life, which would you prefer he/she was saying to you?

People - it is as it ever was: WIN his/her heart/keep his/her heart and he's/she's yours.

I propose a NEW definition of "damaged goods".

Henceforth - "damaged goods" will be "damaged persons", since persons are NOT commodities and therefore not 'goods', and only truly destroyed persons however they have been destroyed, alcohol, drugs, torture, mental devastation, will be referred to as "damaged persons".

Are you with me here?

Mar 26, 2008
FROM UNDER THE BLANKETS
I am sick, sick, ill, sick and I'm staying here until I'm better!
Cancel my appointments!

Call the ministering teddybears!

ABOUT AUTO-REPLIES
"I have one!!
I actually DO have a great autoreply, but UNFORTUNATELY there are those amongst us that do not understand WHAT an *autoreply* is. They seem to think it is something we wrote and copied and send it to particular people, NOT that it is like an answering machine saying we got the message and will email back IF we think we match or anything else. I would have thought *AUTO* explained it."

I have to agree with her! GUYS - AUTO REPLY IS SENT BY THE COMPUTER ALL ON ITS OWN. Once it has been set up, her involvement ends. No she does NOT have to push a button or anything else. Everyone sending her an email, gets the same message.

Understand now?

Mar 27, 2008
YA KNOW
Males get tired of hearing "read my profile" to the point
where they just filter that out. They do NOT go and read it,
of course. I can tell they do this because males under the
age of 40 send me "Hey, wanna have fun?" emails. They
seem to be unaware that I delete all emails from those
under 40 without reading them.

Trust me guys - you do NOT want to receive an email from
me when you do NOT match my criteria. I will not mince
my words in such circumstances.

For example: what do you think this means

Currently not looking.

And how about this:

**Must be between 40 and 60 years of age, 6 foot tall,
unencumbered, furry, nearby, and possess more than
half a brain. Strong enough to be fun but warm enough
to be my teddybear.**

Yeah, yeah, you're going to say "no harm in trying" yes, but
if I find it annoying, you can imagine the other women find
it equally unappealing.

ADJUST YOUR TARGETING

it will save you from so much pain

LINGERING DEBAUCHERY
Having once been "Kittened" does a man ever recover? It is
a point of discussion because I receive emails to this day

from those who have once, or twice, shared themselves with me.

"Then you walked in, smiling and stark naked
- beautifully, beautifully so....
I exclaimed in delighted
(and somewhat aroused) surprise.
We exchanged a few idle pleasantries,
as though neither your presence in the chapel
nor your nakedness were in the least unusual."

How a person lingers in your memory and flits through your dreams leaving a trail of "kitten prints" behind is amazing.

"I watched you cross the graveled alleyway
and enter the large, drab, building
on the other side. There were people
inside that building, people I could
hear but not see. They were clearly
waiting for you, and they were
in a festive mood.
You disappeared inside....
I did not follow farther -
but I very much wanted to...."

I remember. I remember them with kindness. I hope they forgive life and find the peace they seek; in spite of those "kitten prints" I seem to have left behind.

May you find what you seek, my friend.

DISCOUNTING

Men have an unfortunate habit of discounting a woman's anger. "Oh so you're talking to me now?". This makes it seem as if she has no right to be angry and no right to express her anger.

How would you feel if she said "whatever" to you when you're legitimately pissed off at her?

"Just a guy getting his boxers into a twist over nothing. You know what men are. If you don't stroke their 'egos', they can't take it."

"Whatever! Talk to the hand, buddyboy!"

No, you wouldn't like to "receive" so I advise you not to "give".

" I do not like aggressive and forward women, personally or sexually."

Then perhaps you should not be speaking to me at all since to do so is wasting my time.

Whatever, prat!

(I ran the comment by both men and women. Yeah, that's an insult given the context.)

Not ALL men do this. There are men who are not afraid to acknowledge their errors and apologize to the women in their lives. I am not a coward. I can admit mine. I have made a few errors and have apologized for them as is proper.

417

No, it wasn't just the above that inspired this post. Other women have of late been dealing with the same sort of thing. It gets VERY tiresome.

Don't make this your error as well.

Now returning you to your regularly scheduled blog.

BEST COMMENT RECEIVED: "And in some cases, discounting that anger over and over could become hazardous to one's health... **batting eyelashes**"

Mar 28, 2008
SIGNING UP
Maserati is having a drawing to win one of their cars equipped with Bose's best sound system so Grandkitten #1 and I wandered over to Tyson's II to sign up!

While we were there, #1 had her first escalator ride and elevator ride. She loved it! All the shops and all the people - she was fascinated!

We stopped by and signed up, then we wandered over to Levenger's and Crane's and stopped by DeBeers to scope out the diamonds - Mom's a stockholder - and then we swooped into Williams-Sonoma where she nibbled a chocolate chip mini-pancake.

#1 carried her small bags, we had made small purchases in all the stores we visited, very proudly. She was having lots of fun!

Then it was time for her 'invective lesson' as we headed south on the Interstate 95 HOV lanes trying to get down them before they closed in spite of those idiots who do the speed limit in the left hand lane.

A quick stop to pick up a few grocery items and then we were home!

A busy afternoon!
How was yours?

Mar 29, 2008
PICKING BONES
Once again, I'm being reminded that often it is simply just best to say...nothing. Although I do have a few bones to pick, that is what I shall do...say nothing; especially since I do not for one moment believe that my remonstrances will have any effect at all.

This is what happens when sincerity is doubted. You stop thinking you can say anything. You feel you have to tidy away the emotional content, refine your thought and language and in truth - make it all "pretty". Only speaking what they want to hear, when and how they wish to hear it.

thus the lies begin

What course of action do you recommend?
Clear the Air
or
Let Sleeping Dogs Lie

Mar 30, 2008
GLAD I'M CELT
Just finished reading The Bookseller of Kabul by A. Seierstad. Damn, I am SOOOOO glad that my ethnic group is Celtic, both p and q varieties!

Why? Because, they are one of the few groups that prize warrior-women, courageous women, smart women, and strong women - along with the more 'normal' traits attributed to women.

This book is not as 'hard to take' as <u>Burned Alive</u> by Saoud but the systematic physical, emotional, and mental destruction of women is the same.

What is new, is the depiction of how Afghan life also twists and destroys the men who then turn on their own and each other.

For example: little boys are permitted to 'back talk' their mothers and beat their sisters. When these boys are older, they may be told to kill their erring sisters by their mother who is acting upon orders of the father.

War tends to do that, of course, especially when power is sought for its own sake and you forget you're all Afghans in favor of being this tribe/family/sect or that.

These ills are also not confined to Afghanistan or Palestine but also occur in various places around the world where "status" matters more than "accomplishment" and "honor" can be and is purchased.

I recommend the book even though most women will feel the need to hurl it across the room in anger.

BEST COMMENT RECEIVED: "I recently read a similar book, <u>Nine Parts of Desire, The Hidden World of Islamic Woman</u> by Geraldine Brooks. Came close to hurling it across the room several times, and even worse, I was filled with a soul deep sadness upon finishing it. Based on your recommendation though I'm gonna pick yours up too. Knowledge is power...(and YES, thank God my ancestors valued me also)."

MECHANICS
Chapter Five

The Three Date Rule. You have three dates to decide if there is anything possible between you two. Using the tradition form, he invites she out for two dates and she invites him out for the third. The one who invites, pays for the date. A date is a specific event at a specific date, time, and place. It is not "to hang out". When inviting, make it to something your date would enjoy.

Let us suppose he has invited her out for two dates. If she does not then invite him out for the third, he is at liberty to assume that she is not interested in pursuing the relationship. It would be adult of her to tell him so but some women have difficulty being direct and some men have problems with accepting rejection so I am leaving you an 'easy out'.

The Two Year Rule. The three dates have been successful and you two have continued dating each other. You two have gradually revealed yourselves to one another and the gilt is off the lily. It has been two years. Now it is time to say yes or no. In the parlance of the highway robber, "stand and deliver!" Will you or will you not be wed? If not, please part as friends. If yes, congratulations.

This may seem too harsh or too rapid, but consider this – where can you two go from here? You cannot date forever. If marriage is not to be, you should let go and move along accepting that you have at least gained a very good friend, but not your life-mate.

After the first several round of dates, you two may begin to hang out together and socialize as a couple if you choose to do so, but I do not recommend this until you two are affianced. Remember that until you two are engaged to be wed, you are not dating exclusively. The idea that one only dates 'one at a time' is terribly wasteful and limiting. The need to be exclusive is also a mark of insecurity. Do not ask it. Do not agree to it. If your partner disagrees, then he/she is not the person for you. If he/she wants exclusivity, then he/she has to agree to marry you.

The point here is that as you two grow closer together over time, you will find yourself becoming increasingly exclusive of others. It should be happening as a normal gradual process. You two spend more and more time together and therefore do not have time or the desire to see others. If this is how it happens, fine. If he/she demands it at the outset, that is being presumptuous and weak. Just because you are dating does not mean you own him/her. Review what I said about making demands.

Remember the adage:
Marry in Haste, Repent at Leisure.
Do NOT rush the process!

Next week: Chapter Six

Mar 31, 2008
"NO PENIS PIX"
Some might not like the look of men but I am a connoisseur and am deeply 'appreciative' of the well set-up 40-

something and 50-something fur-clad male. Other males can also be quite attractive. *EG*

But males are best "appreciated" in their entirety.

APRIL
2008

Apr 1, 2008

HAPPY APRIL FOOLS DAY!!!

the traditional birthday
of all
cats
large and small

RELATIONSHIPS 101
"I don't think relationships usually fall apart through one
dramatic blow-up. I believe it's the daily grind of "you
didn't take out the trash" or the accumulated arguments
swept under the rug that ultimately stop a couple from
opening their bodies with love and trust. At least, that's my
theory." -BPB*

Yes, the daily drip of poison erodes relationships. And it
doesn't matter if the poison is words or deeds both done or
not done. Once the tender care for each other is lost, the
love begins to fade, the desire slips away, and the
relationship fails.

Because your partner feels you do not value them.

Take a moment to scratch your darling between his/her ears
and give him/her a kiss on the cheek for just as small things
taketh away so to can small things bringeth back.

*referring to: "No way, you asshole."

Apr 2, 2008

CONFLICT RESOLUTION

He got upset about his wife doing something, nothing terrible you understand. She felt attacked and got defensive. He over-reacted in return. She then went completely to an extreme position. He feels like a total moron. She seeks vindication for her position. He tries to get her to move from this extreme position.

And all they do is argue.

The REAL message he was sending her was: I miss you! (I'm lonely, tired, scared, bored, feeling very insecure, and I wish I was home with you.) She didn't understand that. She missed the message.

There are two subjects here - the "apparent subject", what she did, and the "real subject", that he misses her. Always address the "real subject". When done correctly, you can safely ignore the "apparent subject".

The way out of this mess is for HER to send HIM a warm verbal bear hug and tell him that he is her heart's delight with all the passion she has in her. She has to squeeze all of the stuffing out of him and be his glowing golden girl.

The arguing will then end.

REASSURE & REAFFIRM

Apr 3, 2008

-from a Dating Personality test

"The Dirty Little Secret: Deliberate Gentle Sex Master (DGSM) Innocent but fundamentally sexual, You are the Dirty Little Secret.

426

Few women have the confidence for sex mastery, and among nice girls, like you, it's almost unheard of. So congratulations. You've had plenty of adventures, but you've remained a kind, thoughtful person. Your friends appreciate your exploits. They even live vicariously through you.

You seek pleasure, but you're not irresponsible. You are organized and cautious, and you choose your lovers wisely. One, you don't like dirtbags. And two, you like to maintain control. Or at least lose it selectively. You might notice that older men single you out. They have an eye for your sensual nature. Take it as a compliment.

You enjoy making people happy, and it's inevitable that many guys will fall harder for you than you for them. You're not completely comfortable in a serious, long-term relationship right now. Our guess is that the key to extended happiness will be finding a responsible, but kinky, mate."

Some of that is correct!

FLUFFY BUNNY-NESS
You have seen them. Those extremely romantic persons who believe in fairies, tea parties, and making daisy-chains. Come on, you know you have!
They also talk about soulmates, having this 'connection', raw milk, and organic this that or the other. They look for others to 'rescue' them. "My life didn't begin until I met you." and "I will always cherish our love." Rose petals on the bedsheets.

Whatever.

I always question such positions because, for me, cute, charming, and fluffiness should be innate. That is, part of you just like that gap between your front teeth and the fact that you've never been any good at gymnastics. Mathematics, yes; gymnastics, no.

Being innate, your fluffiness does not need to be expressed. You just are cute the same way you are bi-laterally symmetrical. Like the time you went to Home Depot wearing your house slippers and only realized it when you got home, being charming just happens.

There are those who have an almost professional ability to turn their charm on and off like a light switch but these people are often viewed with the gravest of suspicion, as they should be,
since that means your charm is engineered and not part of your DNA.

So the next time you're found giggling with the driver in the front seat like two ninnies, or trying to impale a cricket with a dagger-like letter opener by holding it suspended above said cricket and dropping it, or hopping on one leg while watering the lawn - don't worry.

It's just your fluffy bunny-ness manifesting itself.

Apr 4, 2008

LOVE AT FIRST SIGHT
I do NOT believe in love at first sight.

428

LUST and INFATUATION at first sight, however, DO exist and while LUST is perfectly fine, INFATUATION is not.

People often mistake INFATUATION for LOVE. But the infatuated are in denial and do not see flaws in their beloved while those who truly LOVE see the flaws and would not change any of them for that would make the beloved someone else. The INFATUATED put their love upon a pedestal while the very idea of seeing their beloved atop such a thing makes those who LOVE laugh.

The "hearts & flowers" idea of love is really INFATUATION. It is all high drama and wild emotion. LOVE, however, evolves over time; deepening and strengthening. INFATUATION screams in regardless of character and worth, while LOVE slowly grows from compatibility. INFATUATION rocks your world. LOVE is a recognition of something you always knew.

The deep abiding love that you marry runs through your entire being like Pachbel's Canon in D Major. There are no uncertainties, mind games, and doubts. There is no drama and no wild emotion. Instead, there is a sense of care and mutual respect along with the desire.

Do you see the difference that makes all the difference or do you still believe in "love at first sight"?

Apr 5, 2008

PARTY!!
Last night's M&G at Skinifatz was a BLAST!!! I had a good time although I didn't get to dance.

429

Then today my "partner in crime" AKA "the Good Witch" threw a belated birthday lunch for me today at Mike's in Springfield. Hmmm, 3 ladies and 3 teddybears - sounds like a party to me!! We dined on mince and slices of quince and a Happy Birthday cheesecake! The card was perfect and the presents also just right!

Thank you, Good Witch and the recently promoted at work and therefore richer yet overworked BB, and passionate kisses to each of the three teddybears: Je, 3C, & DD2.

Of course, the question was asked: do we recognize each other when we're all wearing clothes?

PHOTO CALL
Three, or more, unbashful males to stand hip to hip, sans clothing, for a "Here Kitten, Kitten, Kitten! Look what we have for you!" photo. Proper 'attitude' is more desired than physical buffness. Faces will NOT be required as the photo is supposed to be from knee caps to belly buttons ONLY.

Some days - you just have to do it - ya know?
LOL

A CLASS?
It has been proposed, twice now!, that I teach a glass on my techniques. One internet friend from CA asked me to fly out to SexFest and teach a class! Bring a few males for the demonstrations and several hundreds of my books, she said. Alas! I don't have the time and I hate Las Vegas.
It is far too tacky for me.

If enough WOMEN are interested, minimum of 4, in such a class and they are willing to split the costs of a hotel suite, we could do it one Wednesday after the Richmond M&G at Bailey's. Bring your own male.

For those men wishing to volunteer, the requirements are: the ability to be naked in a crowded room without losing hardness, and being able to take it without moving or having to do something. Verbally expressing your delight is permitted. The ability to talk about how it felt, after class, in coherent and precise terms is a plus.

Please leave a comment if interested. Feel free to note down what techniques you're esp. interested in or any concerns you want addressed.

Apr 6, 2008

WHEN NOT WRITING MY MEMOIRS
I have been reading:

Short Stories by P. G. Wodehouse
Sense and Sensibility by Jane Austen
Foreign Affairs by Alison Lurie

- thus moving from the frankly hilarious to the delicately subtle and thence to the deeply pragmatic.

What have you been reading?

TODAY
The SRM turns 53 today. He is not terribly happy about this. However, I still wish him

HAPPY BIRTHDAY!!

And remind him, that Life is Good!

KISSES!!

THE BLUES
We all have those times when nothing, but nothing, fits the mood except the Blues.
From 'smoking barroom' to the more modern strains it is "misery shared is misery halved".

You may not recognize him in this guise, but Jim Byrnes is a bluesman.

And he's right up there with Waters & Wolf in my estimation. But I am not expert. I am just a woman who is a long-time fan of Mssr.s King, Clapton & Cale to name but a few you might know.

I recommend you listen to Byrnes' "The River" from his album House of Refuge produced by Black Hen.

Apr 7, 2008

YA KNOW
Periodically, I get patted on my head by certain persons who are fortunate I let them live. The latest of these incidents occurred when I asked for a translation of the following lyrics

"I got a 13th level halfling fighter-thief
Got 7 hex die on my Backstab."

432

from a song by Deaf Pedestrians. I was informed that my requiring such a translation proved that I am definitely NOT a geek. But that's okay. We like you anyway.

Grrrrrrrrrrrrrrrrrr.

FRUITLESS BUT FUN

Here are a few ideas for when you want to waste time, for example: while waiting on hold.

1. design garments when you can't sew to save your soul.

2. design automobiles, jewelry, china patterns houses, estate layouts - anything really

3. Plan what to do with $220 million.

4. Write music when you aren't musical.

5. Pick a war, any war, and plan your win.

What would you do if only you could? So come on and "empire build" - it beats actually listening to the "you're on hold music".

Life: ya gotta live it!

WAITING TO HAVE SEX

There is a philosophy out there, esp. among women, that sex should be special, meaningful, and only done between committed lovers in the context of having a relationship. So they find it scary and use expressions like "moving too fast", "If I have sex with him too soon, he won't respect me." "He'll think I'm easy." Yadda, yadda, yadda.

433

This is what I call the "hearts & flowers" attitude toward sex and it belongs with tea parties, and playing house with your stuffed animals - i.e. childhood.

A more mature understanding of sex involves being able to appreciate sex for what it is as something both part of and separate from the relationship.

Separate because sex = play. Sex is fun and orgasms are great! If you like him/her and want to take him/her out for a spin - wonderful! Enjoy! Most people would be more than happy to be taken out for a spin. Please be responsible and practice safe sex.

As part of a relationship, sex is an expression of that relationship. If the relationship has problems, the sex has problems and vice versa. Sex can neither fix nor destroy a relationship.

Based on the above, waiting to have sex makes no sense. You have sex if you want to have sex. If you don't, then you don't. You do not have to justify your decision or apologize for your desire. This applies to both genders, btw, even though etiquette demands that the lady retains control. If you respect yourself, your partner will respect you whatever you decide.

Are you with me so far?

Sex is never meaningless, even when it is NSA. Your style tells your partner almost all about you and that may be more than you want him/her to know. Generous or selfish? Real or fake? Skilled or unskilled? Fun or not? Those who truly enjoy sex and their partners cannot hide any of that. Their delight is manifest.

434

Sex even with the same partner is subtly different each time. Pay attention and you will see it. This is one reason why subsequent interludes are usually better than the first. You learn to 'read' each other. You learn how to please each other. This is why once is never enough.

This is the scary part.

You cannot pretend when you're naked. As you come to know each other sexually, your regard for your partner changes - for both better and worse. This mutual increased understanding can be frightening to both of you. How you handle this clearly shows what kind of person you really are. You cannot hide now.

So what's it going to be?

For me, this is when individual men become interesting as friends. Previous to this point, yes, I like them, else I wouldn't even be there. The question now is how will they, and can they, become a part of my life and I a part of his?

Decisions. Decisions.
But if he isn't putting out by the second date, I'm gone, baby! *EG*

Apr 8, 2008

ON BEING FASTIDIOUS
"Possessing or displaying careful, meticulous attention to detail. Difficult to please; exacting." - OED.

Perhaps it is the feline in me, but I enjoy cleanliness, tidiness, and appropriateness in all things. Of course there are times when one plays in the mud, but when playtime is over - clean up, thank you.

But being fastidious is more than just being clean, neat and tidy. It is also being appropriate in behavior, dress, decor, and so on.
Getting it 'just right'. This is not difficult. At first, some thought may be required but soon, being fastidious becomes a habit.

Yes, incidents occur where I have 'made errors' - whereupon I hide my face in my paws, and apologize profusely. I don't need to relate what those incidents are - but yes, they were "buzz killers". It is no matter if others have these moments. "These things happen." It is another thing entirely when I do it.

My standards have been difficult to maintain lately. The grandkittens are here and they have not yet learned the habit of tidiness and will smear Beefaroni in their hair and all over their faces and clothes. Fingerpainting with diaper contents. Not picking up their toys. *Sigh*.

Now I have to go and bathe. Excuse me.

THE MULTI-ORGASMIC MAN
Yes, my lovelies, it can be done! Men can have more than one orgasm per erection. They remain, however, only capable of one ejaculation per orgasm so the trick is to have the orgasm and not have the ejaculation.

Step 1 is to understand that the orgasm is separate from the ejaculation. The orgasm is the flexing of the pc muscle. While the flexing has to occur for ejaculation; a man can have the muscle flex (the orgasm) and not ejaculate.

436

Step 2 is to practice this pc muscle through doing kegels and by practicing edge play.

Kegels - using the pc muscle alone stop and start the stream while urinating.

Edge play - get as close to orgasm as you can without actually tripping over into ejaculating.
The longer you practice this and the closer you can get, the more likely your will become multi-orgasmic.

Your erection might remain firm throughout or it might wax and wane but until you have ejaculated you will avoid the dreaded refractory period. Avoiding the refractory period is a good thing, guys.

Your partner can help you with this practicing by changing movements just before you ejaculate in such a way that she hits your 'reset' button just enough to stop the ejaculation but not enough to ruin the orgasm or to cause you o lose your erection. Helping you with your edge play.

There is another method. This is where he orgasms and ejaculates but she keeps on going and going and going in such a way that she forces another orgasm out of him. Gentlemen who experience 'pain' or 'sensitivity' after ejaculation should be aware that this is a 'false' signal.

The brain is not used to this extra level of stimulation and therefore doesn't know what to do with it and classifies it as 'pain'. The cure is to take deep breaths, relax, and just keep going - you have to go through it to get through it kind of thing.

When you hear of a man "doubling" or "tripling" this is what they are referring to - having more orgasms per erection than a man normally does.

Unfortunately, having multiple orgasms seems to wear them out and they are useless for hours afterward. (dammit!)

PLAYTIME WITH TEDDYBEARS
THE LINGERING WILD

A new mood this time. You are more confident and more eager. Scotch and cookies! Witness that you beat me getting naked and you were first on the bed. Between laughter and kisses we began our dance. Before long you were on your back and I was slowly licking down your body with your sounds of pleasure in my ears. Mmmmm very tasty. Shall I tickle your thighs? Hmmm. Then onto fellatio until you can't take any more without losing it. A slip and slide and then you're inside of me. Oh my yes! I move and ejaculate and orgasm all over your loins; driving, driving, driving until it takes you too over the brink and you crash into your own orgasm. We're laughing and gasping for breath as we stumble out to the sofa for drinks. It is good to see you again, my friend. What? Another scotch for me? How nice! Good thing the ice cubes melted so you couldn't put your idea into operation. Kittens are not fond of cold. Somehow we ended up on the bed again this time you were slowly licking down my body - you do that so well! - mmmmm oral and then oral with manual! Slide inside as I wrap my legs around your hips ah! feels so good! Mmmmm you move so well. More orgasms for me but no? None for you? Oh dear. I'll have to try harder. So I slide around your body, kissing the nape of your neck, caressing your skin, kissing you here, licking you there, a

438

bit of claw, a bit of tongue, a kiss, some murmured words, a little nuzzling until I'm atop you again and moving, moving, moving forcing the pace, changing the movement, more baby. Come on. And You did. You came and then came again. Yes, Twice! This time you didn't make it to the sofa but sat on the floor. I sat cross-legged on a towel spread on your leather sofa, nibbling cookies while you caught your breath. We talked about this and that. You have been thoroughly "Kittened" my friend but do not despair, you will recover soon. Cookie?

Apr 9, 2008

NOTA BENE
All Playtime with Teddybears posts accurately depict actual events. Some allowances have to be made for orgasmic delight, of course, and the names have been removed for obvious reasons but these are the things I enjoy when one-on-one.

Apr 10, 2008

RE-WRITE
While waiting for the Richmond M&G to begin, I re-read several of my books. One seriously requires a re-write so that's been added, along with a few corrections elsewhere, to my agenda.

Sometimes people review their lives and wish for a "re-write" or a "do over". We have all certainly had our boneheaded moments. None of us are without our flaws and missteps. But one cannot re-write one's life. What is done really is done.

But other than these, would you, quite seriously, want to go back and do it all over again not knowing what you know now? Oh sure, if our memories were left intact - no problem. But the memories would be erased in such a reversal. You have to un-do before you can re-do.

I know that HELL NO would be my answer. I'm not going through all of that again.

Who you are is a mix of character and experience with those two operating with and upon each other. You were a different you back then. Chances are, as in the movie Groundhog Day, you'd do the same thing all over again. Without memory, you'd be caught up in the same life again.

For me, the essence of life is to go forward with courage and joy.

Would you do a re-write of your life? Why or why not?

ON OUTING
Socially "outing" someone for something is an act of sanctimony that reflects badly upon the person(s) doing the "outing".

You can attempt to rationalize it all you want. Your rationalizations do not change the fact that you have behaved poorly. And it does not matter if the person being "outed" has made or has not made errors; that is irrelevant. Just because person A has made a mistake does not mean that person B must make a mistake too.

Do unto others as you would have them do unto you.

If you would not mind having all of your dirty little secrets broadcast to the world, then fine - we will be more than happy to tell all we know to everyone who will listen.

Until such time as you want to have other people snooping in your business, keep your nose out of other people's business.

Apr 11, 2008

COMMITMENT
I have heard some women say that men fear commitment. I cannot say the same. In my view, men are no more afraid to commit than women.

It just might be that they are not willing to commit to you for whatever reason.

It just might be that women are too quick to commit.

You simply cannot demand commitment. He/she has to commit on their own, in their own way, and in their own time.

You cannot demand unquestioning loyalty from friends. You cannot demand undying devotion from lovers. For such things do not exist. If you would have friends - expect to be questioned. If you would have lovers you must expect their devotion to evolve over time.

So too you cannot demand total and complete commitment from him/her - the one you would marry.

All you can do is to DESERVE it.

You deserve commitment by being true to yourself, by seeing your adored clearly for who and what he/she really is and accepting him/her "as is", and loving him/her anyway, and by trusting in the bond between you.

The hardest things to do are being true to yourself and yet trusting the bond between you and your beloved. The balancing act this requires is no mean feat. But this is where you prove your worth.

Regretfully, there will be times when your commitment will not be recognized or valued no matter how much you deserve it. There will also be times when another may commitment to you when you do NOT want that commitment from him/her.

In these cases, you will have to accept defeat and move on or help him/her to move on. Either can be difficult, but more so the helping the undesired to move on - especially if he/she or has been 'future-thinking' and dreaming up a happy future life that includes you.

My recommendations:

1. be faster to become friends than lovers
2. be faster to decline than to commit
3. accept reality
4. once mutual committed - stay committed

No one is perfect and in this life, hell & high water will surely come. This is why commitment is so highly valued and desired. But like all human attributes, commitment too will evolve and change over time - hopefully becoming deeper and richer - but of this, there is no guarantee.

No one gender is more or less able to commit than the other. Just this of that person is more or less able or ready to commit to this or that other person. Please notice that all of the above is gender-neutral and is focused upon the individual.

Do not make the mistake of NOT seeing the individual as an individual.

Apr 12, 2008

INTER-MALE COMPETITION
Males tend to compete with other males - and not only 'professionally' but also socially. Even if 'friendly', there remains a bit of an edge to it.

Money is a handy way to assign a value to a male. It is somewhat 'unworthy' but it certainly is convenient. He with more wins.

Women is another but here it isn't just a case of 'quantity' but also one of 'quality'. This area is more subjective because each man's desires differ. Generally speaking women with greater reproductive value, of better social standing, of more wealth, of greater intelligence, of greater beauty, and of better character are rated higher than their less fortunate sisters.

But it isn't only having women but a matter of keeping women. Therefore, married men have a higher social standing than single men. Oh, yes, married men may say they envy the single 'player' male but they don't really mean it; else they'd be getting divorced and spending their lives 'skirt-chasing' too. But they aren't.

And then there are his children. Successful children enhance the social standing of a man since he must have 'raised them right'. Having grandchildren who are also successful is just icing on the cake but what's cake without the icing?

Yes, men do consider 'taller is better' and other physical factors, but those factors aren't as important as what a man does and has when it comes to social competition.

It is fun to watch the 'assessment' when two men meet for the first time

(Women compete too but that's another post)

Apr 13, 2008

NOTE TO PUPPIES
To all of those boys who say "age is just a state of mind" or "age is just a number" - that is immaterial. I do not care if YOU like older women either. All of that is beside the point.

This older woman does NOT want you.

And don't try to tell me how mature you are or that I don't know what I'm missing or it is my loss. You are arguing against a lady's preference and showing me disrespect by NOT accepting my preference for males near my own age. Doing either is not the mark of a mature male.

Arguing with me and showing me disrespect will not get you laid.

Guys - if she's NOT leaping into your arms or bed with flaming desire - you do not want her.
Simple as that.

If you do NOT meet my criteria, you may now stop emailing me. Thank you.

PARTYTIME!!
SEXUAL FEAST

A couple invited me, and whichever teddybear(s) I cared to bring, to a huge party they were having last night. 100 persons from 3 sites converged on The Cottage up in PA for a sexual feast.

And a sexual feast it was! I began with W. W and I are old friends and for some reason, he has but to see me and he's ready. Lovely man. Then there was B. With B. I can be as wicked as I might desire. Nothing is out of bounds with this bear! Wow! The wilder I got, the more he enjoyed it! Next came my host, M - you owe me one, buddy! Catch me later. Now I enjoyed B in the blacklight room and we had an audience watching the play. And it was back to this room we ALL went for a huge group fuck. M. did catch me later closely followed by D. Then it was intermission. During intermission, The Cottage held its 50/50 drawing and I was selected to pick out the winning ticket. This required me to show that I did not have any tickets on me. So a quick strip off of my dress and a rock n roll twirl about clearly proved the point. Then back on with my dress and we got on with the drawing. After intermission I was with one gentleman whose name I unfortunately did not catch - he was great! - and then C.

I ran my knee into one of the bed platforms during this last interlude so it was off to the hot tub for me. C, G and I did some flirty fun while there, but it was midnight. So a quick change and I was on my way home!

6 teddybears in 4 hours and innumerable orgasms!

EXCELLENT PARTY

Apr 14, 2008

MEANT TO BE?
I have my irritations with a few commonly used phrases but "it was/was not meant to be" - really torques my jaws.

I think it is because it removes the power of rational selection from people. They can just shrug off the responsibility for making their own choices this way. They can also shrug off their errors.

Relationships are not easy but they are not all THAT difficult that they require something akin to 'divine intervention', which is what is implied by the expression "meant to be".

Most of the time, the choices we make in our lives determine the subsequent course of our lives. There is nothing 'divine' or 'fatalistic' about it. We make our choices and the consequences just naturally follow.

Certain choices lead to unhappy lives. Certain choices lead to happy lives. A bit of rational thought and you'll know which choices belong to each group. There's nothing 'magic' about this.

446

So before you next use the expression "meant to be" -
reflect a bit and see if you cannot map out what led to this
and how you ended up being where you are today.

How did your choices work out? What choices are now
before you? How can you learn to make better choices? I
can tell you, that making wise choices becomes easier with
practice. Always look at the possible consequences - all of
them! - before you make a decision.

Life can be grand but you have to make it so - you cannot
just say it "was meant to be".

BEST COMMENT RECEIVED: "If it's all fate then where
is free will? Responsibility is the free will's ability to
respond to the negatives or positives which life throws at
us." - from A

THE TEXAS POLYGAMISTS
416 kids and some of their under-age mothers removed
from a sect's "ranch" in Texas - it has been in the news
lately. Perhaps you have read about it.

This is NOT in accordance with polyamory. What this is, is
masculine egotism at its worst.

Polyamory, both polygamy and polyandry, is between
consenting ADULTS who exist in the greater world and
who fully understand the ramifications of their actions.
NOT between confined small groups of people hiding from
authorities like rats in the sewers.

Anytime males begin 'marrying' ignorant youngsters who are NOT of legal 'marriageable' age, you have exploitation and abuse.

How would you feel if your son or daughter was married off at age 13 and 14 to some adult in their 50's? No further schooling, no career - only subjugation and children afterwards and forever more.

These sects go even further - the leader can dissolve marriages and tell her to get with this man over here and expect to be obeyed. Usually she is so beaten down that she will do it.

What kind of a life is that?
How can such an existence and such behavior be considered "godly"?
What possible positive contribution can this kind of thing give to anyone or to any society at large?

This is what happens when you think of people as being 'commodities', women as nothing more than the means of procreation and as trophies in the aggregate "I have more wives than you so I'm the better man", and other persons who should be looking after these girls - aren't and don't, and what happens when women do not behave as the tigresses they should be when it comes to children.

ON PROSTITUTION
The selling of sex for remuneration.

The question is: is he/she selling a SKILL/TALENT or is he/she selling their bodies for another's use as a COMMODITY?

Can it ever be clear cut?

I think that this lack of clarity is the crux of most people's problem with this "profession". Is sex for money actually a profession? Where the client is paying for skilled talent in a specialized area.

Forget for the moment about criminality, morality, and the tawdriness and violence surrounding this job. Just think on this one issue: Skill or Commodity?

Does whether we're talking on the courtesan/gigolo level versus streetwalker/rentboy level make a difference?

I feel it is unfortunate that anyone is reduced to such a level but admit that for some, I cannot think of another job that pays as well for unskilled or semi-skilled persons. The highly skilled, I do not feel we need to worry about as those people have a way of building their own futures. I do admit it is a difficult life to lead.

Decriminalizing prostitution does not solve the problem either. Europe still has the same problems we have with it. Skill or commodity?

For once I have no solution. Do you?

Apr 15, 2008

EXPELLED BY BEN STEIN
"Synopsis
Intrigued by the recent trend of scientists, journalists, philosophers, and teachers who have been ostracized and discredited for daring to suggest that mankind may be the product of intelligent design rather than a random fluke in

the cosmic scheme of things, Ben Stein sets out on a thought-provoking journey to investigate the persecution of the many by the select few. Why is it that in recent years, anyone who dares to question Darwin's theory of evolution is ridiculed and scorned for simply suggesting that there may be evidence that life on Earth could be part of a grander scheme? What is it that frightens followers of Darwin so much they feel the need to violently extinguish any argument that goes against their theories concerning the origins of life? These are just some of the questions that Stein asks as he travels the globe to speak with the supporters of both theories, and ponders the reasons why believing in a higher power has seemingly become a crime in the eyes of the powerful elite. ~ Jason Buchanan, All Movie Guide"

Why are they scorned? Because they are wrong. Duh! Intelligent Design is just another try in a long, long list of mankind trying to make themselves feel "special" and "superior".

And "the persecution of the many by the select few"? You have got to be kidding me! Intelligent Design is the intellectual equivalent of "a fairy came down, waved her little wand (PLANG!) and then said go out and play". Who is actually going to admit to believing that?

Let's bring out the big guns - how can a single cell evolve into a complex multi-cellular being? Every pregnancy does precisely that. From fertilized ovum to baby in 9 months.

Yes, there are thousands of intermediate forms. Of course, you don't see mis-matches because mis-matches between creature and environment die out. Extinction - ever heard of it? Therefore the world WOULD seem to run like "clockwork"

To see how utterly silly all of this Intelligent Design is - simply substitute the word GRAVITY for the words DARWINISM, EVOLUTION and so forth.

"I don't believe in evolution" then becomes "I don't believe in gravity!" Whereupon I'd invite you to step off a three story building.

Neither gravity nor evolution cares whether you believe in it or not. Both will continue to operate as they have - with you or without you.

When it comes to science - hard, cold, impersonal science - the ONLY thing that matters is fact supported by empirical evidence, reproducible experimental results, and the mathematics.

Your personal beliefs are both irrelevant and immaterial. One movie I will NOT be seeing.

PERSONAS
Each of us here presents a certain picture of ourselves. - the social butterfly, the diva, the thorough-going bitch, the he-man, the nice guy, the whatever you will.

But remember, you're only seeing a slice of that person.

Even if you're going to every meet n greet, party, brunch, lunch, whatever available, you only see what others wish you to see. You can surmise but you do not know.

451

For all of my alleged 'openness' there are things I will never talk about with anyone no matter how close to me or how important to me, or I to them, they become.

I am sure it is the same with you.

Stop thinking that you know. Stop pretending that you know. Stop acting like you know.

You don't know.

It is just a persona.

Apr 16, 2008

ABIOGENESIS
In answer to Ben Stein's question in the trailer for his new movie "Expelled" which I was unfortunate to see last night while watching tv...abiogenesis.

All the research is not yet in but the latest information, in the short form, is life began as VIRUSES in a reducing (no oxygen) atmosphere.

Since viruses exist in the gazillions and since viruses are generally speaking mere scraps of molecules and since viruses generally appear dead until they enter a suitable environment anyway, this seems very likely.

Life back then was not measured in heartbeats but rather in chemical reactions.

BTW the no oxygen in the early atmosphere is most important. Oxygen is an extremely dangerous chemical being both highly reactive and poisonous. If the early earth

452

had had an oxygen atmosphere it would have blown the planet apart what with all the volcanoes and meteor impacts going on back then. It was little more than a black and red planet back then - hot lava, cooled lava.

I find the history of earth and life upon it fascinating!

PERSONALLY
I get a kick out of men telling me they're going to "rock my world" or "give me 8 to 10 devastating orgasms".

Oh, goody!
Think you can? *EG*

As to "rocking my world": Fellas, you know I adore you, but really, let's face facts. I have been doing this whole sex thing for 40 years now, I swing, do groups, exhaust the men during gangbangs, and you have no idea how high the bar is set.

As to "giving me 8 to 10 devastating orgasms": is that all? As one lady has said, "not multiorgasmic...polyorgasmic". Plus, you don't "give" orgasms, you "assist" in my having orgasms.(You know this because if she's not into it, she's not getting one no matter what you do.)

I thank you for the thought and for the offer but you know...it isn't nice to make promises you probably cannot keep.

Instead try being witty, say you'd like to try, you'd kill small rodents for the chance (kitten, mouse, you get it), you'd bring scotch!, you'd let me shred your pillows while hiding under the bed (inside joke) - get the idea.

I'm not here for 'the challenge', I'm not here for the 'ego boost' - no. I am here for the FUN!

You with me, baby?

Apr 17, 2008

SINCE I'VE BEEN HERE...
Several things have happened in addition to the attempted blackmail and the very real stalking you understand.

I have met with insincerity, heartbreak, and betrayal but I have also found good and decent people who have become very dear friends - usually where I least expected to. I have found cowards and knaves but also courage of a kind.

I am telling you this because very soon now, this blog will stop. It has served its purpose.
Those who wish to pour over it seeking tidbits of information may do so with my free will. You never did realize that you could, and always could, leave comments did you? Only my stalker was ever blocked from doing so.

And you have witnessed all of it. The joy, the births, the deaths, the triumphs, the fun, and the pain. I let you into some of my life. I have been both demon and the golden girl of one good man's life. But mainly, I have just been myself - unstinting and without pretence.

My friends will know where to find me.

Apr 18, 2008

SHAVING
A recent survey on another site, more devoted to sex than
this one, says 99% of men prefer women to shave their
genitals while 86% of women just want their men trimmed
but not shaven.

Amazing - it is almost like people want to be able to forget
we're animals. If we take off all the hair we'll look like
mannequins and everything will be nice and sterile,
juvenile, and sex will no longer be "two tigers rolling on
Vaseline" but something more pristine.

"this mellow-thighed chick just put my spine out of place"

As for me - come as you are, baby!

Apr 19, 2008

TOP GEAR
There's this absolutely brilliant car show from the BBC
called Top Gear where they have these very expensive toys
that they race around in, telling you all about the cars and
boats, etc. as they drive them about. "Hold onto your spleen
everybody!"

One car they tested had the man saying things like " Oh my
God Almighty" as it screamed from 0 to 60 mph in 2.5
seconds, and then 0 to 100 mph in 5 seconds. The car is a
monster! Unfortunately if you're NOT going around
corners at 100 mph, the handling is so tremendously bad,
you will crash. Ferocious understeer.

It also has a few "issues" - like the throttle sticking open at 150 mph, or the spontaneous bursting into flames, or the broken suspension sending you off skidding into a ditch - but apart from that...it could be fun.

Introducing the Caparo T1 priced at $1/2 million

wish I had one

Apr 20, 2008

WHAT I DO ON THE WEEKENDS
Yesterday's tree felling has resulted in today's fence mending except that it is raining outside. Fortunately, said neighbor is away for a week so we have time to fix the fence before they get back.

There is rope, and then there's rope. Climbing rope is built to have a bit of stretch in it so as to cushion your fall when you reach the end of it. Otherwise you'd snap some bone or other.

But that's not the sort of rope you use to guide a falling tree. In the instance you want no stretch at all.

You know what happened.

RIDICULOUS SEX ADVICE
Some idiot on another site recommended hoisting her up onto the kitchen counter on giving it to her, his words not mine, right there.

Take a look around your kitchen counters. If you move aside the sundry papers, the toaster, the expresso maker, cutting boards, various cooking utensils, the mixer, the block with the knives in it, the paper towel holder, the spices, the cookbooks, etc. etc. etc. - you might have room for her butt.

But what about her head?

I'm sure there's nothing more romantic than slamming the back of your head into the doors of the upper cabinets, or the coffee maker, the cd/radio thing or the telephone thing.

What about the island?

See above about moving all of the 'sundries' out of the way.

This is supposed to be in the nature of spontaneous sex. To prevent boredom and to display your 'adventurous' spirit. Ooookay.

I'm sorry but cleaning the kitchen so as to make it possible to enjoy sex in there does NOT count as foreplay. "Honey, hand me the bleach, please."

I do not know about your kitchen, but mine doesn't have enough room in it for two persons to engage in sexual adventures. Men may want to remember that there are big, long & sharp knives in there too.

Work rooms (utility rooms, garages, kitchens, bathrooms, laundry rooms) should be skipped when considering sex. The environment isn't exactly salubrious, they are filled with dangerous objects and chemicals, and they are usually messy reminders of your housekeeping.

Please stick to the rooms with soft surfaces and large pieces of comfy furniture in them, thank you.

I have enough scars and scrapes on my tailbone as it is.

INTER-FEMALE COMPETITION
There are two kinds, 1. for the best genetics for the children
(biology) and 2. to fulfill issues involving identity &
security (The Queen Bee Syndrome).

If it involves anything "social" as in money and position or
'social standing' - then the competition is for reasons of #2
above and is 'unworthy'. It is not necessary to slaughter
your sisters to achieve anything of that sort. You might as
well just stamp Loser on your forehead and be done with it.
It does not matter if the vehicle of the competition is via
men or jobs - it always reeks to high heaven.

You can see it here where women do not dare say who
they're dating because others will do that poaching thing
and then say 'don't blame me if you cannot hold onto a
man'. Pure "Queen Bee"!
Of course it won't last. He's not the point. Scoring off a
sister is the point - the ONLY point to the exercise. (Sorry,
fellas, but no - it is NOT about you.)

Stopping a "Queen Bee" is easy. Find her weakness and
then make it impossible for her to avoid displaying that
weakness at every opportunity so she ends up dooming, and
damning, herself.

If it involves #1 above, there is some merit to it but not a
whole lot of merit. Since people are not only the product of
genetics but also of nurturing, simply going after the DNA
is insufficient. And there's something very displeasing
about using men merely as sperm banks.

458

Let's face it - only the weak compete.

Apr 21, 2008

EPICENTERS
In any debate/controversy/vendettas/drama - there is
something too often lost. They all seem to somehow
involve certain persons.

Think of the dramas and who is involved - repeatedly.
Focus only upon that. No mitigating circumstances,
excuses, and so forth - only upon the "epicenter".

This all being 'smoke and mirrors' anyway, why would
anyone in their right mind wish to get caught up in such
stuff? Yet, the "epicenter" cannot seem to get clear of the
muck.

The answer is clear-
Should you wish to avoid such nonsense you have only to
avoid those persons.

Apr 22, 2008
DON'T CALL ME BITCH!!
I am not a slatternly roundheeled ghetto guttersnipe and
neither are you!

Calling me any of the current terms, "ho" and any of the
variants of bitch - so they can seem cool and mealy-
mouthed at the same time - "biotch", "beetch" and so on - is
a declaration not of friendship but of WAR!

Talk amongst yourselves however you will, but when
speaking to me, and of me, show some self-respect.

459

YES, I meant self-respect. How you behave, how you dress, how you speak - they all indicate what you think of yourself and how much you think you're worth. How you treat others shows how you wish to be treated by others.

You can have a great deal of fun without having to roll around in the gutter.

I am not a slatternly roundheeled ghetto guttersnipe and neither are you!

Do you not agree?

Apr 23, 2008
OUCH!!
This blog post is gonna get me into trouble!

Okay people, you have been caught by the medical issue or issues currently afflicting you! We got it. You feel good, better, worse, bad. Pick one. This is fine. We have all been there or will all be there. You have our sympathy.

But if your ills are the sum total of your conversation, chat. blog - please STOP!

Because: 1. it is depressing, 2. we've run out of sympathy and now are just tired, and 3. you're giving prospective partners the idea that he/she will be spending every other weekend in the hospital with you which is not fun.

Special note to the women: Yes, men like to feel needed but playing "the wounded bird" to activate their 'protective' circuitry gets old, especially if, in some way, you have brought it on yourself.

460

Children are another matter and I do sympathize with a parent's anxiety. Those facing or supporting those facing a terminal illness also can count on my support.

Yes, I have my medical issues (my right knee) and I tell people when I have a cold (so they stay even further away) but that is NOT all I ever talk about.

The point is: There is MORE to you than what's in your medical chart and/or in your medicine chest. Time to talk about those other things!

Apr 24, 2008
PLAYTIME WITH TEDDYBEARS
FUN! FUN! FUN!
It is so good to see you again! A bit of coy behavior, you're so cute, and some chit chat. Clients being clients. Then it is lying on the bed, mmmmm, furrrrrr, nice and snuggled. No kisses permitted yet due to my lingering cold. I agree that not being able to kiss is no fun but we will see what else we can do. How's your knee? Better? Good! We have oil. A massage and then my next favorite - cunnilingus! You're a msster of the art and I am approaching nirvana. So many orgasms - they just roll through me! Cunnilingus with manual! You wicked, wicked teddybear you! Trying to reduce me to protoplasm? Wow! You just might do that! Slide inside and now you're in my clutches. You will cum for me. Yes, right there. Here we go. 26 for me and 1 for you. We were just about to move this way for more - your knee & a cramp. Hmmm. You've lost weight again btw. Yes, I did notice. But you have been skipping out on your physical therapy. Let's try this way. Yes. That will work! More, more, more! Ah yes! 20 and 1 this time! La, la, la, la, la - what were we talking about? The grandkittens are fine - perfect little minxes. How's your daughter doing? And your

son? I see. Yes, what are you going to do. I have to get the engine rebuilt on the MGB. You look damn good lying naked on a bed, did you know? You're welcome! And now for 'thirds'!

This time I had not messed up my schedule and I had more teddybear!

Apr 25, 2008
FAITH & POLITICS
It has been said that the Democrats have ignored the role of faith in their liberal politics. I say NOT TRUE!

What I say is that your faith is your business, not mine.

Your faith is something private between you and your god and your family. Therefore your faith is far too important and precious to be sullied by being brandished about in public.

This is why I do not agree with holding prayers before meetings, invocations before ceremonies & events, etc. when the meetings, ceremonies & events and so on are SECULAR in their nature.

However, should you yourself wish to pray before such things in private, please go right ahead.

Point 1:
Faith is certainly NOT to be tarnished by associating it with politics! If you remember your history, humans have tried to mingle the two before now and always without any marked degree of success. Religions are always made corrupt when so comingled and the politics are never are never uncorrupted.

462

Point 2:
Modern representative government is supposed to be inclusive whereas religions are only for their adherents and are therefore exclusive. The two are not compatible in their natures.

Point 3:
Nor would we really wish them to be compatible. Think of the penalties. The Army rolling over your house with their tanks because you didn't go to church last Sunday. Being told who to vote for from the pulpit or face excommunication or damnation.

Point 4:
Which religion would be the "official" or "approved" religion? If this religion weren't yours, would you be happy to have to practice an official/approved faith? Would coercing compliance with the dicta of the official/approved faith be right and moral?

Didn't any of you watch the opening scenes of the movie "Elizabeth" starring Cate Blanchett? Where Mary was burning 'heretics' at the stake? Did you miss the point? Look at the brainwashed women of the polygamists! Can you not see that when you comingle earthy power with religious ascendency the religion becomes corrupt and people become slaves?

Not only can we collectively ignore faith, we collectively MUST ignore faith when considering politics.

If you personally wish to be guided by your faith at all times and in all things - that is your business and your right. But you cannot, should not and may not impose your

463

choice upon others for that would be involving yourself in their business and violating their right.

Separation of church and state is NOT a joke. Please do not treat it as if it were one.

Apr 26, 2008
LADIES & THEIR PROFILES
The women aren't all that much better when it comes to crafting effective profiles than the men are. They do one of two things. Either they write an encyclopedia full of detail, TMI, criteria, tales of woe, demands, etc. Or they write a one liner that says "I'm here and I have a pulse." The former sets the bar too high, the latter sets the bar too low. In both cases, the good guys move along.

Honey, if you want the good guys, you're gonna have to work a bit.

1 picture, maybe two, that shows a guy what he might expect. Face pix remain optional.

First section = all about you and what you have to offer. 3 sentences only. Please use spellcheck.

Ex: "Tall, lithe, blithe, polyamorous, witty, and elegant domme who bewitches alpha males, and only alpha males, into becoming willing cat toys as they succumb to their own desires."

Okay, so I told the men all they needed to know in one sentence but I'm a wordsmith.

Then next section is all about him - the kind of man you want. 3 sentences only. Please do NOT be negative and

464

whiny, or a total bitch - unless that is what you're selling.
No encyclopedias!

Ex: "Must be between 40 and 60 years of age, 6 foot tall,
unencumbered, furry, nearby, and possess more than half a
brain. Strong enough to be fun but warm enough to be my
teddybear."

Being a dominatrix required a bit more explanation so I
added the following.

"I am a soft domme and do NOT do pain, abuse or indulge
in humiliation. Basically I want wild, rampant, skin-on-
skin, multi-orgasmic, ejaculatory, full body contact sex on
my terms with someone who can accept my unbridled
sexuality."

It is all about marketing. Know who you are. Know who
you want. Learn how to attract them while repelling others.
Then craft your presentation suitably.

I know you agree with me!

SMITH ISLAND CAKE
Sunday's baking challenge is to be Smith Island Cake. The
recipe is not difficult but it is a rather labor intensive
operation. But Sunday's weather should be just about
perfect for cake baking and I do have my daughter (the
baker par excellence) here so now is the time!

Recipe

1 box cake mix - yellow, prepared as per package
instructions except use only 3 serving spoonfuls of batter

per 9" pan per layer and cook at 350 degrees for 8 to 9 minutes.

Spread liberally with chocolate icing. You must move quickly so the layers do not dry out.

You want at least 10 layers in this one cake.

The trick with this recipe is to not cut the cakes into layers but to bake each layer individually which results in a smoother top and bottom to each layer and increased moisture. Turn the layers out of the pans quickly onto the racks so the layers do not break.

No deviations from the recipe are permitted.
That would not be fair.

Happy Baking!

Apr 27, 2008
END OF BLOG STATS
1325 posts
4752 comments received.
371 watchers
total pages 102

average views per post= 281
average comments per post= 3.59

first post Sept 3, 2005 had 1277 views and gathered 5 comments

lost 10 watchers just in this past week

MY NEWEST BOOK
THE ALTAR CHASE
"If Only -
Dating is very simple. You go somewhere and scope out
those available. You select from them and make contact.
You hold a 15 minute conversation with them and get
phone numbers. You set up dates and go on dates. Sex is up
to her but he is always prepared. You enjoy doing the
rounds until one says "stand and deliver". Then you marry
that person. What's so hard about that?

What is hard is they tell you that you are kind and
wonderful and yet they married the next person they dated
and not you.

This book will try to remedy that situation."
available now at lulu
thank you to my editor!

FOR MEN
Women: a primer for men

"It is a testament to the essential kindness of women that
most men remain unstrangled. This small primer has been
written by an independent woman of vast interpersonal
experience in the hopes that men will remain unstrangled
because they, finally, 'get it'."

All you gentlemen need to know in as few pages as is
possible.
now available at lulu

FOR WOMEN
Men: a primer for women

"if it has tires or testicles, you're going to have
trouble with it"

"There are lots of men in the world. Some are more delightful than others, but most will be very happy if only you'd notice them. Men are neither monsters nor simpletons; they are, like us, a mix of the good, the bad, and the indifferent.

Men pretty much want the same things women want. They mainly want someone to give a damn about them. Men are human beings first and men second. This means that men also have feelings, hopes, fears, dreams and desires.

Men regard women as both the most fascinating and the most exasperating people on the planet. To men, women get upset at the silliest of things and women wonder why they haven't strangled such unthinking persons yet.

This slender book is an effort at a kind of reapproachment between the genders in the hope that more women will have more fun and more men will remain unstrangled."

available at lulu
hey, it's my blog, dammit!

Apr 28, 2008

SUPERB SEX
"Most people have no idea how overwhelmingly good sex, just straight old regular sex, can actually be. This is not a book on relationships. This is a book dealing just with how to have superb sex."

468

Yes, I would know.
available at lulu
and it's still my blog

ORGASMS

You did know that there is no biological imperative for a
woman to have orgasms - so WHY do women have
orgasms? Why are women equipped with an organ whose
sole function is to generate orgasms? Why can women have
so many orgasms one right after another and no end in
sight?

Doesn't seem fair somehow.

My theory is having orgasms binds women and men.
But if you want to know HOW rather than WHY,
read this book!
for both men and women
available at lulu

WWW.LULU.COM

SMITH ISLAND CAKE
Well, we made the cake, see previous post on this subject,
and YES it is labor-intensive.

The main difficulty is deciding what precisely is meant by
"serving spoon". The secondary issue was the thickness of
the batter - to thick, in my opinion.

We decided that two of this particular spoon was the best
amount per layer per cake pan.

We also decided to make the batter a bit more fluid next
time to make it easier to get a smooth layer.

Yes, it tasted damn good!
How did YOURS turn out?

COMING BACK
Could I ever stop dancing naked in the warm rain?
Perhaps once the fire within has died, I suppose I might.
When memory replaces anticipation I suppose I might.
When a lovely teddybear generates as much excitement
within me as a stone cold statue, I might.

But I would miss it.
I would miss the song of my blood, the joy of racing desire;
the pleasure of pouncing!

Then I look into the eyes of my beloved(s) and know - that
day will never come.

I am never going to stop dancing naked in the warm rain!

Apr 29, 2008
THE BOOKS THAT STARTED IT ALL
beguile
All about what I do and how I do it.

available at lulu

"I have actually purchased this book. Very informative. I
enjoyed it and even learned a few new things I still use
now. Y'all should for sure check out her writing."

The Polyamorist

More than one? YES, PLEASE!!

Answers the question: can one sincerely love more than one person?

also available at lulu

COLLECTED WORKS
NOTES of a DOMINATRIX
If you want to save money by NOT buying each of the preceding books - just get the 'pricey' collected works. Each book is $20 more or less so if you buy 4 that's $80 plus shipping. With this one you get 6 books in one with a few extra tidbits and it only costs $40 more or less plus shipping.

Available everywhere - run down to your nearest Borders and order your copy!

GOOD FORTUNE!
I hope that all goes well for you! I would hate to lose you but that's not the reason why I wish you well.

The reason why is for your own sake.
So you can live without fear.
So you can be happy.

Good luck to you!
Always.

Apr 30, 2008

THE CHAT SERIES

In case you missed anything...this, with bits from another blog, has all been compiled. And it is also available at Borders - they had it listed under "international politics" and "history" - HAH!

CHAT -the first year
FURTHER CHAT -the second year
LAST CHAT -the third & final year

answers the question, how much trouble can I get into on the Internet?

IT'S BEEN REAL
and it's been fun - and in certain select case, it has been real fun!

But I have said all I care to say just now so this blog will not be added to for some time to come.

It will stay right where it is and you may consult it as you will and even leave comments if you desire to do so.

I will be around on the site and my friends know where to find me.

CIAO!
I'm outta here!

www.ingramcontent.com/pod-product-compliance
Lightning Source LLC
LaVergne TN
LVHW042136040326
832903LV00011B/274/J